Disconnected Youth?

Other books by Robert MacDonald

RISKY BUSINESS? Youth and Enterprise Culture (*with F. Coffield*)

YOUTH, THE 'UNDERCLASS' AND SOCIAL EXCLUSION (*editor*)

SNAKES AND LADDERS (*with L. Johnston, P. Mason, L. Ridley and C. Webster*)

POOR TRANSITIONS (*with C. Webster, D. Simpson, A. Abbas, M. Cieslik, T. Shildrick and M. Simpson*)

Disconnected Youth?

Growing up in Britain's Poor Neighbourhoods

Robert MacDonald
University of Teesside

and

Jane Marsh

First published 2005 by
PALGRAVE MACMILLAN
Houndmills, Basingstoke, Hampshire RG21 6XS and
175 Fifth Avenue, New York, N.Y. 10010
Companies and representatives throughout the world

PALGRAVE MACMILLAN is the global academic imprint of the Palgrave Macmillan division of St. Martin's Press, LLC and of Palgrave Macmillan Ltd. Macmillan® is a registered trademark in the United States, United Kingdom and other countries. Palgrave is a registered trademark in the European Union and other countries.

ISBN-13: 978–1–4039–0486–7 hardback
ISBN-10: 1–4039–0486–3 hardback
ISBN-13: 978–1–4039–0487–4 paperback
ISBN-10: 1–4039–0487–1 paperback

This book is printed on paper suitable for recycling and made from fully managed and sustained forest sources.

A catalogue record for this book is available from the British Library.

Library of Congress Cataloging-in-Publication Data
MacDonald, Robert, 1962–
    Disconnected youth? : growing up in Britain's poor neighbourhoods / Robert MacDonald and Jane Marsh.
        p. cm.
    Includes bibliographical references and index.
    ISBN 1–4039–0486–3
    1. Youth with social disabilities—Great Britain.   2. Poor youth—Great Britain.   3. Marginality, Social—Great Britain.   4. Poverty—Great Britain.   5. School-to-work transition—Great Britain.
    I. Marsh, Jane, 1974–   II. Title.
HV1441.G7M35 2005
305.235′086′9420941—dc22   2005047301

10   9   8   7   6   5   4   3
14 13 12 11 10 09 08 07

Printed and bound in Great Britain by
Antony Rowe Ltd, Chippenham and Eastbourne

Contents

Acknowledgements

The largest debt of gratitude we owe is to the young people who took time to talk to us for the purposes of our research. We can offer them nothing more than our thanks and our hope that this book goes some way towards doing justice to what they told us. We also very grateful to those agencies in Teesside who helped us with the research and the staff who took the trouble to describe their experiences of working with the problems of social exclusion, in its various guises. The Economic and Social Research Council funded the project and the University of Teesside helped fill the gaps, by allowing some time for analysis and writing, in what proved to be a far lengthier enterprise than originally envisaged. We are grateful to Wendy Bland who provided administrative assistance to the project.

We have been lucky to work in a university where our research interests, as represented in this book, the subjects of the courses that we run and the life experiences of (some of) our students meet so closely. Much is claimed about the important interrelationship of research and teaching. We suspect, though, that it would be difficult to find elsewhere what has proved to be such a productive interplay of ideas between those 'expert' by the fact of academic learning and those 'expert' by the fact of biographical, day-to-day experience. One example: in a seminar, a couple of years ago, two young women students – both residents of one of Teesside's many poor neighbourhoods, recipients of welfare benefits and single mothers – concluded their 'critical assessment' of conservative underclass theory with an overhead transparency projection: 'WE LOVE (signified by a large heart) CHARLES MURRAY!' A case of 'false consciousness'? Possibly, but as we show later, such a viewpoint proved to be far from uncommon among those one might expect least to hold it. Whatever the rights and wrongs from our perspective of students' heated arguments, they deserve credit for the way they have encouraged us to consider close-up the complexities, contradictions and controversies of popular ideas about social exclusion and the underclass.

Colleagues and friends at Teesside have helped enormously in the development of this book – debating its findings and arguments with us, feeding in ideas from their own research projects, reading drafts of the chapters, and so on. Colin Webster has been a constant source of intellectual stimulation and encouragement. Tracy Shildrick deserves special thanks for the same reasons, for reading and commenting on the whole manuscript and for pointing us to good research and new books that we had missed. The number of times Colin's and Tracy's own arguments and ideas crop up in this book (as well as their corrections of ours) far exceeds the number of times they are acknowledged. Donald Simpson, Mark Cieslik, Mark Simpson, Siobhan McAlister, Heather Easton, Robin Haggart and Andrea Abbas have served as readers and valuable critics of particular chapters, or as timely sounding-boards for the development of our ideas. Whilst we never got round to asking Steve Taylor to do much in respect of the book, we appreciate his offer of help and the work he does to make Sociology at Teesside what it is. Further afield, Robert Hollands and Shane Blackman continue to be valued friends and colleagues in the efforts we share to understand 'youth'.

We thank our editors at Palgrave: Heather Gibson for taking this on initially and more recently Jennifer Nelson, Briar Towers and Jill Lake, particularly for their tolerance of our missed deadlines. We are indebted to Bob Coles for being – over many years – an invaluable mentor (to Robert MacDonald) and, in this instance, for taking time to review the manuscript in the ever-diminishing, academic summer vacation. Whilst a friend, he is not shy of criticism. His comments, like those of the others listed above, have improved the book immeasurably. As ever, all faults, errors and inaccuracies remain our own.

Finally, and closer to home, Jane Marsh would like to express her thanks to her family and to her partner, Shaun, for their ongoing support and encouragement. Robert MacDonald would like to record his indebtedness to Jacqui Merchant. If she had not been so supportive and gracious about his badly tilted 'work-life balance' the book would never have seen the light of day. Credit, too, to Jessie, Will and Paddy for only rarely pursuing the 'delinquent solution' when their father was *in absentia*. He dedicates his efforts on *Disconnected Youth?* to his family.

Introduction

Although the facts of poverty frame all that is discussed in this book, it is not one that is concerned with academic debates about measures, rates and definitions of poverty (see Hills et al., 2002; Piachaud and Sutherland, 2002). Nor is it an evaluation of the laudable political efforts of the British Labour government to reduce child poverty, regenerate run-down neighbourhoods or otherwise tackle social exclusion (see Social Exclusion Unit, 2004). Rather, this is a book about the experiences of people as they grow up in some of the poorest parts of Britain; how they live through conditions of poverty and carve out transitions to adulthood in some of the most adverse circumstances. In other words, our ambition has been an ethnographic one: to understand, from the point of view of those at the sharp end, how processes of social exclusion intermesh with processes of youth transition.

The book has at least in part been inspired by the unanswered questions left hanging in a previous title – *Youth, the 'Underclass' and Social Exclusion* (MacDonald, 1997). Although the contributors to that edited collection are best known for their work in the field of 'youth studies', it aimed – as this book does – to address wider-ranging social scientific debates. As Furlong and Cartmel argue (1997: 2), the study of youth provides:

> an ideal opportunity to examine the relevance of new social theories; if the social order has changed and if social structures have weakened, we would expect to find evidence of these changes among young people who are at the crossroads of the process of social reproduction.

In this vein, others that have reflected on our core questions conclude that young people have become disconnected from the normal, moral, mainstream life of society. They are 'a lost generation', part of a new

1

underclass cut adrift from the moralising, socialising conventions of 'respectable' working-class culture and dangerously excluded from the discipline and rewards of working life (see chapter 1). The questioning title of the book betrays our scepticism. Whilst much is said and done about 'socially excluded youth', commentaries based on close-up, detailed, qualitative research with those so labelled are few in number. The core of our book is research of this type; research that explores whether popular theories about social exclusion or a welfare-dependent underclass really do connect with the lived experiences of the so-called 'disaffected', 'disengaged' and 'difficult-to-reach'.

Just as 'youth' is often taken to reveal broader processes of social change and is seen as 'a key indicator of the state of the nation itself' (Griffin, 1993: 197), the conditions of Britain's poor neighbourhoods can be used as 'a barometer for social exclusion. They illustrate sharply the more general problems of social division, inequality, and lack of opportunity in society' (Lupton and Power, 2002: 140). In studying 'East Kelby' in Teesside, in north-east England, our research has focused in on the poorest, most deprived neighbourhoods in one of the poorest towns in Britain. Charles Murray (1994), the champion of conservative, cultural underclass theory, named 'Kelby' as a prime locale where his 'new rabble underclass' might be found. This is one sense in which we understand ours to be a critical case study.

Although firmly grounded in this one place, our descriptions and analysis are not limited to it. Teesside has its own, in some ways unique, socio-economic history and demography (see chapter 2), but the lived problems of poverty that the book reveals are far from being a 'special case'. Kelby has much in common with numerous towns and cities in the old industrial regions of Britain (see Charlesworth, 2000; and Osmond and Mugaseth, 2004, for just two examples) and, to a lesser extent, Europe and North America. Yet qualitative explorations of the realities of life in the thousands of poor neighbourhoods in Britain are rare in contemporary social science. In *Hard Work: Life in Low-pay Britain* (2003), Polly Toynbee makes a similar point about the partial and prejudiced representations of the poor that crop up in British news features and popular television programmes. These dwell on the 'titillating sins of the underclass' (*ibid.*: 12) rather than present more honest, mundane accounts of the mass of 'ordinary' poor people and places:

> Ordinary people who live here and in the thousands of places like this do not figure on the national landscape at all. They are the forgotten, the invisible, only good for tales of mayhem in outlaw

territory. These are the badlands of the national imagination, not ordinary places where nearly a third of the population live ordinary, law-abiding lives. (*ibid.*: 149)

The truth of these remarks is echoed in our findings – albeit that a minority of interviewees did become embroiled in lives that were far from law-abiding. A key conclusion is that, contrary to common (-sense) representations of the singularity of 'problem youth' in 'problem neighbourhoods', young people's lifestyles, transitions and experiences in East Kelby were diverse and heterogeneous. Within the same street we talked to people, like those in Toynbee's book, who were scratching a legitimate income through low-skill, low-paid 'poor work', to young women who were living a socially circumscribed life as 'welfare-dependent' single mothers and to young men who were fully embedded in long-term career criminality as burglars, drug dealers and shoplifters. Some individuals got by through casual and occasionally illicit work outside formal systems of education, employment and training. Others doggedly made their way through post-sixteen education courses and schemes for the young workless, such as the New Deal for Young People. Our attention to the sorts of people, experiences and issues most likely to reveal the existence of the alleged new underclass and the realties of social exclusion is another reason why we describe our project as a critical case study. If we had been unable to find evidence of a new, dangerous underclass – or of an excluded 'lost generation' – in this place, during this period, among these people, it is unlikely to be found anywhere.

The first two chapters of the book set out the intellectual terrain of our study. In chapter 1, we describe how these sorts of ideas and theories have come to the forefront of contemporary social scientific and policy thinking about poverty. The chapter presents a detailed, critical appreciation of the twin concepts of 'the underclass' and 'social exclusion', noting what we feel are some remaining problems and unanswered questions in respect of them.

Chapter 2 locates our study within a critical discussion of current sociological approaches to understanding youth, transition and social change. We conclude that debates about the underclass and social exclusion provide a classic example of paradoxical, ideological ways of thinking about youth that simultaneously see them as vulnerable and demanding of special care and threatening and requiring of disciplinary control. This is not to argue that the contemporary fascination with 'disconnected youth' is simply fashionable, moral panic. Processes of social and economic change have had profound consequences for young people in poor neighbourhoods. The following, empirically-based chapters of the book show this.

Chapter 3 examines how experiences of school relate to the wider realm of young people's lives and their futures, focusing on the important role of schooling in the early shaping of 'inclusionary' and 'exclusionary' transitions. One conclusion that we reach is that, for many individuals, it was impossible to understand processes of school disengagement without also understanding simultaneous and associated processes of engagement with street-based, peer networks.

Chapter 4 uses the concept of 'leisure career' to chart young people's changing 'free-time' associations and activities and how these emerged out of, and impacted on, other aspects of transition. Leisure careers became a crucial influence on wider processes of inclusion/exclusion and we show how, for some, contemporary but under-explored forms of 'street-corner society' played a key role in the creation of some of the most intractable, hardest cases of social exclusion.

In chapters 5 and 6 we return to more direct consideration of school-to-work careers, beginning with an investigation of school-leaving and those elements of the post-sixteen institutional arrangements that were most significant in informants' biographies: post-compulsory education; Youth Training schemes; and the New Deal for Young People programme. Chapter 6 examines the notional end-point of these encounters: getting a job. In charting young adults' enduring commitment to employment yet consistent economic marginality, we contend directly with some of the key assertions of underclass theories and conceptualisations of social exclusion.

In chapters 7 and 8 we turn our attention to, respectively, young people's family and housing careers. While underclass perspectives point to the alleged cultural reproduction of troublesome, benefit-dependent families, government policy targeting of, for instance, teenage mothers emphasises the social inequalities said to accrue to them and, later, to their offspring (e.g. Social Exclusion Unit, 1998, 2004; Hobcraft and Kiernan, 1999; Hills et al., 2002). Chiefly, chapter 7 hinges on an apparent paradox between interviewees' highly conventional, normative perspectives on parenthood on the one hand, and objective indicators which seem to confirm this place as one in which 'illegitimate', underclass families might be found, on the other. In considering housing careers, in chapter 8, special attention is given to the significance of place and the role of social networks in shaping these and to the way interviewees described growing up in some of the most deprived parts of the country.

Chapter 9 turns to a discussion of criminal and drug-using careers. The delinquency, crimes and drug cultures of young men in particular feature high on the list of social pathologies said to be emblematic of life in poor neighbourhoods. A main aim of this chapter is to understand ethnographically the processes whereby a minority of young people in such places evolve careers of dependent drug use and crime and the consequences of these for their broader transitions.

The final chapter of the book summarises the evidence and arguments presented in the previous chapters, weighing these against theories about the underclass and social exclusion. Here particular attention is given to the significance of 'poor work' and the paradoxical effects of social capital and social networks in the youth transitions we describe. Finally, we argue that a more panoramic theorisation of youth exclusion – and more realistic policy development in respect of it – requires us to extend our sociological gaze beyond the twists and turns of individual biographies towards the global–local processes of economic marginalisation and social polarisation that create socially excluded places and populations.

1
Social Exclusion and the Underclass: Debates and Issues

In this chapter and chapter 2 we set out some of the main theoretical and policy questions in which our book is interested. We begin by reviewing two key perspectives on the underclass as an introduction to a fuller critique of these ideas and a discussion of their relationship to more recent thinking about social exclusion.

Underclass theory: a brief recap

In the late 1980s and 1990s a number of writers – coming from different political and theoretical standpoints – implied that young people in poor neighbourhoods were prime candidates for membership of a putative 'underclass'.[1] Those who espoused these popular and influential ideas tended to fall into one of two camps, separated primarily by the way that they explained the emergence of this supposed new division of poor people at the bottom of the social heap (MacDonald, 1997a).

'The other kind of poor people': Murray and cultural underclass theory

Responsible for most of the political heat associated with the underclass idea has been the 'conservative' or 'cultural' thesis. Championed by the neo-liberal American social scientist Charles Murray (1990, 1994), this approach contends that a new anti-social, welfare-dependent, dangerous class has emerged in Britain's poor places. Like its American cousin, the underclass was brought into being by the 'incentives to failure' set by an over-generous, postwar welfare state (Murray, 1984). As in the US, British criminal justice and welfare systems have 'seduced people' into negative social behaviour and immoral outlooks (Murray, 1990: 71). This process has not been a universal one: there is an 'ecology to poverty' (*ibid*.: 69) with Britain's poorest neighbourhoods being the ones in which the 'other kind of poor people' – the underclass – 'are taking over' (*ibid*.: 17).

Three 'early warning signals' of the arrival of an underclass – high rates of crime, illegitimacy and unemployment – are woven together in Murray's thesis, with a model of individual (economic) rationality central to his thinking. In terms of crime, for instance, he says that the likelihood that an offender will be caught, convicted and incarcerated has reduced dramatically since the 1960s. With little obvious disincentive to commit crime, offending has spiralled. Punishment for crime has become too uncertain (Herrnstein and Murray, 1994). For Murray, young men of the underclass are 'essentially barbarians' (1990: 17). They choose criminal lifestyles and voluntary idleness instead of work because weak criminal justice systems and over-generous state unemployment benefits have encouraged them to do so. Given the welfare benefits accruing to single motherhood and the economic unattractiveness of young men as marriage partners, young women of the underclass increasingly choose to have children illegitimately. With more liberal benefit regimes, single motherhood has gone from 'extremely punishing to not so bad' (Murray, 1994: 30). As young women need no longer rely on young men (as husbands) for material support, young men need no longer commit themselves to employment, especially with the opportunity of a life on the dole enlivened and made more lucrative by hustling, benefit fraud and crime. As these young men progressively marginalise themselves from mainstream social and economic life they become still more unattractive as marriage partners and fathers. In this way Murray presents the welfare-draining single mother and the feckless, criminal young man as the key figures in this new cultural landscape.

A central tenet of conservative underclass theory is that a distaste for work and traditional family values is being inculcated into the young, creating a 'lost generation' disconnected from mainstream society (see also Mead, 1997). The female children in underclass families learn to see single motherhood as normal, possible and 'not so bad' and, in time, replicate their mothers' decision to have children outside of marriage. The absence of fathers as disciplinarians, moral guardians and positive role models for male offspring produces a failed generation of disorderly, disrespectful and delinquent young men doomed to reproduce down the generations the same dysfunctional families. Thus, according to Murray, crime, unemployment, illegitimacy and single motherhood bind together in the cultural reproduction of the underclass.

Although his first foray into British debates contained equal discussion of trends in crime, unemployment and illegitimacy, by 1994 it was the last of these three that occupied the central ground of his theory. His most recent contributions – like the previous two, serialised in *The Sunday Times* – confirmed Murray's belief in single motherhood as the engine driving the development of Britain's underclass (2000). And it is this aspect of Murray's thesis that has gained most favour among commentators in Britain. Whilst resisting the terms of full-blown cultural underclass theory, self-styled 'ethical socialists' such as Dennis (1994), Green (1993) and Halsey (1992) have – like Murray and others from the libertarian Right – published tracts for the Institute of Economic Affairs that decry what they see as the devastating social and moral effect of Britain's growing number of 'families without fathers'.

'Outcast poverty': structural underclass theories

The second main position in the British underclass debate during the 1980s and 1990s is what John Westergaard (1992) calls the 'outcast poverty' thesis. Here, the fact of the existence of the underclass is not in doubt; what is disputed are the main lines of causation. Rather than the poor being blamed for their poverty as in the cultural thesis, they are seen as victims of changing economic circumstance and political policy. Industrial restructuring, monetarist economic policy, labour market deregulation and authoritarian social welfare policies from the latter 1970s through to the 1990s are presented *inter alia* as the causal factors behind the emergence of Britain's underclass. Deindustrialisation, not demoralisation, is the key to the formation of an impoverished, welfare-dependent class of people situated structurally below the traditional working class. Runciman's (1990) depiction of the underclass as those who are near-permanently detached from the labour market is a good example of this approach, which universally presents long-term unemployment and, as consequence, benefit dependence and poverty, as the definitive experience of the British underclass.

Despite the political opposition of the authors in these first two camps and their perceptions of the factors that have created this new social group, their writings sometimes contain surprisingly similar cultural depictions – and implicit moral condemnation – of underclass life. Dahrendorf's (1987: 5) account is the best example. He begins forthrightly enough by stating that the 'underclass is not at fault for its own condition' and identifies structural economic developments as formative (particularly the phenomenon of jobless growth and the creation of widespread 'poor work' in the US and UK). The scathing language and metaphors of disease and contagion he then uses to describe the condition of the underclass, however, bear a close resemblance to those employed by Murray. The underclass suffers from 'a cumulation of social pathologies' (Dahrendorf, 1987: 3–5) and represents 'a cancer eating away at the texture of societies'. As with Murray, young people come in for particular blame for their 'laid-back sloppiness' and 'mindless youth culture'. His position seems to be that, in the first instance, economic change is the cause, but subsequently there have developed styles of cultural behaviour, which serve to sustain its existence. It has become a self-sustaining subculture (perhaps similar to Oscar Lewis's (1966) 'culture of poverty') set apart from 'the values of the work society'.

A more thorough, convincing, structurally-oriented exposition on the underclass can be found in the work of the American social scientist William Julius Wilson (1987; 1996). The title of his 1996 book, *When Work Disappears*, betrays the significance he places on economic change in the creation of 'the ghetto poor' (a term Wilson now prefers to 'the underclass'). The abandonment of economically declining inner-city neighbourhoods by more affluent White and Black families, by private business and by public services has increased the concentration of poverty and unemployment in the ghetto. Informal job search networks and employment possibilities disappear, as do role models of Black men who have been successful in legitimate enterprise. As these processes of economic decline and spatial polarisation continue, the ghetto empties out, becoming a 'commercially abandoned locality where pimps, drug pushers and unemployed street people have replaced working fathers as predominant socialising agents' (Kasarda, 1989, cited in Morris, 1994: 90). Over time, the younger, Black residents of the ghetto develop ways of life in *response* to the restriction of legitimate opportunities. The emergence of vibrant, local drug economies is one clear and common consequence of the departure of the formal economy of working-class jobs from inner-city America (Bourgois, 1996). Wilson says:

> in emphasizing the powerful role of the environment in shaping the lives of inner-city residents, we should not ignore or deny the existence of unflattering behaviours that emerge from blocked opportunities ... some of these behaviours, which often impede the social mobility of inner city residents, represent cultural responses to constraints and limited opportunities that have evolved over time. (1996: xviii)

There is an obvious, conceptual parallel here with the position of one of the more serious considerations of 'structural underclass' theory in the UK. Roberts (2001: 113) suggests that:

> even if the original and continuing background cause of social exclusion is a lack of work, it could still be the case that the culture developed in adapting to this situation becomes an additional impediment to the social and economic ascent of those concerned.

So, whilst some of the most important writers on the underclass in the US and UK cite structural economic change as *the* key factor in the creation of new groups of urban poor, they also tend to concur that the subcultural adaptations of these groups to changed economic conditions serve to *further* entrench their social and economic exclusion.

Some problems with underclass theory

Criticisms of underclass theory have been many. One of the most common points to the lack of a clear, shared definition of the concept: 'there are as many definitions of the underclass as there are sociologists' (Macnicol, 1994: 30).[2] Related to this, several writers have noted how underclass theories ignore the differences within and between the groups of people lumped together under this label. It attempts to incorporate such a wide variety of social problems – and the 'problem groups' listed are so heterogeneous (Mann, 1994; Morris, 1994) – that it is difficult to see how it might be useful in describing a social class formation with shared social characteristics and economic relationships (Gallie, 1988). Auletta's well-known, early American version (1982) listed drug addicts, drifters, drunks, drop-outs, bag ladies, released mental patients, street criminals and other hustlers alongside the 'passive poor' and long-term welfare dependants; in essence, a list of those (apparently) culturally different to the mainstream, moral majority.

Similarly, the routes to membership of the underclass can be vastly different (Robinson and Gregson, 1992; Baldwin et al., 1997). Even if we take just one of the sub-groups identified by Murray as plausible members of the underclass – young, single mothers – there are many different factors that might lead an individual to this situation apart from the supposed immorality and rational economic planning he suggests (such as ignorance of sex education and contraception or a short-term perspective on 'life-planning': see Alcock, 1994; Social Exclusion Unit, 1999).

Jones (1997) and Robinson and Gregson (1992) have also argued that underclass theories tend to fall too heavily on one side or other of the 'agency–structure' dichotomy, with conservative theorists particularly notable for their obsession with supposedly disreputable values and behaviours and their blindness to the structural conditions that surround and shape individual action. Murray's (1990) writing on British youth unemployment is a case in point. Insisting that much of this is voluntary, he states glibly that 'the definitive proof that an underclass has arrived is that large numbers of young, healthy, low income males *choose* not to take jobs' (17, our emphasis). In so doing he ignores the mountains of empirical research literature that shows much youth unemployment of the period to be a product not of choice but of a youth labour market decimated by long-term economic restructuring.

The most obvious failing of cultural underclass theories is, however, their sheer lack of empirical substantiation. Many social scientists have been prepared to contemplate the theoretical possibility of the emergence of an underclass or something similar given prevailing economic trends over the past thirty years in Britain (e.g. Smith, 1992). Youth research, in particular, has a privileged vantage point from which to investigate processes of underclass development (MacDonald, 1997a), but at best concludes that the formation of a distinct underclass remains only a possibility, not a current empirical reality (Maguire and Maguire, 1997; Roberts, 1997a; Williamson, 1997). It is difficult to think of any single, serious social scientific enquiry that has located successfully the sort of culturally distinct underclass that Murray claims to have heard about on his few, short trips to some of Britain's poor communities. His research and the few studies that purport to lend weight to his thesis (e.g. Full Employment UK, 1990) are riven with methodological flaws (see MacDonald, 1997b: 177–80).[3]

It is much easier to cite research that disagrees with the central argument that current patterns of crime, parenting and unemployment in Britain are the outcome of separate, subterranean cultures and value systems (e.g. Macnicol, 1987; Walker, 1990; Dean, 1991; Smith, 1992; Heath, 1992; Morris, 1993, 1994; Kinsey, 1993; Payne and Payne, 1994; Holman, 1994/5; Gallie, 1994; MacDonald, 1997c). Neatly summing up the position adopted by those opposed to Murray's ideas, Bagguley and Mann argue that 'the concept of the underclass is a recurrent political and social scientific myth' and that 'because of its inherent theoretical, methodological and empirical flaws [it represents] a demonstrably false set of beliefs' (1992: 122, 125).

What about structural underclass theory? Has it fared better? The main point of contention with this perspective concerns the degree to which Britain's new poor really are wholly and permanently detached from the world of work. There is a danger that writers in this camp may simply re-label the unemployed. Labour market sociologist Lydia Morris (1993, 1994, 1995) has been particularly incisive in charting the changing dynamics of economic life in Britain's post-industrial areas. Rather than identifying a distinct and wholly detached new class, Morris draws attention to the movement of economically marginal individuals between full unemployment and various forms of casualised, underemployment (Morris and Irwin, 1992). As Buck puts it, the long-term unemployed are 'not so much stable members of the underclass, as unstable members of the working class' (1992: 19).

Of course, these debates were being held during the 1990s, drawing on research evidence from that decade and before. In the next section, we will be suggesting that this structural theory of the underclass has neither been proved nor demolished but has merged into a new and broader set of concerns that fall under the banner of 'social exclusion'.

Whatever happened to the underclass? The advent of 'social exclusion'

Since the latter part of the 1990s explicit diatribes against 'the under-class' have declined in political circles in Britain and the US. Academics, too, have been less keen to discuss and debate these ideas. There is far less said about the underclass now. There are different ways of explaining this.

Following Westergaard (1992), it may simply be that the British underclass debate was a passing intellectual fad, now replaced by more modish subjects for academic conjecture. As Morris (1994) notes, we can certainly trace the rise and fall of sociological concern in the problem(s) of the 'undeserving poor' – under different guises and using different terminology – over the past century and before. As might be expected, the chief exponent of the most well-known version of the theory sees it rather differently: 'the last half of the 1990s witnessed a remarkable vanishing act. The underclass, so central to social policy debate from the 1960s through the 1980s, disappeared from national conversation' (Murray, 1999: 1).

'Why', he asks, 'has the underclass disappeared so completely from the national radar screen?' (*ibid.*). In brief, Murray's answer is this. Encouraging downward trends in American crime, unemployment, welfare dependence and teenage birth rates in the 1990s gave the impression that the social problem of the underclass had been resolved. Closer inspection of relevant longer-term statistics, particularly as they apply to key groups such as young Black males in the inner city, reveals that the underclass problem is, in fact, growing. A key example he gives concerns crime. An increasingly punitive criminal justice system meant that by the late 1990s many members of the American underclass were behind bars. America has learned to control the delinquent manifestations of the underclass that most intruded upon the lives of mainstream America. Rather than deal with the root causes of the growth of the underclass – particularly the spread of illegitimacy and Black (and increasingly White) poor, urban enclaves where fatherless families are the cultural norm – mainstream American society is progressively favouring a 'custodial democracy' that seeks to control, isolate and 'wall off' the underclass. For Murray, 'the underclass is out of mind because it is now out of sight' (1999: 29).

Even if true of the US, this seems an unlikely answer in respect of the British context. Such cross-national comparisons are never as easy to make as writers like Murray suggest. The trends in illegitimacy, unemployment, welfare dependence and crime in Britain in the latter 1990s are not the same as those in the US in the same period. Perhaps he is more on the mark with his comments in 1994 on the British debate? He felt then that his iconoclastic argument was receiving a warmer hearing than even four years earlier, as – he claimed – intellectuals and the common-sense 'man in the street' alike observed the playing out of his predictions in the facts of social life. Britain had caught up with America. The problem of underclass culture had come into full view and fewer people felt the need to debate the fact of its existence. Was he right? Is there now less debate and discussion because proponents of the underclass thesis have won the day?

We think not. Criticisms of underclass theories have been widespread and persuasive and earlier we noted only a few of the many dissenting voices and counter-claims. Thus, academic discussion has declined partly as a result of the trenchant theoretical, methodological and empirical critique of underclass theory from within British social science. But this is only part of the answer. As well, a new and apparently less controversial set of ideas has taken the place of underclass theory in British debates about poverty, poor neighbourhoods and their associated social problems. As underclass theory has exited stage right, the 'social exclusion paradigm' has entered stage left (Watt and Jacobs, 2000).

What is 'social exclusion'?

Current usage of the term 'social exclusion' has its roots in French, and then European Community politics and policy in the 1970s and 1980s (Levitas, 1998). Unlike traditional British debates about structured inequality and income poverty, the emphasis in this approach was upon social cohesion. The apparent marginalisation of groups such as the disabled and lone parents and – later – the unemployed and young adults of peripheral social housing estates, was interpreted as a failure of the French state to integrate its citizens into the social, political and moral order (Burchardt et al., 2002). In this republican tradition, '*les exclus*' were seen as both a failure of, and a threat to, social solidarity and cohesion (Silver, 1995). Growing long-term unemployment at European level during the 1980s led the European Union to give primary place to the concept and language of social exclusion in its programmes to counter the negative consequences of globalisation and economic restructuring (Room, 1995; Allen et al., 1998).

Although the British Conservative governments of the 1980s to mid-1990s may have been supportive of this new European emphasis on social exclusion only because it de-emphasised the language of 'poverty' (Burchardt et al., 2002), this cannot be said of their successor. The British New Labour government took up the concept with gusto. On coming to power in 1997, countering social exclusion became the central objective of government domestic policy. As well as providing the rationale for their initial prioritisation of educational policy, it led to a series of area-based programmes targeted at places (typically poor neighbourhoods) – and labour market and training initiatives focused on groups (e.g. young people, single parents, the long-term unemployed) – perceived to be particularly vulnerable to social exclusion. Over the past decade, the term 'social exclusion' has become popular not only with politicians but also with policy-makers, academics and journalists to describe the problems of particular places *and* the people who live in them. The often quoted definition of the Social Exclusion Unit (SEU, 1998b: 1) describes it as 'a shorthand label for what can happen when individuals or areas suffer from a combination of linked problems such as unemployment, poor skills, low incomes, poor housing, high crime environments, bad health and family breakdown'.

The government's enthusiasm for the concept (and the associated funding opportunities) has in large part triggered the avalanche of academic research on social exclusion.[4] The concept has been used to describe quite diverse social groups and social problems. In one year alone, it was applied in separate reports to the situation of women in the labour market (Perrons, 1998), homeless people (Pleace, 1998), drug users (Smith and Stewart, 1998), young offenders (Jones Finer and Nellis, 1998) and unemployed people (MacKay, 1998). And here we see a central problem that confronts those interested in understanding social exclusion: the lack of a clear and accepted definition of the term. Like the underclass concept before it, social exclusion has become a 'catch-all' phrase, popular because it means 'all things to all people' (Atkinson, 1998: 6). Cars et al. (1998: 279) are worried that it is 'a term which could characterise any unwanted social situation', and Spicker agrees that it has a 'very wide remit' that might refer to any individual in a situation of 'disadvantage, deprivation or socially undesirable circumstances' (1997: 133–4).

Nevertheless, it is at least possible to outline some of the key, common characteristics of the concept and in so doing work towards a better understanding of what it might mean. The first point of agreement is that social exclusion is a *broader concept than income poverty*:

> although worklessness, poverty and inequality are certainly all elements of social exclusion, the term does have a wider remit than that. It needs to take on board other elements of social deprivation, including the presence or absence of social support and relationship to the community. More generally it should refer to individuals' participation or non-participation in the whole range of activities that are considered normal for the citizen. (Le Grand, 1998: 4)

Thus, whilst the traditional concerns of students of British poverty are contained within a focus on social exclusion, the phenomenon is typically regarded as multi-dimensional, extending beyond simple income inequality and unemployment. In pursuing this 'wider remit', many commentators have emphasised lack of participation in 'three important spheres of daily life which can trap people in processes of social exclusion: [the] economic, political and cultural' (Cars et al., 1998: 280; see also Bhalla and Lapeyre, 1997; Madanipour, 1998).[5] As Burchardt et al. (2002) point out, however, on this point 'social exclusion' is not wildly different from some older conceptualisations of poverty. Townsend's (1979) classic work on relative deprivation regarded the poor as those who were unable to take part in the normal lifestyles and activities of society.

Secondly, most theories of social exclusion perceive these *different aspects of the phenomenon as being interrelated*. We see this in the Social Exclusion Unit's (1998) emphasis on 'the combination of linked problems' that typifies the condition of social exclusion. Although various commentators give different weight to one or other of these spheres in creating social exclusion, most stress lack of access to employment and the resultant poverty as fundamental in shaping wider forms of exclusion (e.g. Cars et al., 1998; MacKay, 1998). Again, this is typical of Townsend's (1979) approach to poverty, but what is perhaps different here is that the majority of theoretical discussions of social exclusion emphasise the *cumulative* impact of problems in the economic, political and cultural spheres. For instance, Cars et al. argue that, in isolation, social exclusion in any one of these will seldom lead to exclusion in another, but 'when combined they become a strong force pushing people into the processes of social exclusion' (1998: 281).

Littlewood and Herkommer suggest that the 'accumulation of exclusionary effects is most obvious and in fact most visible in the case of its *spatial concentration*' (1999: 16, our emphasis). Thus, the third common element of most conceptions of social exclusion is that 'they widen the focus in another way – beyond individuals and household to communities and neighbourhoods' (Hills, 2002: 228). This socio-spatial focus is to the fore in the work of the Social Exclusion Unit. The coalescence and concentration of multiple social problems in Britain's poorest places have created 'several thousand neighbourhoods and estates whose condition is critical, or soon could be' (1998: 1). Such neighbourhoods have experienced all the 'joined-up' problems of social exclusion and have undergone the spiralling decline that concentrates the problems of poor areas and further separates them from more prosperous ones (Lee and Hills, 1998; Power, 1998; HM Treasury, 1999; Lupton and Power, 2002). Thus, 'the poorest neighbourhoods have tended to become more run down, more prone to crime and more cut off from the labour market' whilst most areas have 'benefited from rising living standards' (Social Exclusion Unit, 1998: 9). This focus highlights the uneven distribution of life-chances and deprivation by area. One of the key dimensions of the social exclusion literature in Europe and the US is thus the geographic polarisation of social constraints and opportunities and the increasing physical and social segregation of affluent and poor areas (with the 'gated communities' and inner-city ghettos of American cities being frequently cited examples; Davies, 1990). The fact that the neighbourhoods of the rich and the poor sometimes exist cheek by jowl heightens the intensity and visibility of social polarisation by place (Toynbee, 2003).

We can now glimpse the fourth distinctive aspect of discussions about social exclusion: a concern with *who*, or *what, is doing the excluding*. Some formulations (e.g. Parkin, 1979) draw on the Weberian idea of social closure and see social exclusion as the outcome of the efforts of one group 'to secure for itself a privileged position at the expense of some other group through a process of subordination' (Burchardt et al., 2002: 2). Jordan's (1998) economic theory of exclusive groups is a good example of this approach. He draws attention to the political economy of social exclusion: how the poor are made so by the organised interests of the economically powerful. Wholeheartedly in this vein, Byrne takes issue with those sociologists (such as Bauman, 1998) that see the new poor and unemployed as now completely irrelevant (as consumers or as producers) to the needs of post-Fordist societies. For Byrne, the socially excluded remain an essential reserve army of labour in such societies (see chapter 6).

Even if they do not go as far as Byrne in seeing social exclusion as a necessary and inevitable feature of such economies, many would agree that processes of economic restructuring are chiefly responsible for the growth of social exclusion in late capitalist societies (e.g. Brown and Crompton, 1994). In tune with more structurally oriented under-class theory, the emphasis here is on the socio-economic causation of social exclusion. The economy is not the only arena in which we can see powerful social forces at work in the creation of exclusion. Others have, for instance, described convincingly the way that the housing market can add to the physical and social polarisation of the poor and the affluent (e.g. Byrne, 1995; Power, 1998; see chapter 8).

The fifth common feature of discussions of social exclusion/inclusion is that they 'are words that draw attention to processes' (Hills, 2002: 228). Becoming socially excluded is a *dynamic process* that happens to individuals over time. Many advocates of the concept therefore employ longitudinal methodologies to chart the changing experiences of individuals and their households across the life-course (e.g. Kiernan, 2002). This focus on the dynamic, processual nature of social exclusion allows researchers to 'take into account the experience of changing situations, of precarious conditions, of being periodically excluded and included' (Littlewood and Herkommer, 1999: 14). Thus, when we talk of an individual as being excluded or otherwise we are more likely to be talking about *the changing degree* to which they are able to participate in society rather than hard-and-fast divisions between the included and excluded. There is an important difference with underclass theory here, as Littlewood and Herkommer point out: 'exclusion is a process, where underclass is a more or less stable situation which results from the exclusionary process' (1999: 14).

Related to this is a concern, sixthly, to observe the potential *inter-generational effects of social exclusion*. A common interest in dynamic, life-course processes, the multiple, cumulative causes and effects of exclusion and their neighbourhood concentration mean that some – understandably – concern themselves with the extent to which the disadvantage associated with social exclusion is passed on from one generation to the next (Hobcraft, 1998; Lee and Hills, 1998; HM Treasury, 1999). There is a clear parallel with conservative underclass theory here. We have noted how the latter tend to emphasise the cultural inheritance of values and behaviours that further entrench the poverty of children born into the underclass and doom them to replicate the same problem families. Those working within the exclusion/inclusion paradigm tend to be more careful about asserting this sort of 'culture of poverty' argument as causative, preferring instead to use large-scale, quantitative data sets to delineate the complex associations between a range of indicators of family and childhood exclusion and later disadvantage (e.g. Hobcraft and Kiernan, 1999; Hobcraft, 2002; Kiernan, 2002).

Some problems with 'social exclusion'

These six themes give a composite description of the concept of social exclusion. Different social scientists emphasise different aspects of the idea and other reviewers sometimes offer different listings of the main components (e.g. Littlewood and Herkommer, 1999). We have also hinted at some of the potential problems with the concept. We will return to a fuller discussion of its usefulness in chapter 10, but for now let us highlight one or two concerns, particularly in relationship to related theories of the underclass.

Although numerous attempts have been made to clarify its meaning, like 'the underclass' before it, it remains 'a contested term' (Hills, 2002: 226). Part of the attraction of the language of social exclusion to politicians and journalists is exactly that it can be used – like 'the underclass' – without intellectual rigour as an easy, imprecise shorthand (Kleinman, 1998). It is attractive because it conveys and appeals to 'common-sense' understandings of the world. An added benefit for New Labour rhetoric is that it appears to drop the victim-blaming ideological and moral connotations that tainted underclass theory.

We say appears to because, for writers such as Kleinman (1998: 9), 'the term "social exclusion" is often used interchangeably with the discredited concept of the "underclass"'. Hall puts it nicely: 'Murray has probably had his day now, but social policy in Britain and the constellation of anxieties and initiatives that circle the preferred term "social exclusion" still bear the imprint of the underclass debate' (2002: 3). Ruth Levitas (1998), one of the strongest critics of the social exclusion paradigm, argues cogently that New Labour thinking on social exclusion fuses competing (and contradictory) political philosophies. Sometimes the dominant theme is the social inclusion of economically marginal groups through paid work, as epitomised by 'welfare to work' programmes such as the New Deal. Levitas calls this the 'social integrationist discourse' of social exclusion (or SID). Less frequently, redistributive policies in the interests of the poor are to the fore of government, as in New Labour's pledge to end child poverty in twenty years through various taxation strategies (the RED discourse). But never far from the surface of the New Labour approach, she argues, is the suspicion that the socially excluded – like Murray's underclass – are morally or culturally responsible for their predicament (this Levitas names the 'moral underclass discourse', or MUD). On coming to power in 1997, Tony Blair announced the government's intention to 'tackle what we all know exists – an underclass of people cut off from society's mainstream, without any shared sense of purpose'(cited in Kleinman, 1998: 7). Although talking of social exclusion here, the following extract from another Blair speech (*ibid.*) reiterates Murray's core ideas:

> It's a very modern problem, and one that is more harmful to the individual, more damaging to self-esteem, more corrosive for society as a whole, more likely to be passed down from generation to generation than material poverty.

A number of writers have also attacked New Labour's ambitions to combat social exclusion via 'social integration' into paid work (e.g. Holden, 1999). Lee and Murie neatly sum up the complaint:

> When social exclusion is closely linked to the labour market a dichotomy is immediately created whereby all those outside the labour market are perceived as excluded whilst those in work are seemingly included ... such a restrictive view of exclusion ignores inequality of incomes and conditions *within* the labour market. (1997: 90, our emphasis)

Two criticisms are implied here. One is that a focus on social inclusion *as social integration* into employment takes our eyes away from more entrenched social divisions such as by social class (see Byrne, 1999). As Levitas (1996: 18) notes, 'the positions into which people are "integrated" through paid work are fundamentally unequal'. Furthermore, emphasising the movement of the unemployed into jobs may have the corollary of de-emphasising the continuing need for wealth redistribution to tackle the poverty faced by those who for whatever reason remain on benefits (Kleinman, 1998).

A second criticism of New Labour's 'social integrationist' discourse is that there is no guarantee that employment will terminate a person's experience of social exclusion. 'Solving' unemployment does not 'solve' social exclusion. The equation of 'in employment' with 'socially included' underpins programmes like the New Deal for Young People, geared, evaluated and funded as it is towards shifting young welfare claimants into jobs. The problem is, though, that many of the jobs into which the unemployed might be helped remain so poorly paid that the new worker remains unable to afford 'normal' patterns of economic (and social) participation. For this reason Byrne (1999) argues that 'welfare to work programmes' represent the state's attempt to force people into 'poor work' in the interests of capitalism. For him, they *add to* rather than resolve problems of social exclusion. This argument becomes even stronger if we consider the insecurity of many of those jobs accessed by those leaving unemployment.

This criticism has chiefly been directed at more political and policy-oriented uses of the concept of social exclusion. Some academic approaches have, however, also come close to replicating this conceptualisation of social exclusion as lack of employment. In a rare attempt to operationalise the concept for empirical research, Burchardt and colleagues (2002) identify four dimensions by which we might measure social exclusion: participation in relation to consumption, to production, to political engagement and to social interaction.[6] Typical of most empirical attempts to research social exclusion, they use the opportunities provided by large-scale, longitudinal data sets (in this case the British Household Panel Survey) to track the changing circumstances of individuals and households as revealed by repeated waves of questionnaire surveys. Their method is one in which 'lack of participation in any one dimension is sufficient for social exclusion' (31). Admittedly the authors go on to examine the degree to which individual's experience of these different dimensions of disadvantage overlap and change over time, but there remains the potential here to count a person as 'excluded' simply because they are not economically active at any one moment.

So, whilst Burchardt and her colleagues are to be applauded for their attempts to put into practice a clearer concept of social exclusion, problems of definition and measurement remain. So far there have been very few studies like this that have sought to research social exclusion in a rigorous way. Even fewer in number are ethnographic studies that seek to understand the descriptive and explanatory value of this concept by taking as a starting point the lived experiences of those people and places that might best reveal the meaning of social exclusion.

Conclusion: unanswered questions

In summary, we suggest that underclass theory – even the more contro-versial, neo-liberal variant offered by Murray and his followers – has neither collapsed under the weight of social scientific critique nor been borne out by research or self-evident social developments. Following Levitas (1998), our view is that underclass theory has become subsumed into the even more widespread and influential political, policy and academic discourse of social exclusion. As we have seen, some of the central ideas of the latter are the same as those of the former. We would also argue with Bagguley and Mann (1992) who suggest that the social scientific engagement with underclass theory in Britain has served to demolish its claims. There are many remaining questions to be answered. The closing pages of this chapter outline these and, in so doing, help explain the perspective of our research on social exclusion and the underclass.

So, whilst our study had underclass theory in its critical sights, that is not to say that we started from the common academic position that underclass theories – even the controversial version offered by Murray – are *necessarily* mistaken. Much of the research that purports to *disprove* underclass arguments has not been methodologically or conceptually sufficient to that task (MacDonald, 1997a; Roberts, 1997a; 2001). Let us take methodological problems first. Putting it baldly, critics of under-class theory have tended to look in the 'wrong' places, at the 'wrong' times, at the 'wrong' people with the 'wrong' methods. Payne and Payne use findings from a large-scale survey of the young unemployed of the 1980s to reject the underclass thesis but, in a telling caveat to their study, they say:

> This is not to deny that in some parts of the country there may already exist minority underclass cultures ... Indeed, if such minority cultures do exist, they are not likely to be identified by large surveys ... which rely on conventional methods of sampling and data collection. (1994: 18)

The point is that many of the cross-sectional surveys of the alleged underclass rely exactly on this sort of sampling. They tend either to select respondents from official but partial records such as electoral rolls and the national census (which is thought to have missed approxi-mately two million people in 2001: *The Guardian*, 1 October 2002) or use dedicated social surveys (as in the case of many of the studies of social exclusion we report). It is quite feasible that those individuals *most likely* to be part of an underclass – or to experience the most extreme forms of social exclusion – are the *least likely* to be either listed on such records or to respond to questionnaire surveys. Even if they were to, it is debatable whether individuals would be keen to tick off answers that depicted them as immoral, indolent and criminal. Resultant findings are therefore likely to be biased against uncovering the alleged underclass. Payne and Payne conclude that underclass culture is unlikely to be 'a general phenomenon amongst the unemployed' (*ibid.*, 18) and most surveys of the socially excluded tend to reach the same conclusion (e.g. Gallie, 1994). But this is not what Murray claims: 'there is an ecology to poverty. Cross-sectional surveys of poor people or of the unemployed are useless in either confirming or disconfirming this hypothesis' (1990: 69). Showing, via incomplete surveys, that most of the poor and unemployed in general do not share underclass characteristics does not mean that some people in some places at some times might not evolve 'underclass cultures'.

If we are to engage properly with underclass theses, and to gather research material that might serve to answer fully its central questions, what is needed are studies which are able to explore in depth the values, activities and outlooks of the most likely members, in the most likely places and during the most likely periods in which underclass phenomena might emerge. Such an approach could provide a promising addition to our *qualitative* understanding of social exclusion and go some way to answering Jordan and Redley's (1994: 156) call for a 'new orientation in research on social exclusion' that would give more room to the 'survival strategies and cultures of resistance' of the poor and economically marginal. Only ethnographic studies at neighbourhood level and of the 'micro experiences of the excluded themselves' (Glennerster et al., 1998, cited in Foster, 2000: 320) are likely to provide the evidence necessary to support or reject underclass theories or to develop richer theories of social exclusion.

Such an approach would also be able to grapple with some of the more conceptual claims and counter-claims in the underclass debate. Ken Roberts provides one of the most careful considerations of the value, or otherwise, of conceptualising the underclass *as a class*. He asks whether underclass theory passes the normal 'class tests': 'first, whether those concerned occupy distinctive work and market situations; second, whether they are a demographic entity with characteristic life chances; and third, whether they have developed a characteristic type of consciousness and political proclivities' (2001: 113).

The hypothesis has little difficulty with the first test, he says. The group concerned are those with severely disadvantaged market situations who are 'unlikely to obtain employment' and whose 'distinctive work situation is having none' (*ibid*.: 113). These are the long-term and/or recurrently unemployed who are the focus for much policy intervention against social exclusion. Roberts suggests that weighing the evidence against the second test produces a less certain answer. Whilst he acknowledges the main argument set against more structural underclass theories – that there is no hard-and-fast divide between those in standard employment, casualised jobs or who are unemployed – he feels this does not invalidate underclass analysis. Class boundaries are often blurred. That its membership comprises disparate groups and that people join via different pathways is also not untypical of classes in formation, he argues. The crucial question, he goes on, is the life-chances that befall those born into this class. He refers to Rutter and Madge's famous study (1976) of cycles of disadvantage not, as most critics of the underclass idea do, to emphasise the intergenerational social mobility of those born into severely disadvantaged families but the opposite: the continuities of disadvantage and exclusion that around half of such people, according to that study, will face in later life. Extrapolating from this and other evidence, Roberts predicts that if the British working class continue to experience widespread worklessness over the coming decades, it is probable that an inter-generationally immobile, core underclass will separate out from the working class.

He admits, however, that underclass theory falls heavily at the third fence. There is currently no evidence available to show that those who might be classed in this way exhibit distinctive class or political consciousness. Some localised, sub-cultural life-styles and coping strategies have been unearthed by ethnographic studies but that these are peculiar to the underclass, widespread among them or political is not the case. That clearer examples of underclass politics and consciousness might emerge in the future is, he acknowledges, pure conjecture.

Overall, then, Roberts concludes that the evidence for the existence of an underclass *as a class* is mixed. We cannot be definitive in our verdict on the underclass question because the process of formation of such a class in Britain would take some decades more. But, he says, it is:

a real future possibility ... an underclass will be created if poor parents rear low-achieving (in education) children who leave school then become chronically unemployed themselves. The creation of an underclass will require those concerned to interact with one another more than they interact with members of other classes, which is likely if they are concentrated in particular districts, and in doing so they are likely to develop a distinctive culture. This may tolerate and transmit skills required for criminal activities and work in the unofficial economies, and lifestyles which the wider society rejects. The consolidation of the underclass will require the second generation to rear yet another generation of heavily disadvantaged children by when the class will be a demographic entity with characteristic life-chances... the above future-gazing is not pure guess work, it is based firmly on our knowledge of the normal condition for, and processes of, class formation. (2001: 117)

Roberts' clear and unusually tolerant discussion of the underclass thesis helps us because it demonstrates the central questions and concerns of both structural and cultural variants *and* the social exclusion paradigm: how economic change and its consequences for poor neighbourhoods – particularly persistent unemployment – might bring forth social and cultural adaptations that harden into ways of life and which themselves become further obstacles to individual progress; the importance of neighbourhoods and their social networks in shaping the legitimate and criminal opportunities and life-styles of the poor; the role of education in reinforcing disadvantage; and the significance of family and parenting in the reproduction of life-chances marked by social, economic and cultural exclusion.

And it is these questions that lie at the heart of this book. In 1994 John Macnicol conjured with the question 'Is there an underclass?' Although he has been one of the most avid critics of underclass theory, he reflected that 'no thoughtful visitor to the now blighted inner city areas of Britain or America, whether Meadowell [in north-east England] or Chicago's South Side, could deny that *something* new and frightening has happened' (1994: 30). We agree. Something profound has certainly changed in the social, economic and community life of Britain's poor neighbourhoods. That the idea of an underclass – or the more recent paradigm of social exclusion – can help us to understand what these changes are, how they have come about and what they mean for young people is, in our view, less certain.

2
Young People, Transitions and Social Change: Researching Disconnected Youth

Introduction

The late 1990s and early 2000s were a favourable period for youth research in the UK, in terms of the amount of academic research funded by research councils and charities and the apparent willingness of government to support applied, youth research (Jones, 2002).[1] This interest in youth studies can be explained, at least in part, by a long-standing, ideological representation of youth 'as/in trouble' (Hebdige, 1988). The twin discourses of 'care' and 'control' have shaped popular, political and academic representations of youth and informed the governance of this social category through successive waves of state intervention (Griffin, 1993). Since the emergence of youth as a recognised age category in the early industrial era, social commentators have constructed young people as a vulnerable group in need of special treatment and care in a hostile adult world and, simultaneously, as an uncivilised, threatening presence requiring discipline and control (Gillis, 1974). Geoff Pearson (1983), for instance, sees societal reactions to the perceived disorderliness of working-class young men in the nineteenth and twentieth centuries as a long-running 'history of respectable fears'. For Stan Cohen (1980), popular reactions to the Mods and Rockers sub-cultures of the 1960s can be understood as media-fuelled moral panics about these new, young 'folk devils'.

Social exclusion and 'status zer0 youth'

Contemporary debates about 'the underclass' and social exclusion provide a classic example of these paradoxical, ideological ways of thinking about youth. Within conservative theses, the archetypal protagonists in the development of this new dangerous class (Morris, 1994) are disaffected, deviant, work-shy young men ('essentially barbarians', to cite Murray 1990) and irresponsible, promiscuous, immoral young women who, together, do no less than threaten 'the survival of free institutions and a civil society' (Murray, 1994: 127). Here, young people in poor neigh-bourhoods *are* the problem to be fixed. More structurally-oriented underclass theses, and much of the policy discussion of social exclusion, position such people as the victims of socio-economic change, as *having* problems to be combated by the multiplicity of policy interventions that now bear down on young people in poor neighbourhoods.

Yet, as we saw in chapter 1, such approaches often implicitly express the same sort of disquiet towards the perceived unconventional values and disorderly life-styles of those at the bottom. The concern of gov-ernment and academics about those sixteen- and seventeen-year-olds 'not in education, employment or training' is a case in point (see Social Exclusion Unit, 1999a). Britton et al. (2002) suggest that at any one time 214,000 young people nationally are likely to be NEET, to use the favoured policy acronym. Istance et al. (1994) estimate that around 20 per cent of the age group are likely to fall into what they prefer to call 'status zer0'.[2] Raffe's study (2003) in Scotland suggested a figure of over 30 per cent. Because of earlier disadvantages, some young people are more at risk of becoming 'status zer0' than others (for example, Black and minority ethnic young people, those with disabilities or special needs, care leavers, young lone mothers, working-class school-leavers). Being 'status zer0' is also said to predict later disadvantage. Not being in education, employment and training at age sixteen is reported to be the most powerful predictor of unemployment in young adulthood and it is also associated with teenage pregnancy and criminal and drug involvement (Social Exclusion Unit, 1999a; Bynner and Parsons, 2002).

'Status zer0' is seen, then, as an important gateway for escalating 'troubles' and has been the single issue which has most exercised, and which most clearly represents, contemporary British policy-making about excluded youth (a focus which, in chapter 10, we suggest is mis-taken). On the one hand, this is a group portrayed as disadvantaged by the restructuring of traditional, class-based pathways to adulthood and excluded from the social and economic advantages that accrue from post-sixteen learning and skills development (i.e. a vulnerable group in need of care). At the same time, these 'idle hands' pose the threat of trouble: a danger that demands intervention and control. Even sensitive sociological accounts, close to the empirical realities of 'status zer0', reflect this twin concern of 'youth in/as trouble':

There is a risk of scare-mongering about the wider social consequences (in terms of, for example, homelessness, drug misuse and criminality) resulting from such long-term marginality to mainstream structures of economic opportunity, but that does not mean they will not materialise... Status zer0 young people, if renewed effort is not made to integrate them into training and labour market structures, may be the first generation for whom the underclass is a social reality rather than a political and ideological device. (Williamson, 1997: 81)

These sort of respectable fears about the social exclusion of young people have been central to recent programmes of youth research in the UK. The majority of projects within both the recent ESRC and JRF programmes (see note 1) were, to different extents, interested in the transitions of vulnerable young people and in processes of social inclusion/exclusion. These central themes are reflective of the broader priorities of these research funders and of a New Labour government that, on coming to office, was keen to make 'evidence-based policy' in respect of the 'one challenge' that stood above all others: 'tackling the scourge and waste of social exclusion' (Mandelson, 1998; see chapter 1). Tellingly, several of the reports first published by the Social Exclusion Unit (SEU) concerned youth issues (1998; 1999a; 1999b) and Coles (2000b) has described the SEU as the midwife of youth policy in the UK.

This chapter will review some of the key recent studies about youth, the underclass and social exclusion. This is embedded in a broader, but necessarily selective, discussion of some key theoretical debates in youth studies. Our argument will be that a broad, holistic understanding of transition is crucial for a proper, in-depth analysis of the processes whereby some young people become 'included' and some do not (see Coles, 2000a; MacDonald et al., 2001). Finally, we discuss the distinctive nature of our research and suggest that this sort of youth study provides an excellent vantage point from which to critique policy analyses of inclusion/exclusion and to engage with broader social scientific debates about social and economic change and reproduction.

Understanding youth transitions

Paradoxically, this materially favourable period for youth studies in Britain has also been one in which it has recently come under considerable intellectual attack, much of it from within. A central theme is that the dominant conceptual approach of most British youth research – the sociological study of youth transitions – is no longer helpful in describing the changing situation of young people (if it ever was). We disagree. In order to set out what *we* mean by the study of youth transitions – and the value we see in this approach – we review here the apparent crystallisation of two traditions of youth research in Britain and some recent criticisms of the concept of transition.[3]

Two traditions of youth research

Bob Coles (1986) was probably the first writer to note how, in the mid-1980s, youth sociology was splitting into two separate trajectories. That youth sociology has developed into two distinct perspectives and that this hampers a more encompassing, useful study of youth are ideas that have now become axiomatic (Jones, 1988; Griffin, 1993; MacDonald et al., 1993; Gayle, 1998; Hollands, 2002). A similar argument applies in the 'new sociology of childhood' with, for instance, contributors arguing for a qualitative understanding of children's agency and cultures in their own right (as opposed to conceiving children as passive recipients of socialisation on predetermined paths of transition) (James and Prout, 1990; Morrow, 2004).

The two youth perspectives can be characterised as the *youth cultural studies tradition* (chiefly associated with the influential work of the Centre for Contemporary Cultural Studies at the University of Birmingham in the mid-1970s) and the *youth transitions tradition* (perhaps typified by the ESRC's '16 to 19 Initiative' at the beginning of the 1990s). As the 1970s gave way to the 1980s, several factors influenced the turn away from theoretically-driven, ethnographic studies of youth sub-cultural style and resistance (e.g. Hall and Jefferson, 1976; Hebdige, 1979) towards more empirically and policy-oriented accounts of school-to-work transitions (e.g. Roberts, 1984; Walker and Barton, 1986). One factor was the emergent, critical assessment of the CCCS's work. In what is still one of the most insightful critiques of sub-culture theory, Gary Clarke questioned

> the value of decoding the stylistic appearances of particular tribes during a period in which young adults are the prime victims of a state policy of manufactured unemployment... the time has come to turn our eyes away from the stylistic art of a few. (1982: 1)

Empirical changes in the youth situation also motivated a shift away from cultural studies towards more 'social problems' oriented approaches (Griffin, 1993). From 1980 onwards – with the advent of Thatcherism, the 'collapse' of the youth labour market, soaring youth unemployment and the expansion of youth training schemes – the academic gaze settled on the changing *structural* situation of young people and the steps they took from school to work (or unemployment and schemes). With the demise of punk apparently signalling the end of the post-war parade of resistant sub-cultures, youth *cultures* seemed less interesting and pressing to sociologists (and their funding bodies) than young people's 'fractured' transitions to adulthood. According to Roberts:

> youth's new condition led to a boom in youth research, mostly policy-oriented research, which was weak on theory but strong in counting and profiling those experiencing education, training, jobs and unemployment, then charting their next steps. (1997b: 62)

In the 1980s, then, the study of youth transitions became the main preoccupation of youth sociology and the questionnaire surveying of cohorts of school-leavers, rather than ethnographic observation of sub-cultural groups, became the dominant methodology. The early 1990s brought some reanimation of youth cultural studies, largely as a response to the reanimation of youth culture itself. This 'new cultural turn' has coalesced around a common interest in vibrant and diverse club cultures and the proliferation of fragmented and ephemeral youth cultural styles, 'scenes' and 'neo-tribes' (Redhead, 1993; 1997; Thornton, 1995; Bennett, 1999, 2000; Malbon, 1999; Muggleton, 2000). These authors distance themselves from the class-based theory of the CCCS (and the more general interest in social inequalities found in transitions research). Postmodern theory and participant observation are distinctive features of this new trend in youth cultural studies. That said, some of the latest and most interesting work 'after sub-culture' has signalled critical re-engagement with, rather than rejection of, those older youth cultural theories that were rooted in an understanding of social divisions (see Hodkinson, 2002; Hollands, 2002; Pilkington and Johnson, 2003; Shildrick, 2003; Bennett and Kahn-Harris, 2004).

This division still maintains and youth cultural studies remain marginal to the main(stream) thrust of the field. The ESRC 'Youth, Citizenship and Social Change' programme was again dominated by transitions studies, even though the early research agendas argued that youth culture and identity would be integrated as core research themes (Bynner et al., 1997). It is important to stress that we describe *general trends* here. The separation of 'structural' from 'cultural' analysis has never been absolute whether at the level of individual projects or in the field of youth studies as a whole. For example, some of the work associated with the CCCS placed particular emphasis on combining cultural ethnography with a structural analysis of youth's economic and political condition (e.g. Hall et al., 1977; Willis, 1977). A number of studies that had the restructured youth transitions of the 1980s and 1990s as their main subject simultaneously used qualitative approaches to access the lived, cultural experiences of youth (e.g. Griffin, 1985; Brown, 1987; Hollands, 1990; Bates and Riseborough, 1993; Blackman, 1995).

By the turn of the century, however, the perceived marginality of more 'lively', ethnographic and theoretically-driven studies of young people's cultures and identities – and the perceived hegemony of 'dry', quantitative, empiricist and policy-driven mappings of school-to-work transitions – led some in the field to argue that youth studies has come to a parlous, near-moribund state (Jeffs and Smith, 1998; Cohen and Ainley, 2000; Miles, 2000). According to Miles, such trends threaten the 'very authenticity of the sociology of youth' (2000: 11).

These critics offer different prescriptions for 'the way forward'. Most of them, though, would agree with Cohen and Ainley that youth studies needs to carve out 'a third space between a narrow empiricist focus on transitions and a quasi-anthropological concern with exotic instances of youthful deviance and difference' (2000: 88–9). Whilst there is much in their separate critiques with which we would concur, we are more concerned with assessing their depiction of 'the problem' of youth studies. They argue that the overriding failing of youth sociology over the past twenty years has been its preoccupation with 'transition'. Cohen and Ainley (2000: 80) lambaste what they perceive as the 'narrowly restricted' economism of a 'series of repetitive and redundant...transitions studies'. Miles argues that:

> The tendency...to adopt a structural perspective on transitions has been counter-productive, primarily because of its failure to prioritize the actual views, experiences, interests and perspectives of young people as they see them...[T]he most damaging problem with the 'transitions debate' is that it has tended to take young people out of the youth equation...treat[ing] young people as troubled victims of economic and social restructuring without enough recourse to the active ways in which young people negotiate such circumstances in the course of their every day lives...(2000: 10)

Fergusson et al. (2000) are less damning, but also question the idea that there is now a mainstream transition and that the post-sixteen years are made up of orderly, logical and linear stages towards adulthood. A significant minority of teenagers in their study followed flexible, non-traditional pathways through the multiplicity of options now available in post-sixteen education, employment and training markets. Cohen and Ainley make a similar point: 'young people simply do not view work and study in the linear sequential way implied...images about "pathways" and linear transitions from school via further study and then into the world of work and an independent adult way of life do not reflect the actual experience of growing up' (2000: 83).

Contrary to these critics, we would wish to *reassert* the value of the transitions perspective. The model of transitions studies that these writers attack is one that we do not recognise as holding the sort of sway in the field that they suggest. What they present is a narrow and largely outdated picture of the nature of transition studies that underplays the theoretical potential of contemporary studies of youth transition.

The restructuring of youth transitions in the UK

In simple terms, youth transitions can be understood as the pathways that young people make as they leave school and encounter different labour market, housing and family-related experiences as they progress towards adulthood. The relative influence of individual choice (i.e. a young person's active decision-making) and social structural constraint (e.g. the 'structure of opportunities' prevailing for young people in a particular place and time) has been much debated in youth studies – as elsewhere in sociology – and is reflected in the ongoing search for the most appropriate metaphor to describe the general shift from childhood dependence to adult independence (Jones and Wallace, 1992). 'Trajectories', 'pathways', 'routes', 'journeys' and 'navigations' find favour with different authors, with versions that suggest greater degrees of individual agency becoming more prominent in the latter part of the 1990s (see Evans and Furlong, 1997; Hodkinson and Sparkes, 1999; Cieslik and Pollock, 2002).

Few disagree, however, with the general argument that the nature of youth transitions in the UK has altered radically over the past thirty years. Of primary interest to youth sociologists, particularly during the 1980s and early 1990s, has been the economic aspect of transition: what has become known as the 'school-to-work' career. Numerous accounts have plotted how young people – differentiated by social class, gender, ethnicity, locality and education – follow different paths during the late teenage years as they leave school, enter the labour market and seek adult statuses and identities (e.g. Banks et al., 1992). All stress how school-to-work careers – especially for working-class youth – have been transformed by a series of interrelated social and economic developments (Roberts, 1995; Mizen, 2003). These include: the virtual collapse of the youth labour market (from the early 1980s) and the sharp decline in the number of jobs and apprenticeships for skilled employment for young people; persistent, regionally concentrated, structural unemployment, particularly during the 1980s and early 1990s; the introduction of wide-spread youth training provision and employment preparation programmes; a range of 'reforms' which have reduced young people's entitlement to state welfare benefits; and the expansion of opportunities in Further Education (FE) and Higher Education (HE) for young people who might previously have been unlikely to continue in post-compulsory education.

Of primary importance in understanding the restructuring of youth transitions is the first of these. The others – to some degree – have been developed in response to the decline in labour market opportunities for young people. To describe the consequences of these changes for young people, sociologists have variously conjured with notions of 'long', 'broken', 'extended', 'protracted', 'uneasy' and 'fractured' transitions to describe the resultant extension of the youth phase. Young people now experience longer periods of dependency on parents and have delayed access to the identities and activities which were previously regarded as signifying adult status (e.g. earning a wage, leaving the parental home, the establishment of long-term partnerships, parenthood). Youth transitions in the UK are beginning to emulate more closely transitions in continental Europe and the US, and Jones and Wallace (1992) suggest that, increasingly, British youth also 'enjoy' a 'post-adolescent' life phase, free from the traditional demands of adulthood.

Individualised transitions?

Most would agree with the empirical description presented above. More contentious are the theoretical conclusions that have been layered upon it. Those keen to argue that we have moved, or are moving, into a postmodern era look to the young for evidence (e.g. Featherstone, 1991; Fornas, 1995; Epstein, 1998; Wallace and Kovacheva, 1998). Examining the youth phase for breaks with traditional patterns of social reproduction and scrutinising young people for signs of new consumption- (rather than class-) based identities might substantiate theoretical claims about the decline of grand meta-narratives of modernity (cf. Lyotard, 1984; Baudrillard, 1988). As noted earlier, various studies of contemporary youth culture in the Britain are written from exactly this theoretical perspective.

Most influential in youth transitions research of late have been the ideas of Giddens (1990; 1991) and Beck (1992), who concede that social life has undergone profound change but are less willing to accept that we have experienced a complete, epochal break with the modernist period.

Summarised by Cieslik and Pollock (2002: 3), the argument is that the social divisions associated with modernity no longer have such a hold on young people's identities, outlooks and activities:

> In the place of these collective guides and traditional institutions are much more individualized identities and biographies where individuals have a greater scope beyond traditional markers of class, race and gender to create complex subjectivities and lifestyles.

According to Beck, contemporary risk societies are typified by greater opportunities for individual action and decision-making but which, because of this, involve increased risks. Young people are required to adopt calculative, strategic and reflexive personalised strategies towards the new risks and opportunities of the post-school world rather than to follow the obsolete 'solutions' traditionally associated with their collective class, ethnic or gender identities. In this context of 'reflexive modernisation', individualised transitions predominate.

Furlong and Cartmel (1997) consider theories of reflexive modernisation, the Risk Society and individualisation as they pertain to youth. They agree that life-chances and lifestyles have become more individualised, fragmented, risky, unpredictable and *apparently* disconnected from the collective sources of identity and action associated with the Fordist heydays of the 1950s and 1960s. Opportunities for choice are myriad and recurrent; in particular, the opening up of access for greater numbers of 'non-traditional' students to FE and HE has been emancipatory. They conclude, however, that more complex, extended transitions present risks which are disproportionately borne by those sections of the youth population with the least resources with which to deal with them (Bates and Wilson, 2004). The *sense* of individual autonomy engendered by such transitions obscures the fact that existing social divisions are only being reproduced in different ways. We return to these ideas in chapter 10.

Wider aspects of transition

Critics of youth studies, and of the concept of transition in particular, have complained about its 'bland discussions, most commonly of trends in employment and education patterns' (Miles, 2000: 10). It is certainly the case that if any one topic dominates UK youth research – over the past few decades and still – it is the study of school-to-work transitions.

That said, the last ten years have witnessed attempts both to broaden the subject matter and to give greater theoretical space to the agency of young people in the making of transitions. The sociological concept of 'career' (Becker, 1963; Berger and Berger, 1972) has been used to explore the way that individual decision-making, informed by the cultures from which young people originate (and the sub-cultures they originate themselves), interacts with the structured opportunities facing people as they move through the youth phase to create individual, and shared, paths of transition (Coles, 1995; Hodkinson and Sparkes, 1997). There is more to becoming adult – and to understanding youth – than movement into the labour market. Broadening the focus allows us to see the interdependent influences on transition of school-to-work, family (e.g. from being a child to being a parent) and housing careers (e.g. the movement to independent living) (Roberts, 2000; Heath and Kenyon, 2001). For instance, with delayed access to the material resources provided by steady employment and entitlement to full state welfare now delayed to the age of 25, the attainment of other key markers of adult status, such as the formation of independent households, partnerships and new families may also be postponed (Jones and Wallace, 1992). Alternatively, such status passages may be 'decoupled' in that the achievement of one (such as parenting) is no longer (perceived as) dependent on the other (e.g. the getting of steady employment) (Jones, 2002).

That youth research should strive towards a more holistic study of transitions, over a period more extended than the years immediately following school-leaving, has, then, become a common call of late (Coles, 2000a). For instance, the ESRC programme of youth research included projects that examined aspects of school-to-work (e.g. Dolton et al., 2002), housing (e.g. Ford et al., 2002) and family careers (e.g. Quinton et al., 2002). Some, including this one, strove to unravel the interrelationships between these different aspects of youth transition (e.g. Lister et al., 2002; Thomson et al., 2002a). Although we agree with Roberts (2000: 6) that 'it is impossible to explain what is occurring elsewhere until the sub-structure of young people's lives (their school-work and family/housing transitions) has been analysed properly', we also recognise the importance of studies that have pushed the boundaries of transitions research even further. Valentine et al. (2002) and Skelton (2002), for instance, identify sexuality and dis/ability as sources of identity and disadvantage in the marginalisation of young people. Our study also stresses the importance of criminal and drug-using careers to understanding some youth transitions (Johnston et al., 2000; Stephen and Squires, 2003) and the interconnection of these with what we might call 'leisure careers' (Shildrick, 2000; see chapter 4).

That transitions research is dominated by the study of school-to-work careers has not been the only complaint made about this body of work.

Broadening out the subject matter, giving greater emphasis to young people's agency and exploring the more complicated patterns that are then observed, will not dispel all criticisms. For instance, a point made by several writers has been that the concept of transition implies the pursuit of orderly, logical steps that cohere into a linear, progressive movement towards adulthood. Instead, transitions are marked by false starts, backward steps, unpredictability and circularity (Furlong, 2000; EGRIS, 2001; Bagnoli, 2003). One of the present authors noted this in an earlier youth study:

> it is often immensely difficult to identify a coherent, unitary or linear trajectory from the mess and jumble of individual's biographies. Life is not as simple as the step-by-step model implied in this approach. (MacDonald and Coffield, 1991: 92)

Similar observations have been made by others (e.g. Craine, 1997; Hodkinson and Sparkes, 1997; Raffo and Reeves, 2000). Johnston et al. (2000), for example, show how young people are often involved in fast-changing and multiple training, educational and labour market statuses *over time*, and participate with some of these different activities *at the same time*. The recent critics of youth transition studies (e.g. Skelton, 2002) are also correct that some still operate with normative models of a 'better', 'successful' path to adulthood that all should follow – irrespective of the value placed on such routes by different social groups of young people – deviation from which signals 'failure', or at least the risk of 'failure' (e.g. Dolton et al., 1999)

In short, we agree with many of the separate, critical comments ranged against the concept of transition. We disagree, however, with the view that this means sociologists of youth should abandon transition studies. Because sociologists have reached for a variety of adjectives ('long', 'fractured') to try to convey the way that transitions have been restructured – or that other periods of the life-course also involve important transitions – does not mean that we need to follow Jeffs and Smith (1998) in despairing of the whole idea of transitions *per se*. Discovering *empirically* that the transitions that some young people make are messy and complicated, and that the steps taken sometimes lead sideways or backwards, does not require that we jettison the *concept* of transition. Concluding that transitions have been extended into other life-phases, and that the destinations to which they lead are now less clear and less easily obtainable for some, does not mean that they are any less interesting (as implied by Cohen and Ainley, 2000).

For us, 'transition' is useful as a general, overarching concept; a metaphor that does not presume a particular sort of content, direction or length at the level of individual experience. It is a heuristic device valuable in organising our enquiries. Because the details of individual youth transitions are often unpredictable and change in relation to wider societal and historical developments this presents empirical questions for sociological investigation. The primary sociological, political and policy relevance of the study of youth lies in the fact that youth *remains* a critically important period in which life chances are established.

Processes of transition, exclusion and inclusion

The concept of transition predisposes us towards studying youth as *a life-phase* and the shifting social, economic and cultural processes that shape it. This is what gives 'youth' any meaning. As Roberts puts it: 'youth is a life stage, neither the first nor the last, and as such is inherently transitional' (2000: 3). Experiences in childhood, of course, impact dramatically on the later outcomes of individuals. It is in youth, however – when individuals first encounter the wider institutions of social and economic (re)production outside of their family of origin – that the nature and direction of this transition solidifies and becomes difficult to change (Jones, 2002). Whilst the consequences of the school-to-work, family and other careers that make up youth transitions are not completely irrevocable, most find it difficult to escape them in adulthood.[4] Of course, youth sociology is more than the study of individual fortunes. For us, the appeal of youth sociology is that it offers a privileged vantage point from which to glimpse processes of social structural formation and transformation and, as such, to generate analyses of theoretical relevance beyond the confines of youth studies.

There is an obvious homology between many of the core debates about the concept of transition and the concept of social exclusion. Both emphasise the importance of understanding processes, particularly economic ones, in shaping individual's life-chances and destinations and yet both also seek to cast the analytic net beyond labour market experience to allow a more holistic, 'joined-up' analysis. The importance placed on locality in discussions of social exclusion echoes a long-standing concern in youth research to investigate how local socio-economic and cultural conditions influence youth transitions (e.g. Ashton et al., 1982). We have seen how underclass theories and discussions of social exclusion have paid particular attention to the youth phase, and to young people as a social group, in the reproduction of social disadvantage and in the production of new social divisions. In summary, then, we remain convinced of the value of the study of transitions, broadly understood, in our attempts to engage critically with underclass theses and to comprehend processes of social exclusion/inclusion. These sets of theories suggest the central questions of our book. Have particular sections of the youth population become disconnected from mainstream opportunities and life-styles? To what extent do popular and influential theories about disadvantaged youth really connect with their lived experiences of transition? In order to answer them we undertook research which focused on the people, places and processes in which social exclusion might take its most extreme form and in which 'underclass' cultures are most likely to be found (Roberts, 1997a; MacDonald, 1997a).

Researching 'excluded' youth: a critical case study

Our research was conducted in the council estates of 'East Kelby' in the conurbation of Teesside, in north-east England. This place provided the opportunity for a critical case study of youth transitions in a context of severe social exclusion.

Deindustrialisation on Teesside

Teesside is a place that, in the latter part of the twentieth century, went from 'boom to bust in quick time' (Foord, 1985) as the 'old economy was swiftly and ruthlessly torn apart by international competitive pressures in the 1970s and 1980s' (Beynon et al., 1994: 9). Virtually full employment in skilled, relatively well-paid manual jobs (for men) gave way to widespread unemployment. The reduction and restructuring of steel, chemical and heavy engineering industries – the historic mainstays of the local economy – led to a remarkable jettisoning of jobs. Between the mid-1970s and mid-1980s one-quarter of all jobs in (what was then called) the county of Cleveland were lost. In the same period, half of all those employed in manufacturing and construction were made redundant (Cleveland County Council, 1986).

Detailed accounts of the restructuring of Teesside's economy and its social consequences are available elsewhere (Foord, 1985; Hudson, 1986; 1989b; Beynon et al., 1989; 1994; MacDonald and Coffield, 1991). An over-concentration of employment in a narrow range of large, manufacturing industries was bolstered by a state regional policy that purposefully sought to limit employment diversification in order to safeguard labour supply to ICI and British Steel. This made the local economy particularly vulnerable to the (inter)national recessions of the early 1970s and to increased global competition in manufacturing production. By the 1980s,

Teesside – once world-famous for its industrial prowess – became notorious for having among the highest levels of unemployment in Britain.

The past twenty years have seen a partial recovery of employment, with local fortunes mirroring national cycles of economic recession and expansion. Efforts to encourage inward investment in the north-east of England, from overseas and other parts of the UK, have provided some employment gains, but worries remain about whether these branch plants will merely become the 'disposable global outposts of multi-national corporations' (Robinson, 1990: 53). Although employment in traditional industries remains vital, key companies – such as Corus (the Dutch-owned successor to British Steel) and ICI – remain vulnerable and have periodically initiated new rounds of redundancies during the 1990s and 2000s. As with the national economy, service sector employment has grown rapidly and now provides the majority of jobs bringing about an increasing feminisation of the workforce (Brown, 1997). This development has particular resonance in a place like Kelby because the historical 'dominance of male-centred extractive and heavy manu-facturing employment was accompanied by a near-total lack of waged employment opportunities for women' (Beynon et al., 1994: 21). As these authors go on to explain, however, much of the new service (and manufacturing) sector employment is part-time, low-waged, low-skilled 'routine work taken up by women eager for a wage despite the condi-tions' and who need to combine employment with domestic work (*ibid.*: 155). Service sector work is also now increasingly vulnerable to global relocation, as recent high-profile instances of the exportation of call-centre work to the Indian sub-continent attest (Denny, 2003). As in many other 'post-industrial' urban centres, 'non-traditional', hyphenated forms of employment proliferate: temporary-work, part-time work, casual-work and self-employment replace the long-term, full-time jobs typical of this place in the long, postwar boom (Beynon, 1997; see chapter 6).

The increased and continuing availability of this 'poor work' in service and manufacturing sectors has not been sufficient to eradicate unemploy-ment and, since the economic crisis of the 1970s, Teesside has consistently recorded levels of unemployment of at (at least) twice the national average. As a consequence, Teesside has been the subject of repeated rounds of government programmes for socio-economic regeneration (e.g. an Urban Development Corporation, City Challenge, the Single Regeneration Budget, New Deal for Communities, Sure Start) and the town of Kelby is possibly the only in England to have simultaneously been dealt the full hand of government Employment, Health and Education Action zones. Although the reasons for its decline may be 'most untypical'

(Hudson, 1986: 13),[5] Teesside is a place that displays the socio-economic *consequences* of deindustrialisation in ways that will be familiar to students of the failure of 'old industrial regions' and 'rust-belt' cities of Britain and elsewhere (Beynon et al., 1989; Hudson, 1989a; Byrne, 1999). That said, the speed and scope of economic change here have been particularly dramatic. We can think of few other places in the UK that have experienced such a rapid reversal of fortunes and such an extreme upheaval in the organisation of economic life.

East Kelby: social exclusion *in extremis*

Because Teesside is 'one of the most de-industrialised locales in the UK', Byrne worries that it is a 'limiting case' for sociological analysis (1999: 93). For our purposes, the opposite is true. We chose to locate our research in East Kelby exactly because it appeared to be a place that displayed the problems and processes associated with debates about the underclass and social exclusion in extreme form.

Most of the council housing of East Kelby was constructed post-1945, close to the steel foundries and chemical plants in which many of the original residents worked. Our pseudonyms for these five wards (Orchard Bank, Primrose Vale, Meadowfields, Riverside, Brookville) have retained the pastoral air of their real ones, named after the farms and green land on which these estates were built (Lock, 1945). About 30,000 people live there currently. Gladstone characterises Teesside as 'an industrial area: no more, no less' (1976: 39, cited in Beynon et al., 1994: 22) and, like Kelby itself, these are neighbourhoods that wholly owe their existence to the needs of recent capitalist development. Astonishingly, the population of Kelby amounted to only 40 people in 1820 but, as a near-contemporaneous account describes, 'the field for labour [that was] suddenly opened up by the discovery of iron' inspired a 'breathless and tumultuous... change in the conditions of the district' which became 'swamped under a great rush from all parts of the country' whose 'main objective of life [was] to be at work' (Bell, 1985: 2–3). During the nineteenth century Kelby was the fastest growing town in England, with slum houses thrown up to accommodate the massive influx of manual workers arriving to work in the 90 new iron foundries that ringed the Tees (Briggs, 1963). By the mid-twentieth century many of these streets in the old core of the town were demolished and households moved to new 'garden village', suburban estates like those of East Kelby.[6] Further evidence for Kelby being a 'company town' can be found in the fact that preference in council lettings on these estates was given to employees of ICI (Beynon et al., 1994: 64).

As recently as the 1960s, the economic success of Teesside underpinned social cohesion and stability. Kelby was a place that 'worked', albeit in ways that reinforced classic, industrial divisions of labour and gender relations. By the end of the century, when this research took place, East Kelby had become a place redolent of 'social exclusion'. The town of Kelby has the highest concentration of the most deprived wards in the country. The economic shocks of the 1970s and 1980s hit the residents of East Kelby particularly hard, producing 'pockets of severe social stress' (*ibid.*: 122). All of its five wards can be now characterised as 'poverty wards' (Glennerster et al., 1999). In a list of the 8,414 wards in the country, two of them – Primrose Vale and Orchard Bank – rank in the top five most deprived (and all are in the top 5 per cent) (DETR, 2000). In other words, East Kelby is a very disadvantaged part of a very disadvantaged town.

East Kelby has some of the lowest levels of educational achievement and progression to post-sixteen education in the country (see chapter 3). Rather than continuing in education, or entering training or employment, many school leavers enter 'status zer0'. In 2000, between 25 and 35 per cent of East Kelby young people were in this position six months after leaving school (Kelby Partnership, 2003). Joblessness[7] persists at high levels in Kelby and East Kelby. For instance, in 2003, 53 per cent of Orchard Bank residents were counted as jobless (compared with 32 per cent nationally (*ibid.*; see chapter 6). In addition to problems of educational underachievement and joblessness, of all the families with dependent children in Kelby, 53 per cent are headed by a lone parent (compared with 40 per cent nationally, according to the 2001 census) (see chapter 7). Poor health blights the area too. The average standard mortality ratio for 1994–98 (which compared actual deaths with what might be expected against a national average of 100) showed Kelby to have a figure of 114. Primrose Vale had the highest mortality ratio in the town at 169. Car crime, burglary and drug-related offending blighted Teesside during the 1990s (Kelby Borough Council, 1999; Johnston et al., 2000) and Kelby is still regarded as one of the worst areas in the country in these respects (Home Office, 2003).

In short, East Kelby suffers from all the 'joined-up' problems of social exclusion and has undergone the spiralling decline that concentrates the problems of poor areas and further separates them from more prosperous ones (Wilson, 1987; Power, 1998; Lee and Hills, 1998). East Kelby contains good, if extreme, examples of the 'several thousand neighbourhoods and estates whose condition is critical, or soon could be' (Social Exclusion Unit, 1998: 1). If we are unable to locate the sort of deviant and dangerous cultures described by underclass theory in the places that we looked, among the people that we talked to, using the methods that we selected, it would be unlikely to find them anywhere in Britain.[8]

Research participants and fieldwork

The fieldwork, which was undertaken between late 1998 and mid-2000, had three strands. The first was 40 interviews with people who worked with young people and/or problems of social exclusion (e.g. probation officers, drugs workers, New Deal advisers, youth workers). These 'stakeholder' interviews had a number of purposes, but were chiefly to facilitate access from them, as 'gatekeepers', to young people who might take part in the research.

The second strand of fieldwork comprised a form of participant observation, whereby one of the authors spent time with groups of young people in youth clubs, unwaged groups, Family Centres and 'on the street'.[9] Dropping into these places on a regular basis, over a year, chatting informally with those present and spending time travelling around East Kelby by bus proved to be an effective way of getting recognised by, and to recognise, some of its young residents. It helped develop at least a degree of acceptance of us by young people. A number of interviewees were recruited in this way. More important was the opportunity for casual observation of, and discussion with, young people. The resultant field-notes helped to contextualise, and weigh up, the claims and comments of interview-based accounts.

The third and main element of the fieldwork was a series of qualitative, semi-structured interviews with 88 young people, aged between 15 and 25 years (although some were older than 25 by the time of second interviews). These biographically focused interviews explored experiences of transition to generate holistic, narrative accounts of the processes that led young people to their current situation. They also surveyed individuals' views of the future and their neighbourhoods and solicited discussions of what the research literature told us were the most important topics for theories of the underclass and social exclusion. Interviews usually lasted for at least an hour, but often were considerably longer, were audio-recorded and transcribed verbatim. They mostly took place in people's homes, but also in the offices of training programmes, in Young Offenders Institutions, in schools and colleges, workplaces, and so on. They were usually conducted on a one-to-one basis but occasionally with a pair or small group of young people, if this was most convenient for informants.

Those we interviewed can be understood as a theoretical sample (Brewer, 2000). Individuals were recruited purposefully so as to reflect a wide range of experiences pertinent to social exclusion. The sample is, therefore, not statistically representative. It included, for instance, youth trainees, lone parents, employees, young offenders, school pupils, clients of drug advice centres, the unemployed, college students and New Deal participants. The sample spanned the 15–25-year-old age range and included 45 females and 43 males, allowing for some comparisons by age and gender. Virtually all were ethnically white and from working-class family backgrounds (i.e. typical of the population of East Kelby). They were recruited via the first two fieldwork strands and through 'snowballing', whereby an interviewee would suggest possible others. The fieldwork strove to follow the British Sociological Association's guidelines on research ethics (Brewer, 2000). None of the research was covert; we believe participants took part on the basis of informed consent and we have attempted to preserve the confidentiality of accounts by anonymising all real names (e.g. of people, of agencies and of places within the immediate environment of the study).

Second interviews within a year of the first updated us on the progress of the sample and probed further about emergent findings. Techniques to limit 'sample attrition' (e.g. entry to a cash prize draw for those who undertook two interviews) helped us to re-interview 60 per cent of the original sample. A few declined but most of those 'lost' were so because they had had changed address and/or phone numbers. We gave informants several opportunities to take part in repeat interviews, but there is an ethical question about the extent to which research should endlessly pursue individuals who might prefer not to be contacted again. Notwithstanding the general problems reported in reaching 'excluded youth' for research or policy purposes (Merton, 1998; Bentley and Gurumurthy, 1999; Britton et al., 2002), we feel that we generated a sample that was large and varied enough (for a qualitative study) to give a relatively rare insight into processes of social exclusion from the point of view of a social group most affected by them.

Analysing biographical accounts

The recent turn toward biographical methods in social science has been inspired by interest in 'the changing experiences and outlooks of individuals in their daily lives, what they see as important and how to provide interpretations of the accounts they give of the past, present and future' (Roberts, 2002: 1). Given our earlier conceptualisation of transition, the fact that interviewing was our main methodological strategy and our preference for understanding processes of exclusion/inclusion from the point of view of those experiencing them, our choice of a generally biographical approach seems obvious. A fuller, more sophisticated exposition of the sociological promise of the biographical method is presented by Chamberlayne et al. (2002). Their study of social exclusion in Europe shares many of our primary research interests and elegantly details the sort of approach to which we have aspired:

> Biographical studies of individual citizens are a valuable means of exploring the conditions of life in rapidly changing societies. In particular, these studies can illuminate the experiences and problems of *transitions* from one social situation and milieu to another... although our focus was on individual 'life journeys' our aim from the start was to explore the connections between these and their larger social contexts... (Rustin and Chamberlayne, 2002: 2)

This final point is a critical one. The twists and turns of individual life-stories are not the outcome of pure human agency, nor are they purely individual phenomena. The interrogation and comparison of detailed accounts of individual's lives – in this case of 'socially excluded' young adults – allows us to comprehend the shared social conditions and objective constraints against which these life stories are made and how these were perceived and responded to in similar and different ways by our informants.

Biographical research, like qualitative research in general, is characterised by relative openness (Roberts, 2002); by interview methods, for instance, that allow for the discussion of issues not pre-figured in the researcher's agenda of questions. So, whilst our own interview schedules were geared towards central debates in respect of the underclass and social exclusion, interviewees often led us into discussion of topics that were not expected. The quantitative and qualitative significance in the interviews of discussions about heroin use and its impact on social life in these neighbourhoods was, for instance, a real surprise to us (see chapters 8 and 9).[10]

These interviews gathered informants' understandings of their earlier lives, how things happened as they did (the content and sequencing of events) and their experience and explanations of them at the time and now, in retrospect. The first stage of analysis of these longitudinal processes involved constructing 'life-grids' for each individual (Easton and Heggie, 2003). These mapped biographies, year by year from late childhood/ early teenage, by six 'careers' that appeared from our reading of the transcripts and from relevant previous studies (e.g. Johnston et al., 2000) to be important in understanding patterns of transition: that is, school-to-work, family, housing, criminal, drug-using and leisure careers (subsequent chapters focus on each of these). To each of the 'cells' created by this grid we added abbreviated notes and striking bits of quotation that seemed to capture what was going on in the interviewee's life at that time.

These 'life grids' proved a very useful aide-mémoire for us in our efforts to think about each case (i.e. summarising many pages of transcript) and every case (rather than just the most memorable ones) and to check the details of their particular life histories when we came to write about them. Importantly, they provided the opportunity to 'see' informant's lives in the round, to consider their current situation in relation to previous experience and, significantly, how events and 'critical moments' (Thomson et al., 2002b) in one sphere of their lives (say, in respect of family career) might have knock-on effects elsewhere (e.g. in terms of school-to-work career). This form of analysis – casting backwards to explain current life-situations and looking to the future from current vantage points – reflected the form of questioning in interviews and allowed for insights into multiple processes of transition over time understood from the informant's point of view.

Alongside this form of biographical, quasi-longitudinal analysis we undertook a more standard, cross-sectional, qualitative comparison of key themes *across* the interviews, following the inductive principles of grounded theory (Bryman and Burgess, 1994). It was geared towards getting a clear(er) picture – from several thousand pages of highly detailed, 'raw' transcripts – of how individuals experienced and talked about the process of growing up in poor neighbourhoods. This coding, 'cut up' and comparison of sections of transcript gave access to recurrent themes and divergent responses from all interviews. Using biographical and cross-sectional analysis, proved to be, we think, a particularly powerful way of understanding youth transitions.

We acknowledge, however, that the easy description given above brushes over long-standing debates in qualitative methodology (and some newer ones about the particulars of biographical methods). For instance, it hides a complicated, unobservable process whereby we necessarily gave priority to some interview extracts rather than others, at times favoured our own interpretations over those of individual interviewees and presented as evidence in this book only a small portion of the things that were said to us. On the same theme, we have chosen to use directly in this book only a very small portion of what was told to us by 'stakeholder' interviewees. This partly reflects limitations of space, partly a conclusion post-fieldwork that this was best understood as contextual 'data', and partly a political preference to prioritise the accounts of young people themselves, not those with a vested interest in 'managing' youth transitions and the problems of 'excluded youth'. This population and the place they are from have plenty of voices speaking against them (with Murray, in particular, springing to mind). Less often are their own accounts heard. Like other research in the ethnographic tradition, then, we are open to the charge of partiality (Brewer, 2000).

This leads us to the other, most important methodological question that bears on research of this sort: the epistemological status of interview accounts. In brief, we do not take the strong realist view that young people's accounts provide a direct, unproblematic representation of the empirical events and experiences to which they refer. Nor, however, would we follow those social theorists who would 'deny there is something beyond the accounts that people give' (May, 1993: 107): that is, the constructionist position that holds that interviews are only really of value in understanding the discursive and conversational techniques used by people to create accounts. Our position is, we think, close to what Hammersley calls 'subtle realism' (1992: 53). That is, we accept that more goes on in interviews than the telling of the truth of lived experience. For instance, our interviews – however loosely structured – demanded implicitly that informants recall and recapitulate particular events, experiences, memories and feelings in ways that at least attempted to make some sort of narrative sense (to them and us). This post-hoc narrative structuring is then, at least in part, a construction of the interview (even if they had undertaken such story-telling on other occasions).[11] Putting aside the simple problems that people sometimes forget things, that – as we noted earlier – youth transitions are often messy and jumbled and that some people are more skilled storytellers than others (Thomson et al., 2002b), there is an understandable tendency for human subjects to create accounts which position themselves in particular (usually 'positive') ways. 'Vocabularies of motive' (Mills, 1940) – the reasons given for why individuals acted in particular ways in particular situations – may then be little more than post-hoc excuses; self-interested justifications for what others might perceive in negative ways.

Like Thomson et al. (2002b: 351), we feel 'unable to solve the methodological riddle of distinguishing between a life that is lived and a life that is told' and take the sort of pragmatic stance that Roberts (2002) says is common to most biographical research. We accept that some interviews contained commentaries (at times pretty obvious to us) that primarily functioned to provide moral self-justification and/or promote a particular form of self-identity. As in Simpson's study (2003), some of the clearest examples of this came from people who had lengthy records of crime. They expressed a moral hierarchy of offending (the details of which were constant across his and our study) that justified individual's own crimes, no matter what they were, as 'less bad' than another named crime higher up this list.

We also insist, however, that our interviews provide a route to understanding the transitions of these young people in this place. As Hammersley (1992: 54) says, 'we must be concerned with the truth or otherwise of accounts...and judge this as best we can'. Our judgement of the relative truthfulness of these interviews rests on various contentions: the 'triangulation' or general (but not complete) fit between the 'findings' of our different strands of fieldwork; consistency within and between young people's accounts; the opportunity for checking, probing and contesting provided by our relatively open interviews with young people; the similarity of our findings to those of other studies of similar groups in similar places at similar times (e.g. Johnston et al., 2000);[12] the view of 'expert groups' (e.g. local practitioner audiences) that, in general, our findings are accurate; and – most significant to us – the sheer force of emotion and verisimilitude that accompanied the giving of many of these interviews. Of course, any final judgement about the authenticity, validity and partiality of this research rests with the reader.

Conclusion

Despite the relative silence in academic and policy discussions in the late 1990s and 2000s about 'the underclass', young people in Britain's poor neighbourhoods remain central to apparently more politically acceptable descriptions of them, and their locales, as 'socially excluded'. The restructuring of transitions for working-class young people has opened up new opportunities, through extended participation in education, but economic and social marginalisation remains a key feature of the youth phase for many and a destination for some. Notwithstanding the numerous criticisms ranged against transition studies, a broad concept of transition remains, in our view, a valuable way of understanding the way that individual agency, local cultures and social structural constraints come together to challenge or reproduce familiar social divisions and inequalities in early adulthood.

The demonisation of working-class young people said to be socially and economically disconnected is certainly not a new phenomenon and the past 150 years are replete with examples of new labels – and policies – being applied to such groups (Pearson, 1983; Morris, 1994). We also argue, however, that there is more to contemporary fascination with 'disconnected youth' than fashionable moral panic (Westergaard, 1982). Processes of social and economic change have had profound consequences for youth in poor neighbourhoods and the coming chapters – beginning with an exploration of schooling in poor neighbourhoods – show this.

3
Missing School: Educational Engagement and Youth Transitions in Poor Neighbourhoods

I was easy led, very easy led. I'd do anything anyone told me to do. I'd just do it...because I didn't *mind* going to school. Like, I didn't *hate* the lessons. If I was there, when I did go to a lesson, I'd do it and I'd enjoy it. It's just I couldn't be bothered or someone'd say, 'Away, let's nick off. Let's go here today' and I was, 'Away then!'

(Liam, 27, unemployed)

Introduction

We now turn more concertedly to our own study. This is the first of seven chapters that draw on our research to explore the experiences that one set of young people had of growing up in poor neighbourhoods. Here we examine the important role of schooling in the shaping of 'inclusionary' and 'exclusionary' transitions. Education has long been recognised as a key social institution that does much to reinforce social inequalities as well as providing opportunities for some for social mobility. One of the central dilemmas for the contemporary sociology of education remains 'whether education is really concerned with cultural reproduction (maintenance of the cultural status quo and inculcation of "societal values") or cultural interruption (changing the social order; providing the means to new identities and challenging the conventional outcomes of education)' (Coffey, 2001: 72). And whilst this research is not a study in the sociology of education as conventionally understood, questions about young people's schooling are crucial to our attempt to comprehend youth transitions in this context.

Central to the discussion will be young people's experience of schooling in poor neighbourhoods and the way that such experiences relate to the wider realm of young people's lives and their futures. This case study material is drawn from an area which has had some of the lowest levels of educational achievement and post-sixteen progression, compared with national figures. Biographically focused interviews proved invaluable in documenting how young people experienced, oriented themselves to and acted in relation to schooling in poor neighbourhoods. In turn, these accounts are central to our understanding of how early processes of inclusion and exclusion are set in train.

Schooling in poor neighbourhoods: the local educational context

Plewis argues that 'all the research evidence points to there being rather small differences in schools' outcomes once you have properly allowed for differences in pupil intake' (1998: 106). According to Darton et al. (2003), the key differences are to do with poverty and class. Indeed, the House of Commons Education and Skills Committee concluded that it is unarguable 'that poverty is the biggest single indicator of low educational achievement' (2003: 3). Given this, we can imagine how the five secondary schools and three special schools that served the wards of East Kelby at the time of our fieldwork might struggle to raise educational standards and outcomes.

At the time of the study, 60 per cent of pupils from one East Kelby ward could claim free school meals, a proxy measure of poverty, against a national average of 19 per cent.[1] In 2000, nationwide nearly 50 per cent of pupils achieved five or more GCSEs graded A–C (this is a common but contested measure of educational success in the standard examinations for sixteen-year-olds: see Lauder, 1999; Gillborn, 2000; Ball, 2003). In that year, the 'best' East Kelby school recorded a figure of 20 per cent with the 'worst' showing only 4 per cent reaching these grades. In the nearby, middle-class suburb of Ackthorpe, 74 per cent of pupils at a state secondary reached this target (DfEE, 2000). Ofsted reports (1998) talk of pupils entering secondary education in East Kelby with low achievement and being unable 'to recover from their poor start', of the 'important challenge of...ensuring pupils regularly come to school' and of 'a significant number of pupils who have little regard for education'.

Government targeting of 'failing' schools (Coffey, 2001) has resulted in the demolition of two of the secondary schools that our interviewees attended, to make way for a new, part-privately financed City Academy. Further policy initiatives in East Kelby have included an Education Action Zone (EAZ) and the piloting of the Educational Maintenance

Allowance (EMA) programme to encourage school-leavers to go on to college (see chapter 5) (Plewis, 1998; Crowther et al., 2003).[2]

Schooling for the lower classes: incentives to disengagement

What did our interviewees say about their experiences of school in this context? Perhaps the most striking thing about their accounts was their similarity to numerous descriptions of working-class educational disengagement and disaffection that have been published over the past three decades (e.g. Willis, 1977; Ball, 1981; Brown, 1987; Riseborough, 1993; Mac an Ghaill, 1994; O'Donnell and Sharpe, 2000), despite the reforms of the education system that have been attempted since the mid-1980s (Cohen, 1997). Ball (2003) argues that the imposition of the national curriculum, increasing testing of pupils, resultant league tables and the marketisation of schooling has intensified processes of educational sorting and differentiation in Britain, *compounding* working-class disadvantage in education. In our study, positive reflections on school were few and brief (of which more later). Criticisms and complaints were numerous and extensive.

'Colouring dinosaurs' and being 'under that mark'

Bell (2003: 496) argues that it is not just pupil poverty that determines unequal educational outcomes: 'poor neighbourhoods are associated with lower quality teaching'. Although some interviewees described some of their teachers as overly authoritarian, too quick to condemn and unlikely to provide academic encouragement,[3] the most hostile comments were reserved for the quality and content of teaching rather than the teachers themselves. This theme is one of those that had a depressingly familiar ring to it. Regardless of repeated attempts over the past 25 years to 'vocationalise' the curriculum for 'less academic', working-class pupils (see Mizen, 2003), it was seen by the majority here as 'pointless', 'meaningless' and 'menial'. In their view, being in a low-achieving school, especially being in a low-achieving class in a low-achieving school, resulted in their receiving education of a low quality. Although quick to play down their own intellectual abilities, interviewees also resented the fact that apparently little emphasis had been placed upon providing them with educational challenges:

> All they were learning me when I left school was adds and takeaways and that was in secondary school. The maths teachers used to take us weight training — didn't do maths. So I just thought 'sack it' [give it up].[4]
>
> (Lisa, 24, non-employed mother)

We never got no homework... Five years, I was never given it. Towards going for my GCSEs, I had to actually ask for homework... in the first few years, I was in the bottom set and I think they just didn't bother with us... That's what I feel, they just didn't bother about us. All the other classes were getting homework constantly and we just never got any.

(Simon, 19, factory employee)

Sustained misbehaviour meant that some were routinely referred to a 'learning support base' where the standard of work required was even more basic than the mainstream education described above. This was a source of great amusement for Broderick and his friend:

Broderick: I got put on that thing... where you're colouring dinosaurs...
Paul: Yeah, the learning support base... it's like a special needs bit to, like...
Broderick: For the demented and that [*laughter*]... I think it was, like, three times a week. I'd miss certain, some lessons and go there and colour in and that and stuff like that...
JM: And what kinds of pupils went in there?
Broderick: Naughty ones, dumb ones, demented ones... Yeah, you don't do nowt! [*more laughter*]. Just sit there and that. They just give you these books.
Paul: Big box of fat wax crayons [*loud laughter*].
Broderick: Yeah, like that... Sectioned off we were, from the other school, with all these doors and that!... Weren't allowed to sharpen your pencil too much. Nowt like that [*laughter*].

(Broderick, 18, unemployed, and Paul, 16, YT trainee)

The perception of not being an educational priority was widespread among the interviewees: 'I was in lower sets... I think maybe *under that mark*, there didn't seem there was enough encouragement' (Anthony, 23, part-time college student; our emphasis). This allegation that academically weaker pupils are neglected in East Kelby classrooms is supported by Simpson and Cieslik's evaluation (2000) of the local EAZ. They conclude that a latent function of its mission to improve educational standards in poor neighbourhoods has been a concentration of resources towards 'the more able and "borderline" pupils at the expense of the less able' (2000: 13). In targeting support to those deemed most capable of reaching GCSE grades A–C (at the expense of those deemed unlikely to make this benchmark), the EAZ might be accused of *entrenching* practices that add to processes of educational underachievement (i.e. our interviewees reported school experiences *prior* to the introduction of the EAZ). This is not to imply that covert internal selection for educational support is limited to EAZ schools. Sarah, now a 23-year-old mother and university student, had attended a school with a more academic reputation in another part of Kelby. She reflected:

> If you didn't show the slightest bit of talent you never got pushed, do you know? If you couldn't be bothered, they didn't bother with you. They'd never like, 'Oh come on, you can do this if you try' or anything like that...they get all them people who're clever or the slightest bit clever, push them, so they get all them who pass which makes them look good but the others, they're just not bothered about, where it should be them that they're bothered about really. Well, I think so.

Getting 'tortured', fitting in and informal peer culture

Alongside critique of the quality of schooling encountered in East Kelby, interviews contained extensive discussion of the way that informal social relations between pupils served to structure their experience and assessment of secondary education. For instance, a large minority of the sample had been victims of bullying that ranged from low-level name-calling to more intense, prolonged victimisation (O'Donnell and Sharpe, 2000; Ridge, 2002). For some, 'getting tortured' (to use the local parlance) wholly explained their affective and physical disengagement from school.

Simon was difficult to contact. His mother, who works for a local voluntary youth organisation, suggested him as a possible interviewee. After three 'failed' appointments (which Simon had 'forgotten about'), it became clear that he was perhaps not as keen to talk to us as his mother was. Simon seemed depressed. He was nervous, avoided eye contact and spoke very slowly and quietly, often forgetting what he had said moments before. Although wary of pathologising this young man, we feel these reflections from field-notes are relevant to our present discussion. This is what Simon said of his schooldays:

> Hated it...I used to get bullied quite a lot by one lad. I wasn't, like, the most popular lad at school so I didn't enjoy it. I'd have done anything to get out...My nickname at school was 'Dozy Simon'. Everyone thought I was thick and stuff...I thought if I'd have gone to one of the teachers [to complain about the bully], he'd have just done it

more... At one point I was beginning to think I was depressed, really depressed about it and... basically I was one of them lads who kept meself to meself and didn't talk to very many people or things like that. I just put me head down and got on with it, you know? Just tried to keep myself quiet so no one'd talk to me or owt like that... Sometimes it just got on top of me and I just didn't wanna go, you know?... And basically it ruined my chances up 'cos most of the time I was off [absent from school] and ... I could've done better at school.

Simon described *leaving* school as 'the happiest time of my life'. He left with five GCSEs (at low grades). His post-school career was typical of many (see chapters 5 and 6): temporary jobs in factories and fast-food outlets, unemployment, participation in New Deal for Young People and – significantly – a return to Further Education college to re-sit GCSEs. Despite detesting his school days and having apparently supportive parents, Simon had felt unable to confide his experiences of bullying to anybody. He concluded his interview by saying 'I don't think anyone knows... except for you!'

We also talked to people who had been bullies. They described bullying as just one item in the repertoire of activities sometimes practised by informal peer groups in the pursuit of 'having a laugh'. Being part of a 'crew', and bullying those who were not, made for momentary 'mad laughs', to use the words of Paul and Darren. Informants also recognised, however, that allegiance to such peer groups often involved the mutual reinforcement of (sub)cultural orientations to the formal business of school that could have broader consequences in the longer term.

Discovery and discussion of alienated pupil sub-cultures has been a staple of educational ethnography for years. One of the most useful discussions can be found in Brown's (1987) critical engagement with the classic work in this field: Willis's *Learning to Labour* (1977). Rejecting Willis's depiction of working-class kids' cultural engagement with school as falling on one side or the other of a resistance/conformity dichotomy, Brown describes the plurality of 'different cultural responses *among* working-class pupils' (1987: 22). He argues that locally differentiated, working-class culture generates alternative, cultural predispositions towards education which are then moulded by the school's own systems of educational differentiation and labelling. A possible example of this is Broderick's throwaway comment, earlier, that '[I] didn't do no work 'cos I was in all the bottom groups' (emphasis added). Apparently, being relegated to the school's lowest ability stream combined with an incipient alienated orientation to generate for Broderick a more fully blown anti-school attitude.

The number and type of 'frames of reference' displayed by pupils in a given context will reflect the different forms of local, working-class culture, the recent socio-economic history of the place, the internal systems of the school and, we would add, the consequences of educational policies (e.g. as in provision of financial EMAs to encourage pupils to 'stay on'). Brown's study identified three main forms: a 'positive', normative acceptance of school (typical of those pupils his informants described as 'swots'); a 'negative', alienated rejection (the 'rems') and, between them, an alienated but instrumental orientation to school ('the ordinary kids'). According to Brown, Willis missed the theoretical and empirical significance of this latter group in his fascination with 'the lads' and their more obvious cultural resistance to the school. Brown's 'ordinary kids' balanced a discourse of 'school irrelevance' against a collective understanding that 'getting on' after school required an instrumental engagement with education.

Brown's critique resonates with the findings of our own study. It helps us grasp in a more nuanced way the different cultural forms of '*being* in school and *becoming* adult' (1987: 31) that exist in East Kelby and the provenance of these in relation to local working-class culture and history and the changing structure of opportunities perceived by young people (of which more later). In returning to Brown's book during the writing of this one, we were struck by the uncanny similarity between the accounts and explanations of educational disaffection given by the 'rems' and those presented here. The contours and details of their narratives were virtually identical, despite being separated by several hundred miles, nearly twenty years and some rather important socio-economic changes in the interim (Brown's study was undertaken in South Wales in the early 1980s). We consider the significance of this observation in conclusion.

In addition, at least some of the narratives of school experience we gathered seemed similar to those of Brown's 'ordinary kids'. In fact, much of what our interviewees said about school can be understood in terms of the competition, played out day to day in the classroom, between a generally alienated but instrumental orientation to school and a complete disengagement from its formal purposes and strictures. The choice to pursue a more instrumental approach (to 'get your head down' and make personal effort towards academic progress) was balanced against strong informal sanctions in the opposite direction. Those who worked hard in class, completed homework or revised for exams risked 'getting tortured' (at worst, severe bullying and exclusion from friendship groups). Being 'a swot' was an identity to be avoided, suggesting that – in contrast to Brown's findings – *any* display of educational engagement was treated as signalling conformist acceptance of the school deal. Consequently, saving face amongst peers group was often viewed as more important than striving to achieve higher GCSE grades:

> *Claire*: It's peer pressure as well. You wanna have a laugh and a joke and you don't wanna be the swot of the class, 'cos they're doing all the work.
> *Emma*: Yeah, 'cos you just get tortured. You'd just get tortured at school. It's hard at school, isn't it?
> *Claire*: The people like that had no friends.
>
> (Claire, 20, non-employed mother, and
> Emma 25, non-employed mother)

Going by these accounts, oppositional pupil cultures were widespread and held a powerful claim over the social identities developed by young people in and towards school. The efforts of the school or pro-school pupil groups to orient behaviour towards academic goals were weak in comparison:

> [School] was all right when I first started. I just started mixing with the wrong people, experiencing drugs about thirteen [or] fourteen...I mean, I was stood outside the headmaster's office all the time...Smoking, fighting, nicking out of lessons, everything. I just didn't take no notice of the rules or nowt...I just wanted to be like the others, you know what I mean? Just like a little gang that used to knock about together: if they done it, you done it.
>
> (Adam, 20, inmate of Young Offender Institute)

Several interviewees claimed[5] that they had wanted to work harder at school but found this difficult given the low-level disruption of learning caused by the implicit imperative to 'mess about' and the informal sanctions operated against those seen to be bowing to the formal school demand of academic work: 'there was a couple of us in our class who just wanted to do work, but like you get all that, don't you? "Swot, swot!" and you get yourself tortured' (Allan, 21, unemployed). Significantly for our broader research interests, 'inclusion' in the formal life of the school could mean effective 'exclusion' from informal friendship groups. It was not just young men who described this insistence on 'messing around' and 'having a laugh'. Although national-level trends and debates would predict clear gender differentiation in forms of educational orientation and achievement (Weiner et al., 1997; Coffey, 2001), there was little evidence here to suggest that young women were pushing ahead of young men in terms of academic achievement or adopting notably more instrumental attitudes to study.

We are not convinced, however, that pupils' cultural orientations to school are as stable as implied in Brown's analysis. Sometimes the same individuals recounted narratives of school that contained episodes of *both* instrumental engagement and complete disaffection, occasionally reversing the sequence of such episodes that would be predicted by other studies. That is, some of our informants described a process of instrumental accommodation in the latter years of compulsory schooling, following earlier disengagement. Others were currently attending Further Education College after earlier, dismal school experiences:

> Nobody was learning owt, 'cos everybody was still messing about and stuff like that. But some of us, like, we got into year 10 and 11 then we started to settle down and, still a bit of talking here and there but...
>
> (Samantha, 16, college student)

Those who saw the instrumental rationale of education but simultaneously felt the countervailing pressure of counter-school peer groups faced difficult choices. Walking a line between them was virtually impossible. Rarely were young people confident enough to assert their commitment to school over the risk of being 'tortured'. Leanne (16, a recent school-leaver) was one exception:

> When they [friends] started nicking off, like quite a lot, I was going into my fourth year and it was an important year for me, so I just said, 'No, I'm staying'. They used to ask me every day, 'Are you nicking off?' I said, 'No, I'm going into school today.' 'Oh, you snob!' I said 'I have to'... It didn't bother me, 'cos I had, by this time, I had loads of friends so like one friend wouldn't matter losing...

Although Leanne's case was unusual even here we see the importance attached to popular opinion and friendships in school. She explains her ability to resist the cajolery of truants *because* of her attachment to a new, wider friendship group that remained committed to school. This extract introduces one of the most obvious consequences of young people's general, negative experiences of schooling, and their attachment to counter-school peer groups in particular: their physical escape from the school.

Truancy: the path to social exclusion?

Interviews with teachers and youth workers in the area reported truancy to be a major problem and published statistics show East Kelby schools to have over twice the rate of authorised and unauthorised school absences compared with schools in more affluent parts of Kelby a short distance away (DfEE, 2000).

According to the government, 50,000 pupils truant every day (cited in Hayden, 2003) and reducing these figures has been identified by the Social Exclusion Unit as 'a crucial part of the government's wider strategy to tackle and prevent social exclusion' (1997: 3). Indeed, its very first report concerned school truancy, with its first page warning that:

> Truancy and exclusions have reached crisis point. The thousands of children who are not in school on most schooldays have become a significant cause of crime. Many of today's non-attenders are in danger of becoming tomorrow's criminals and unemployed.

Experiences of truancy in our sample were widespread. A minority had never done it or had only infrequent unauthorised absence from school (19 from 88 interviewees). 29 interviewees reported being 'occasional truants' (i.e. they missed school quite often but not extensively). We concentrate our discussion on those 40 people that we classed as 'frequent truants' (i.e. persistent and extensive unauthorised absence that sometimes amounted to weeks, or even months, at a time).

Explaining frequent truancy

The factors that shaped young people's alienation from school emerged as the key motivations behind frequent truancy and matched those reported in other recent studies (e.g. Cullingford and Morrison, 1996; Osler et al., 2002). Some frequent truants had difficulty in pinpointing exactly what it was that they disliked about school. It was the whole experience that they found dull and uninspiring:

> I was going every day in the first and second year... I just got fed up of going in every day... There was nowt specific I didn't like about it, it was just, I dunno, the thought of getting up every day and having to go in school and sit there bored all day. I just didn't fancy it.
>
> (Louise, 17, unemployed)

In a similar vein, school was described as 'boring', 'the same stuff all the time', a 'waste of time', and our interviewees complained about being 'just not interested' and unable to 'get into it'. Some struggled to cope with the difficulty of schoolwork and feelings of failure could be avoided – at least in the pressure of the moment – by escaping school. Mally attended a special school where, despite the close support of teachers, his poor literacy skills frustrated and embarrassed him to such an extent that he often missed several days each week:

> I was looking at my timetable and I seen all that and I said, 'I can't do all that, I can't do this'. So I thought, 'Oh, I'll nick off' ... My reading's all right, it's my writing's terrible. I mean I could be there [in a lesson] and I'd be the last one trying to, you know, write something and it just really gets to me that I can't write ... They did, they helped me a lot and half the time I'd been nicking off. It's really my own fault I'm not learning owt ... I can't blame the teachers. All I can blame is myself, for getting shot out or nicking off. It's me own fault.
>
> (Mally, 19, unemployed)

Conversely, one young man, Fox (19 and on New Deal), explained his frequent truancy at the age of eleven and twelve in terms of school work being too simplistic, banal and regimented: 'we were all separated into ourselves and we all had to do this basic work that was really boring. "Spell this. Write that. Read that". Although I love reading, the books they had us reading weren't that interesting'. In later years, Fox[6] returned to regular attendance when he began to find the curriculum more interesting:

> Well, what it was, was I always liked Maths and History, and at 3rd year we started doing World War One work, and I started to love the work so I used to go then more often and then in fourth year, I was surprised that I was put into the top class for the year and ... it was just arrogance of being in the top class. I thought, 'Well, I'm being referred to as one of the best here. I'm gonna have to start working harder' so I started coming more often, well, I used to come every day ... It was a bit of faith was shown, so I just thought I'd put in a bit more commitment then.[7]

For others, their pattern of non-attendance reflected directly the pattern of their victimisation by bullies (Carlen et al., 1992; Osler et al., 2002; Ridge, 2002). Here self-exclusion was self-preservation: 'I was just like sick of getting bullied and name called and this, that and the other, you know?... I just got sick of it and I didn't wanna go in (Simon, 19, factory employee).

Perhaps the most common explanation given by those who regularly missed school was peer influence (Darton et al., 2003). The thought of losing face among peers (by resisting calls to truant) appeared particularly daunting. A sense of belonging to peer groups was often valued above a clean record of school attendance or the acquisition of good GCSE grades. Interviewees spoke about being 'easily led', 'trying to be like the rest', 'following', 'copying' and 'listening' to the 'wrong crowd' and being the 'odd one out' if they resisted the pull of counter-school norms. Going against the flow was rarely considered an option, even when school was experienced as enjoyable (as described by Liam, in the chapter's opening quotation).

Finally, a prominent minority discourse contradicted directly the instrumental claims of education: having a good education and possessing GCSE qualifications would *not* necessarily enhance their later job prospects (Brown, 1987). If little was to be gained from regular attendance, why not truant? Broderick puts it bluntly:

> They'd [Broderick's parents] argue about it. Our Neville [his step-father] come home and he'd say 'Hasn't he been to fucking school again?'...He'd just go 'He'll never get a job when he leaves school 'cos he's never there'. *Why?* So if you go to school for a full five years, you're definitely getting a job when you leave? *All that – full of shit – no!*
>
> (Broderick, 18, unemployed)

Missing school: regrets, claims and counter-claims

Towards the end of the interviews we asked young people to look back over their lives and to consider whether they wished they had done anything differently. Typically, interviewees compared their current circumstances with schooldays. Favourable reflections on schooling itself were rare. Our interviewees seemed only to value informal aspects of their school experience. They reminisced nostalgically about the value of school as a site for making and seeing friends, for passing the time in a (not too) regulated way, for having fun (e.g. O'Donnell and Sharpe, 2000; Ridge, 2002). As Darren put it, 'we used to go to school and have a good laugh, like sit in the class and have a good laugh and that, didn't we?' Brown (1987) describes how, in comparison with young people's later experiences of unemployment, being in school was valued because it provided opportunities for sociability and 'a sense of social worth, dignity and *predictability*, even though they [were] not academically successful' (1987: 49, our emphasis). With their schooldays behind them, our informants had encountered a world that seemed less certain, more risky, more serious:

> I still wish I was at school, 'cos now you have to get out, if you're not going to college . . . I have to get out, find a job and it's just hard. You have to make all your own decisions and everything. When, when I was at school, I just got out of bed, got dressed and off and now I just . . . I wish I was back at school.
>
> (Clare, 16, recent school leaver)

School life provided a rhythm to the days and relatively few choices (apart from whether to attend or not). On leaving school, broad, taken-for-granted friendship groups began to peter out (see chapter 4). Normally, the post-sixteen options many had moved into since then – Youth Training, the Further Education College, the workplace – did not provide the same opportunities. People – themselves included – came and went too quickly to establish new bonds (see chapter 5). Those who were long-term unemployed, single mothers or young offenders had even less obvious opportunities for socialising. Occasional meetings in the street or in the Post Office queue, or sharing a prison cell, provided an unsatisfactory replacement. The most poignant expressions of this sense of loss of easier times were given by young men who, at other points in the interview, presented a harder face. Here are three young men interviewed in Young Offenders Institutions:

> I wish I was back at school – with all my mates and have a good laugh. I don't see many of them in here.
>
> (Richard, 20)

> People used to say to you that you would miss it [school] when you left, that you'd wish you were back. I ignored them. I used to think 'I hate school'. I was obviously wrong, given how I feel now. I miss waking up in the morning, hearing the bell, going into school. I miss me mates . . . yeah, there's mates and routines in here but it's different. A different set of circumstances.
>
> (Gazz, 20)

I miss school. I wish I was back there...Why? I don't know. It would be nice to go back, be back there. Be younger again.

(Andrew, 18)

This sense of loss was combined with a regret for not having worked harder at school and became one of the most regular, predictable responses across the interviews as a whole. The same finding has been reported widely in youth studies (e.g. Lloyd, 1999; Hall, 2002; Gunter, 2004) but has rarely received much consideration. On the face of it, with the *benefit of hindsight* the majority seemed to have bought into the orthodox educational contract: working harder at school would have delivered better qualifications which, in turn, would have increased the chances of getting better jobs. This was a message that they had heard often enough from teachers but which had been ignored or questioned by many of them at the time. Numerous recent studies report this same instrumental orientation to the value of educational qualifications amongst British youth (e.g. Ball et al., 2000a; Coffey, 2001; Evans, 2002). In one short extract Catherine, a nineteen-year-old New Deal trainee, describes three competing discourses that ran through many of these interviews before reaching her conclusion ('qualifications have no instrumental value, 'people like me fail anyway', 'qualifications do have instrumental value'):

I didn't think they'd [GCSE qualifications] do me any good and then I thought I'll do crap in it. So I never done 'em but I wish I'd done 'em now...Dunno, they'd help me get a job better, and most jobs want GCSEs.

It would be easy for us to conclude our consideration of this question here, given the dominance that educational instrumentalism has achieved in policy discussions *and* the predominance of this sort of resolution in young people's accounts. The teenage kicks of early school disengagement were now regretted as they faced the difficulties of the post-school world. Looking back from their current vantage points – and trying to understand the course of their lives since school – the majority of young people seemed to conclude that they had been wrong and the teachers right. Only in retrospect were they beginning to see the vocational value of education.

Yet this is not the whole story. Many who declared these sorts of final regrets had earlier in the same interview described their school experiences in very negative terms and expressly *denied* the relevance of educational qualifications to post-school careers. This is an intriguing conundrum for those of us interested in understanding the subjective engagement of 'socially excluded' young people with their schooling. How do we explain it?

'Brain box, works in a cake shop'

First, let us consider counter-claims to the 'education = jobs' equation, a viewpoint held strongly by a significant minority of the sample. Several of these people referred to individuals who had been among the school's high achievers (the 'swots' or 'snobs') but who had since experienced faltering school-to-work careers. Gail described a group of girls who, despite doing well at school, had still found themselves in dead-end, low-paid jobs:

> Well, Caroline – she's on the dole. She was dead brainy and they thought that she was something, she's just on the dole now . . . or if they've got a job they haven't got a good job 'cos one of them, brain box, works in a cake shop. What's *that*? It's not as if she's actually *done* something and gone . . . I thought she'd go to college and you know and all that, but she isn't, she works in a cake shop in East Kelby!
>
> (Gail, 17, non-employed mother)

Similarly, Darren and Broderick describe the current status of one of their school's academic stars:

> *Darren*: It's mad really . . . 'Cos there's a lad – Timothy Spence – he got five A's, I think it was. What was it? Three A's, two A stars?
> *Broderick*: Oh, he got all sorts him, didn't he!
> *Darren*: Working in Morrison's now.
> *Broderick*: I know, yeah.
> *Darren*: That's what I mean. He got the best scores, right? And he's working in Morrison's!
> *Broderick*: Packing fruit! [*laughs*].
>
> (Darren, 16, unemployed, and Broderick 18, unemployed)

Of course, this discourse of educational irrelevance may simply be a rhetorical attempt to justify individuals' previous misbehaviour in school and their subsequent lack of labour market progress. If even the best-qualified, hardest working pupils can be presented as 'failing' later, what point is there in striving for academic success, particularly when this would carry the cost of working against the normative pressures of school-based peer groups?

Because ours was not a statistically representative sample of school-leaving cohorts we are unable to assess directly the effect of GCSE pass rates on later outcomes. One method of investigating these questions, though, is to consider the post-school careers of those with the highest levels of school qualifications (i.e. those six interviewees who passed five GCSEs at grades A–C), against those of the majority who appeared to have no (n = 34) or lower levels of qualification (n = 48).[8] To what extent *does* the orthodox educational deal work for young people in East Kelby?

In this study, some, albeit limited, evidence suggests that those six with higher educational attainment had more conventional school-to-work careers (i.e. all but one were engaged in some form of post-sixteen education or training until the age of eighteen and all gained further qualifications as a result). Overall, though, there was remarkable similarity between the *longer-term* post-school careers of these six and the rest. *All* informants reported erratic, complex and economically marginal transitions, consisting of much swapping between training and education courses of mixed quality, spells of unemployment and episodic engagement with usually low-paid, low-skilled and temporary jobs (see chapter 6). In scanning the current labour market destinations of the sample as a whole, it would be impossible to identify those six people who had achieved the most 'success' at school: their transitions and outcomes were too similar to those with no or only modest educational qualifications.[9]

Summary and conclusion: continuities in educational disengagement

Although just a few years – sometimes only months – had passed since leaving, young people's positive reflections on school were limited to nostalgic memories of easier times, free of the risks and uncertainties they now faced. These were weighed against recollections of discouraging teachers, the perceived pointlessness of the curriculum, the shared sense that people like them were not an educational priority, the torments of those who were bullied and powerful peer sanctions against school engagement. Interviewees recounted their tales of school with the resilient tone of the 'taken-for-granted'; a weary, sometimes jocular and occasionally questioning acceptance that this was their lot. Anger was rare. We are aware, of course, that we are presenting a depressingly familiar account of working-class disaffection from school. Why spend time reporting all this?

First, continuity in social experience can be intriguing in its own right, especially where the experience in question is set in a markedly different socio-economic context from that which helped explain working-class 'failure' in education in previous decades (Furlong and Cartmel, 1997). Willis (1977) explained this in terms of the cultural correspondence between inherent, class-based tastes and impulses, the masculine counter-school cultures of the 'lads' and – crucially – their later destinations in the sort of 'real', manual jobs held by working-class men in that time and place. Youth unemployment in the 1980s and 1990s had a devastating impact on the structure of opportunities facing all working-class youth, not just those young men destined for low-skilled factory jobs. O'Donnell and Sharpe (2000: 45) suggest that 'it no longer made sense for [working-class pupils] to adopt the cocksure attitude to job prospects of the lads of Willis's study'. By the time of Brown's study (1987: 174), the closing down of routes through post-school employment to 'respectable' working-class adulthood was beginning to undermine the instrumental orientation of 'ordinary kids' to school:

> The material bases of the frames of reference exhibited by the ordinary kids (and rems) can now be seen to reflect past processes rather than current practices. It is making it increasingly difficult for the ordinary kids to see why they should continue to 'make an effort' in school if it is no longer the basis for personal survival in the labour market.

Moving forward in time we think we see in these accounts from East Kelby further evidence of the diminishing hold that this form of 'ordinary' working-class, instrumentalism has on young people's orientations to school. This frame of reference seemed less common than in Brown's study and less capable of withstanding the counter-claims of a more disaffected, disruptive point of view that directly contested the 'education = jobs' equation. Our admittedly imperfect research design showed – *in this context* – that this argument had some merit. There was little substantial difference between the post-school careers of the most and least qualified.

This finding contradicts a barrage of statistical evidence from national-level research that demonstrates a strong correlation between educational qualifications and later outcomes (e.g. Jones, 2002). Have we, then, accessed a particularly unusual, unrepresentative sample of young people? Have we missed those individuals who progressed more success-fully through school, gaining better qualifications that helped secure more rewarding post-school careers? Certainly, the levels of qualification our interviewees possessed are unusually low by national standards. They are, though, comparable to those typically gained in East Kelby schools during this period. (To reiterate, in 2000, the 'best' East Kelby school had 20 per cent of its sixteen year olds gaining five GCSEs at grade A–C; the 'worst' had 4 per cent.) We do not claim our sample to be representative of young people in general, but think it is broadly typical of young people in this place at this time (see chapter 2). More importantly, it is a sample that allows us to focus in on that minority of the youth population that do not share in the patterns of educational engagement and progression displayed by the majority.

Following Brown, we argue that differential patterns of school engagement need to be understood in relation to the changing structure of opportunities that await school-leavers in their localities (see chapters 5 and 6). O'Donnell and Sharpe (2000: 87) found 'social class-based anti-school sub-cultures [to be] less strong than previously' with few expressing the contempt for education typical of Willis's 'lads' or Brown's 'rems'. The difference between O'Donnell and Sharpe's findings (from London) and our own is explained in part, we think, by the relative employment opportunities available to working-class young adults in these two places. The contemporary paucity as opposed to historical abundance of decent, working-class jobs for young adults in East Kelby has effectively undermined the traditional educational contract which served to incorporate the majority of working-class pupils into begrudging acceptance of the instrumental value of schooling. Serving in cake shops or stacking supermarket shelves does not, in their view, require GCSEs.

A few of the sample had clung to a belief in school, 'got their head down' and managed to resist pressure to disengage. Several arrived at the instrumental thesis *after* leaving school. This latter group often appeared to be voicing desperate, inchoate attempts to understand their lack of progress in largely individualist terms ('If only I'd worked harder at school...') (Raffo and Reeves, 2000; Evans et al., 2001). The uncertainties and hardships of post-school life bred nostalgic memories of school days and after all, they kept hearing 'the qualifications = jobs' mantra repeated by a succession of college tutors and YT trainers. Furlong and Cartmel (1997) refer to this as the 'epistemological fallacy': the flux, complexity and widened 'options' typical of contemporary youth transitions engender subjective feelings of individual agency among those stuck in them. Consequently, 'failure' is interpreted as an outcome of an individual's own choices and actions. The objective persistence of the socially patterned nature of working-class young people's *collective* outcomes from school (dis)engagement is normally visible only 'from above' and over the longer-term (as in a study like this one).

Of course, we must allow as well that some individuals had, through experience, discovered that qualifications were of use after all. Qualifications have not been stripped of all relevance in this locality. They are often requirements for entry to the plethora of post-sixteen educational 'options' that now soak up many school-leavers (see chapter 5).

The fact, however, that educational qualifications appeared to play an at best minor role, by this point in their lives, in the shaping of overall transitions for these young adults is best explained by reference to the particularities of this local labour market and the cultural knowledge, tastes and aspirations of this group (Hudson, 1989a). Ironically, these interviewees were distinguished not by anti-employment attitudes, as suggested in conservative underclass theory (Murray, 1990), but by what we might call *hyper-conventional* views about the value of jobs (see Chapter 6). As Ball et al. (2000a; 2000b) explain, 'learner identities', which incorporate personal perceptions of the attractiveness of learning and the value of educational qualifications, take shape in relation to young people's variable encounters with formal schooling and 'the economic, political and ideological trajectories of their families, and communities [and the] political economies of their neighbourhoods' (Apple, 1986: 5, cited in Ball et al., 2000b: 59; Rees et al., 1997). That de-industrialised localities like this continue to provide jobs for this age group, albeit now in the form of severely casualised employment that pays no regard to educational credentials, helps to explain the ready abandonment of formal education by some young people and their often dismissive attitude to it.

A second reason for recounting the informants' school experiences is that they reveal processes that are crucial to answering our broader questions about longer-term patterns of exclusion/inclusion. In general terms school disaffection and absence are, of course, likely to limit individual educational achievement (and therefore the chances of trading in school qualifications for entry to 'better' post-sixteen options) and to increase the chances of later social exclusion. The evidence from these young people in this context suggests, however, that we might understand school disengagement, in part, as an *effect* of social exclusion; i.e. of attending schools in poor neighbourhoods that 'failed' (some now demolished) and imbued in interviewees a strong sense, to use Simon's words, of not being 'bothered about'.

Yet there is one important implication of these accounts that we have not drawn out in any detail. We refer to the apparent non-determinacy of early experiences of educational dis/engagement and give two examples. First, frequent truancy was explained in quite different ways and had different meanings for interviewees. This means that we should be cautious about interpreting it as an irreversible step towards – or *cause* of – later social exclusion, criminality and unemployment (as implied by the Social Exclusion Unit, 1997). Recurrent unemployment was experienced by virtually all interviewees regardless of their propensity to school truancy.

Secondly, our study uncovered many instances of the lasting, negative impact of schooling on young people's attitude to education. As Ball et al. describe:

> many of those outside of education and training post-16, the 'others' to the 'learning society', carry with them learner identities often severely damaged by their experiences in compulsory education. More learning is the last thing they are interested in. (2000a: 8)

We give examples from our research in chapter 5. But interviews also revealed many instances of people who, over time, moved in and out of education. Learner identities are not set in stone. For individuals like Fox, virtual abandonment of formal schooling at the ages of twelve or thirteen did *not* predict educational disengagement at fifteen and sixteen. Some of those with the grimmest memories of school life, like Simon, returned to college some years later. Equally, early instrumental orientations to school could be supervened by later, full-blown alienation.

A further, clear message from this discussion is that we cannot understand typical patterns of disengagement from school without appreciating the same informants' simultaneous affiliation to peer groups that operated in and outside of school. These were defined by a set of values and practices that stood against the ethos and expected behaviours of formal education and became – for some but not all – the forum for the establishment of criminal and drug-using careers (see chapter 9). This is why we believe a more holistic approach – one that incorporates investigation of young people's leisure, social networks and, in particular, their affective engagement with the informal youth cultures of 'the street' – is a necessary part of any attempt to understand these processes of transition and social exclusion. These are the subjects of our next chapter.

4
Street Corner Society: Leisure Careers and Social Exclusion

Corner Boys are groups of men who centre their social activities upon particular street corners...they constitute the bottom level of society within their age group, and at the same time they make up the great majority of young men in Cornerville...most of them were unemployed or had only irregular employment. Few had completed high school...

Whyte (1943: xvii)

They don't want to do a qualification...There are high levels of absenteeism, truancy. It [studying] has no relevance to them. They simply don't care ... the most important things to them are not their relationships with schools or teachers, but their relationships at night-time. *Friendships and street corners are the main thing*. Total apathy. They never do their homework. Drugs and sex – that's what their life is.

Karen (who works with school-leavers deemed not 'work-ready': our emphasis)

Introduction

We now turn our attention away from young people's differential engagement with school to consider their leisure lives and social networks and how these relate to wider process of inclusion and exclusion. As we described in chapter 2, more holistic youth research has striven to understand young people's housing and family careers as well as their school-to-work experiences (Coles, 2000a). Relatively few studies simultaneously consider criminal and drug-using careers (see chapter 9), and fewer still incorporate an investigation of youth leisure as part of the task of charting and understanding transitions. Although young people's leisure lives were not imagined by us to be significant in this respect, they certainly became so in the course of fieldwork and analysis. In this chapter, we discuss young people's accounts of their changing free-time associations, peer networks and leisure activities and their significance in explaining their current life situations. We use the concept of 'leisure career', which has had some airing in the leisure studies literature (Rapoport and Rapoport, 1975) but which has been discussed rarely in youth research (Roberts et al., 1990; Roberts, 1999).

From street corner society to commercial leisure

For the large majority of the sample, much of their free time during their early teenage years – that is, the time outside the demands of school and part-time jobs – was spent in the company of friends outside the home in the public spaces of East Kelby. Young people would meet after school, on weekday evenings and during the weekends, congregating at particular sites to spend time talking, walking about the area and generally 'hanging around'.

This is not a particularly novel point to make. Even casual observation of the estates of many British cities and towns would reveal exactly these sorts of youthful public gatherings. Numerous policy and press reports have described young people's collective occupation of public space and the 'problem' that this presents for local communities (see Coles et al., 1998). Reports about area regeneration or local policing (e.g. Kelby Borough Council, 1999) regularly identify the alleged antisocial behaviour of groups of youths 'on the street' as a pressing problem for local residents. Describing three socially excluded neighbourhoods, Page says, 'large numbers of unsupervised children and teenagers who gather in groups were a feature of all estates' and that 'on all estates, and across all age groups, the biggest single issue identified by respondents was the antisocial behaviour of children and teenagers' (2000: 37). A previous study of East Kelby found that adult residents identified 'crime' and 'young people' as the two issues which impacted most negatively on quality of life and that these problems were perceived as synonymous (Brown, 1995).

As we described in chapter 2, there is a long history of respectable fears about 'troublesome youth' (Pearson, 1983; Muncie, 1999). The impulse of respectable, adult society to corral and control those engaged in apparently unproductive, street-based leisure – especially working-class young men – has culminated, of late, in the increasing imposition of

'Anti-Social Behaviour Orders' (Abrams, 2004) and night-time street curfews (Jeffs and Smith, 1996) on British youth. At the time of writing, Kelby has become the latest British town to introduce street curfews for under-sixteens (*Kelby Evening Chronicle*, 5 March 2004).

Surprisingly few sociological studies have, however, sought to get to grips from young people's point of view with what Paul Corrigan labelled three decades ago 'the largest and most complex youth subculture': young people hanging around and 'doing nothing' (1976: 103). Of late, a number of writers have attempted a less hostile, more sociological understanding of these contemporary but under-explored forms of 'street corner society'. Chiefly, they stress the importance of unsupervised time in the formation of teenage identities or the way that the street becomes a contested site between relatively powerless young people, adult society and the formal institutions of the state (e.g. Wacquant, 1993; Valentine et al., 1998; Stenson and Watt, 1998; Hall et al., 1999; Pavis and Cunnigham-Burley, 1999; Robinson, 2000; Brent, 2001).

'Just streets to walk down': early teenage leisure in poor neighbourhoods

Our fieldwork generated two findings that are significant given the usual way that the street-based leisure of teenagers is presented in most policy and press reports.

First, street-based socialising was a common way of spending leisure time for young men *and* young women in their early to mid-teens. The 'invisibility' of girls to 1970s and 1980s youth cultural studies was in part explained by the gendered segregation of youth life-styles (young men occupied the masculine world of the street, young women were confined to the privatised, 'bedroom cultures' of the home) and the consequent methodological difficulties of researching young women (McRobbie, 1991).

According to interviewees' contemporaneous and retrospective accounts (and what we observed), this physical separation of young women's and men's leisure arenas no longer holds in East Kelby (and, surprisingly, most of the few that had avoided this street-based socialising were young men). Gillian (16) was typical. During the evenings she and her friends would 'just probably walk about the streets or just sit in the house and just talk...most of the time we don't hang around near houses or nowt. We just meet in, like, fields and that'. Similarly, Lucy (16) talked about how she and her best friend Abigail would 'just walk about the streets...like, round Primrose Vale, through the park and that and we'd walk to each other's houses or summat'.

'Hanging around the streets' was a social activity that was central to early teenage leisure. It provided the opportunity for informal and independent socialising away from adults and with friends and potential boy/girl friends. Hall and colleagues (1999: 506) explain the pull of the 'street' in the same way:

> This is free space, where attendance is neither necessary (as at home) nor compulsory (as at school) but chosen. It is also a social space, where relations are not marked by familial obligation or by official authority, but by friendship. Clearly, this space is for leisure, but it does not follow that what takes place there is unimportant... it is in the course of such informal interaction, away from parents and teachers, that significant aspects of young people's personal and social identities are affirmed, contested, rehearsed and reworked.

Street corner society was also valued because of the lack of affordable, alternative leisure outlets for teenagers:

> *Lucy*: If you had money you could to the pictures [cinema] or bowling and places like that... but mostly we can't afford to.
> *Abigail*: Mostly we just sit on the benches in the park, 'cos there's nowt for us to do... Everywhere to go costs money and if you haven't got any money, then really you can't. There's not much to do at all.

Whilst these neighbourhoods are relatively well served by youth clubs, few attended, regarding them as suitable only for younger children. Richy put it like this: 'you can't go into a youth club at seventeen! 'Cos they're all young 'uns, aren't they? All there is is — it's a lack of every-thing. There's nothing to do, just streets to walk down and stuff like that.' The Prince's Trust (2004: 2) found that 'almost half of all socially excluded young people... believe there is a lack of things for them to do' in the areas where they live.

This leads us to our second main finding. Across the interviews there was a clear understanding that young people, especially in groups in public spaces, were commonly taken to signify a disorderly and delinquent presence to be complained about, surveyed, moved on and dispersed by adult authorities (chiefly the police).[1] Interviewees, however, did not *define* street-based leisure as a forum for delinquency (beyond occasional underage drinking and possibly cannabis use) and were keen to dissociate themselves from this perception. In their view, everybody took part, not just those they knew to be the 'hard lads' or 'bad lads' (an argument confirmed by our study). Several informants made a point of saying that they congregated away from shops and houses (in fields, parks, at 'the beck', 'behind the old baths') to avoid causing trouble to local, older residents and the perception that they might be doing so. This is not to argue that participation in street corner society played no role in the formation of criminal careers. As we argue later, street-based leisure was, in virtually all cases, a necessary but *not* sufficient condition for the establishment of these.

Truancy time: 'pin-balling about the estates' and early instances of offending

Although boredom and the perceived irrelevance of schooling were prime motivations for truancy (as we described in chapter 3), absconding from school did not lead to unremitting excitement, despite the quantitative increase in leisure time it afforded. The long days of truancy were described as boring and direction-less: 'just doing anything' to pass the time. Part of the pleasure of street corner leisure in the evenings derived from the fact that it signified a release from the daytime confines of school routines. For those who were frequent truants, not only were the evenings spent on the streets of their estates but much, and many, of their days. They spent them 'hanging round' street corners, 'dossing about' in alleyways or the stairways of high-rise blocks, wandering around the shops in the town centre or even sitting at the back of the Kelby law court buildings. Although occasionally a solo venture, most frequently it was done in pairs or small groups, who would sometimes congregate in the house of whoever's parents were out at the time.[2] Some minor thrills could be had in 'hiding' from parents, police and 'school bobbies' (i.e. Education Welfare Officers) and in devising elaborate strategies to avoid teachers and circumvent school registration procedures.[3]

Liam, now 27 and unemployed, described the general experience of truancy time with a neat turn of phrase: '[we] used to just pin ball about the estates, go walkabout all day'. In later years some questioned why they had been so keen to abandon school in favour of this sort of purposeless drifting:

> I dunno, when I think back, I mean, all the time I spent sitting at home being bored and hanging round the streets being bored, I think to myself, 'Well, I wouldn't have been bored if I'd have gone in [to school].
>
> (Louise, 17, unemployed)

For only a proportion of even those we class as frequent truants did truancy time signify the moment or opportunity to initiate delinquent activities. Whilst there is obviously a strong association (Graham and Bowling, 1995; Cullingford and Morrison, 1996), we need to be wary of analyses that imply a tight, causal fit between dodging school and criminal offending (Social Exclusion Unit, 1997). Whilst the majority (n = 16) of those with more sustained, criminal careers (n = 20) had been frequent school truants (and of these, most described at least one spell of school exclusion), a substantial minority (n = 14) of those classed as frequent truants (n = 40) reported no offending whatsoever. As noted in chapter 3, our biographical interviews contained numerous instances of individuals attempting to pursue 'mainstream' school-to-work careers after lengthy periods of school disaffection and absence.

Furthermore, whilst some frequent truants did enliven truant time with first forays into recreational drug use (Simpson, 2004) or petty offending, these often did not harden up into more sustained offending. Occasional or one-off instances of shoplifting, usually in early teenage or before, were commonly reported, but imbued with little significance by interviewees. Fox, for example, laughed about getting 'locked up in the police cells at the age of ten for nicking a couple of Lego men from a toy shop'. At fourteen, Susan had stolen items of clothing (her 'going-out gear') whilst on shopping trips with her mother (unbeknownst to her). People wanted things they did not have the money for and, as Stevo put it, shoplifting was 'for a laugh, like'. This sort of offending whilst truanting was regarded as a common, relatively trivial and passing feature of early teenage years. Getting caught by parents or police was often enough to deter it.

Growing up and going out: pubs, clubs and alcohol

As the informants approached their later teenage most left street corner society behind and began to participate in the more commercialised, alcohol-based leisure activities aimed at young adults (see Hollands, 1995; Roberts et al., 1990; HMSO, 2000; Chatterton and Hollands, 2002). Leanne (16) described this general shift in leisure career:

It's, like, the 12–13 year olds who are drinking on the streets and 15–16 year olds who are in the pubs. You see 'em all down the town. They're all getting too old to go on the streets, they go out [into town] now... it's just somewhere to go. But I don't think it's a good thing 'cos they're underage. I shouldn't say this 'cos I'm the same! When I started going —— I feel more older and, like —— Just going to a disco. I love discos and that, and coming in late.[4]

The move from the street to pubs and clubs tended to coincide with the cessation of compulsory schooling. Young men became able to present themselves as old enough to enter licensed premises; some females made this move at even earlier ages. As Lucy put it, 'All you need to get into *The Capital* [a night-club] is a short skirt, knee-high boots, a little top and loads of make-up'. Other young women (and men) postponed 'nights out on the town' because they feared being turned away from pubs and clubs for being underage. The potential violence that can accompany such nights out was also a deterrent for some young men (see chapter 9).

By this age many – but not all – had started jobs or training schemes that provided the income necessary to participate in youth nightlife. Contemporary accounts of youth leisure tend to emphasise aspects of (sub)cultural differentiation in explaining young people's consumer 'lifestyles' (e.g. Bennett, 2000; Miles, 2000; Chatterton and Hollands, 2002). More prosaic factors often influenced youth leisure in these poor neighbourhoods. Other studies have described the 'leisure poverty' of the young unemployed (Banks et al., 1992: 59). Here sheer lack of money sometimes prohibited participation in desired leisure pursuits (such as going to the cinema, night-clubs or ten-pin bowling), leaving some materially excluded from the sort of leisure life-styles that others now enjoyed: 'We just sit in watching the TV or if it's pay day [i.e. bene-fit payment day] we get a few cans and a video' (Louise, seventeen, unemployed). Progress in school-to-work careers also allowed the development of new friendship groups via workplaces, training schemes or college courses and separation from those made at school. As Sam (16) put it, 'we're actually getting further and further apart as we're getting older'. Friends from school and the neighbourhood would be seen around, but for those who spent working days away from their immediate locales, the physical sites for maintaining day-to-day social contact had gone.

Thus, for most interviewees teenage street corner society gave way to more mainstream, commercialised leisure life-styles afforded by young adults' increased age and income. The hub of leisure life gravitated from the immediate neighbourhood of their outlying estates to the pubs and clubs of the town centre. This general pattern of leisure career was not followed by two groups that are of significance for current debates about transition and exclusion: 'disengaged' young men and young mothers. In the next section we concentrate on the first group, leaving more detailed discussion of young motherhood and its social and economic consequences for chapter 7.

Street corner society and social exclusion

JM: What sort of thing do you do in the evenings?
Broderick: Drink, cause havoc, fight.

Several of those men who were in the late teens and early twenties described how 'hanging around' the estates was *maintained* as their dominant form of leisure throughout the teenage years and into early adulthood.

Unlike counterparts from school days who had at least some form of progression into continued education or the labour market, these repeatedly unemployed young men lacked the sites through which to establish new, more socially varied or geographically spread social networks. For them, friendship groups had hardened up, become more tightly knit and almost wholly based on the immediate neighbourhood of home (Campbell, 1993). They associated with other similarly placed men from their immediate neighbourhood and often referred to themselves by the names of particular estates or parts of estates (e.g. 'the lads from the top end of Brookeville'). They were largely excluded – materially – from the pleasures of youthful nightlife in the pubs and clubs of the town centre (see Chatterton and Hollands, 2002).

One of the main problems became filling time. Even though many had missed much of their formal education, the fact that they should have been at school flavoured days wandering around their estates with a little excitement. Choosing whether to attend or dodge school also gave some sense of autonomy and some difference to the days. Now there was little else to do but spend every day and every evening 'hanging around'. Matty (20) was asked how he filled his unemployed days: 'Don't know, just hang about with a few lads. Round our way. Just come out to Primrose Vale, hang about with 'em, playing football or anything. Just hang about.' Ian Loader's excellent study *Youth, Policing and Democracy* (1996) describes how young people's localised identities and persistent use of public space can be a reflection of wider, 'marginalising' transitions. Although this was a study of a different locality (Edinburgh), his description tallies very closely with our own:

> Denied the purchasing power needed to use, or even to get to, other parts of the city (and most importantly the city centre) unemployed youths are for the most part confined to the communities in which they live...as a result, the 'locality' tends to retain a prominent place in the lives of marginalised young people, both as a site of routine

activities and as the basis of their identities...hanging around the streets becomes a culturally inappropriate way of killing endless time. (1996: 112–13)

Across the fieldwork (as in Loader's research), interviewees operated with subjective, mental maps of their area that subdivided it into separate neighbourhoods and locales, each with their own reputations (i.e. greater or lesser associations with crime and risks to personal safety; see chapter 8). In an evocative turn of phrase, one youth worker told us that local young men 'penned themselves into their own patch'. Interviewees – particularly young men of the sort that we are focusing on in this section of the chapter – displayed affinity with their 'own' area (and sometimes hostility to the young men of other nearby locales).

Forrest and Kearns ponder the implications of globalisation for place-based identities (a question we return to in chapters 8 and 10). They say, 'intuitively, it would seem that as source of social identity the neighbourhood is being eroded with the emergence of a more fluid, individualised way of life. Social networks are city-wide, national inter-national and increasingly virtual' (2001: 2129). Their intuition may play out for 'cosmopolitans' elsewhere, but it does not for the 'locals' of East Kelby. The sense of territoriality, belonging and attachment to a neighbourhood peer group, was a rare constant in the lives of young men who, with the passing of their teenage years, had been left largely unemployed and disconnected from the progress that other young adults had made. Danny was 21 and serving a sentence in a Young Offender's Institution (YOI):

JM: Are you still in contact with people you went to school with?
Danny: No, I've moved on from there now.
JM: So, who do you see when you go out?
Danny: Just lads off the estate and that. From round Orchard Bank —— there's a few lads in here [the YOI] from the estate as well.
JM: And most of the lads you knock about with, would you say that they're involved in crimes as well?
Danny: Yeah, yeah.

Continued engagement with street corner society was clearly a gendered process. Whilst some young women, like Annie below, had similar experiences of disaffection from school (e.g. Annie had been a frequent truant and eventually absented herself permanently, leaving school with no qualifications), none in our study continued with street leisure into their late teens or beyond. As we will show in chapter 7, processes of disengagement from street corner society for young women (and some young men) – the 'time to grow up', as Annie puts it – often coincided with important steps in their housing and family careers (chiefly the onset of parenthood and the establishment of independent living). Her interview was interesting because it foregrounds the power of local social networks in shaping individual identities and possibilities. Here Annie directly frames an account of how she strove to overcome 'the Orchard Bank attitude' in departing from her previous life-style to return to education to become a university student via an Access course, with a comparison of her boyfriend's *deepening* immersion in prevailing, neighbourhood street culture and the apparent attraction of a particular form of masculine identity in this process:

JM: What were your friends' reactions when they knew you were going to college?
Annie: Oh, 'you're the only one that's got a head on your shoulders' and all this. I mean there was a few bickering and bitching, you know: 'Bet you think you're summat, don't you?' You know what I mean? Why? Why do I 'think I'm summat?' I mean, I'm from Orchard Bank like anybody else. It's just happened that I've grown out of that Orchard Bank attitude basically.
JM: What do you think that Orchard Bank attitude is like?
Annie: I dunno. It's just so easy to get in that role. Get into that drug scene, the burglaries. I mean it's there, handed on a plate. It's like the norm in some cases. At a young age you don't know what you're doing. Like, I didn't know what I was doing when I was at school. I just thought it was a laugh. I mean if you're knocking around Orchard Bank, it's easy. 'Oh, we're going to stand around the shops, are you coming?' 'Oh yeah, yeah'. I was like that in school. I didn't wanna know in school. But I just never went onto drugs and I never went onto burglaries. But I was hanging around, like. Then I got into babysitting [a part-time job] and that, otherwise I would have been [still] hanging around the streets.
JM: And 'cos you had a boyfriend, a long-term relationship, that probably affected the way you spent your time ——
Annie: Yeah, well he used to knock about the shops but he used to be the quiet one, the sensible one, but he used to be there. And whereas now it's totally different, it's like 'All right Sammy, you all right?', you know what I mean? He's one of the lads, like. He's 'the man', you know, sort of thing. That's what they're like. I tell him 'Oh, you're stupid'.

JM: So does he still hang around with his friends from Orchard Bank?
Annie: Yeah, yeah, yeah, yeah. And I think maybe that's our battle.
I mean, I'm not saying he should grow away from them. I mean, my
friends are from Orchard Bank but there's a time to grow up, there's
a limit.

'Disengaged' young men and the emergence of criminal and drug-using careers

We have argued that the widespread street socialising of East Kelby
children and teenagers should *not* be read as indicative of their social
disaffection and incipient delinquency. For some, however, such street-
based networks *did* provide the forum for early drug experimentation
or delinquency and became, for a proportion of these, long-term alternatives to regular participation in formal education, training or employment
(Pavis and Cunnigham-Burley, 1999). In chapter 9 we map in more
detail the *consolidation and development* of more serious drug and criminal
careers (and explain what we mean by these terms). Here we concentrate
on the processes that led to the *emergence* – for some of these disengaged
young men – of these sorts of transition. For this group, long-standing
participation in strongly localised, street-based peer networks was both
a cause and effect of their exclusion from the social and economic
mainstream. Sustained involvement over years led them progressively
away from opportunities that may previously have been open to them,
thus entrenching their exclusion.

In general, sustained criminal careers were initiated as a group response
to the tedious days opened up by frequent school absence (nine of the
eleven interviewees who had been imprisoned had been frequent truants)
(Cullingford and Morrison, 1996):

> Just me and this other lad used to nick off all the time . . . Just go and
> hang about the town —— that was me starting days of crime and that,
> yeah —— shoplifting and pinching bikes, that's what it was.
>
> (Danny, 21, YOI inmate)

In earlier years aimless leisure had been spiced with occasional wrongdoing (at this age, typically illicit smoking, drinking and drug use and
a bit of shoplifting). Nearly always these were group activities, carried out
by friends known from the neighbourhood and school who mutually
nurtured a critical attitude to the latter. As Little (1990) points out, at
this early stage of criminal careers (and later), the actual doing of crime

was a relatively rare activity in the sense that, even for the most persistent offenders, criminal acts accounted for only a small amount of time in a typical day or week.[5]

The shift from relatively widespread, occasional wrongdoing (typified by instances of shoplifting) to less common, more purposeful, acquisitive and other crimes was associated with *persistent* physical absence from school and *continued* commitment to street-based peer groups. The thieving of saleable items from garden sheds, garages and cars was the next most common offence of those listed by the sample and also appeared to be the offence to which (some) shoplifters graduated in their criminal careers. Still of school age and still filling truant time, these were as much leisure-time crimes as anything else (Stephen and Squires, 2003). Although Richy said that he had often 'mooched [stolen from] sheds', he did not consider himself 'a bad lad, a real thief'. Acquisitive crime did raise cash, but the main motivation was to relieve boredom: 'when you pinch summat, like a barbecue set you can sell on for £10, you can buy yourselves a few bottles of cider, can't you? You can cure your boredom then.' At this stage, theft can be understood primarily as leisure; exciting, thrill-driven moments in otherwise dull days. Barney (20, in YOI) describes how stealing motor-bikes had been a 'big thing' in his teenage years:

> We'd go all through the night, you know what I mean? Over a back wall and have a motorbike away. We'd always pinch them in the summer [too], drive them around on the field. We've got the bikes to take chase if the police come after us and that would make for a good buzz.

Reference to 'the buzz' was very frequent in attempts to explain earlier criminality and given as the sole motivation behind the few instances of vehicle theft reported to us. Asked about this, Gazz (also a 20-year-old, YOI inmate) commented:

> No, not bad crimes, not bad stuff. Just jumping in cars which were nicked. Not nicking them. Just jumping in with the lads for a spin round. Looking back, I can't see why I did it. Daft stuff. Just the buzz. Like these two bottles of pop I nicked – and a can of aftershave – that's my two shoplifting ones. I didn't really need them. I just did it. For the buzz I suppose.

As we describe in chapter 9, some young men graduated from these thrill-seeking, leisure-time crimes to crimes more oriented to raising cash.

Again, loyalty to street-based peer networks was an important part of this process. Although, Matty (now 20) had done well at school with a good academic reputation (in another part of Kelby) a combination of events and processes conspired to set him on a different course. These partly relate to the death of his father when Matty was fourteen, subsequent rows with his mother and a shift from occasional, petty offending to more frequent and serious criminal activity. At fifteen, Matty decided to attend a different school, closer to home in East Kelby. This meant that he began to spend more of his leisure time with a set of young men from his own estate and his schoolwork deteriorated dramatically:

> Then I went to Orchard Bank school. Most of my mates round our end [his part of the estate] went there so I knew I'd fit in straight away — I was in all the top classes anyway. I was expected B's and C's for my exams — but I didn't sit them. I got in trouble again — I started getting in a crowd round our end again, burgling — it was other people, who'd been shot out of [expelled from] schools already — I was still going [to school], it was just on a night-time, started burgling and all that, with the wrong crowd . . . So I was always up in court — Then in the end, couple of months before the exams — I dunno, I just took their advice, and they were egging me on and I ended up staying off [truanting from school] and then just left the whole thing altogether . . . I just listened to them. They said, 'It's no good, you're wasting your time going to school, it's crap' . . .   Half of them are in jail [now] or on the gear and that, drugs.

Looking back, virtually all those with more committed criminal careers referred to their attachments to estate-based, street youth culture in explaining their transitions to crime. Long-term participation in illicit and dangerous activities (that brought excitement, some income and social standing amongst friends) inspired a strong camaraderie that served to separate further those on this track from the wider set of peers that they knew in their schooldays. This in itself served to perpetuate criminal and drug-using careers. Abandoning them would mean abandoning what in many cases was the thing that they had come to value most in their lives: their friends. With the passing of time and the rolling-on of criminal careers, these informants came to recognise that detachment from their social networks was critical if their attempts to desist from crime were to be successful (see chapter 9).

Matty was explicit about these effects. At fourteen, he had been – in comparison with others in the sample – a successful school pupil following a largely unremarkable path. By fifteen, he was burgling local houses. He was adamant that the fact of living in Primrose Vale had made him vulnerable to the blandishments of criminal associates, which, in turn, had denied the possibility of effective engagement with employment after he left school. His post-school years had consisted of periods of Youth Training and short-term employment interspersed with time on the dole. He was currently serving a three-year period of probation for burglary:

> *JM*: So you had a habit of hanging around with the wrong people? Why was that, do you think?
> *Matty*: Dunno. Probably because I grew up around the area. It's the only reason I can think of.
> *JM*: Do you still see the lads you went to school with?
> *Matty*: Yeah, now and again. They're on the dole now mostly, or at college. Just the dole most of 'em. Half of 'em are in jail. God knows where they are, on drugs or something.
> *JM*: When you left school do you think you could have done everything different, like get a job and maybe you might not have got involved in crime?
> *Matty*: I was in that crowd at the time. No matter what you done, if you're in that crowd you just stick with 'em really. So you'd have just ruined that job anyway. If you leave the crowd before you get the job – that was the only way it could have changed you, I think.
> *JM*: You said before it was because of where you grew up?
> *Matty*: Yeah, you can't get out of it unless you move out of the area. It's the only way.

Summary and conclusion: youth culture, peer groups and transitions

According to our evidence, investigation of young people's social networks and leisure careers constitutes an important part of the task of understanding the exclusionary transitions of some young people. Other aspects of transition – such as school-to-work, family, housing, criminal and drug-using careers – shaped leisure careers. Steps taken in these arenas are, in turn, strongly *influenced by* young people's shifting leisure activities and peer associations. Two sub-samples of young adults differed from the predominant pattern of leisure career that we described: young mothers (see chapter 7) and 'disengaged' young men. As a precursor to chapter 9, we have focused here on the latter group and investigated how their leisure activities related to particular social networks and how, in turn, these influenced broader exclusionary processes, particularly through the generation of criminal and drug-using careers.

Compared with earlier years, the web of associations of these young men had become smaller, more tightly defined and composed almost entirely of others in the same social and economic situation. Leisure activities at this stage in their lives were limited in range, constrained by poverty and focused, on a daily basis, on the immediate neighbourhood. This combined hardening up of social networks and closing in of leisure activities has implications for this group in terms of individuals' capacity to alter the course of their transition. This was chiefly, we argue, because these changes brought with them a closing down of the range of self-identities available to young men in their situation (Little, 1990).[6] As Matty put it, 'No matter what you done, if you're in that crowd you just stick with 'em.'

Collison (1996: 428) wonders 'what form of masculine identity is open to the young men of the (ex-)working-class now described as an underclass'. He argues that out of the double-bind created by 'the contemporary priority given to consumption' in a context of 'persisting structural exclusions', such young men commit to the sense of active agency, excitement, loyalty and status to be gained from risky, criminally-oriented street culture: 'there is a level of ontological security and trust to be found on the street which obviates some of the uncertainties and insecurities of being male on the margins of civil society' (Collison, 1996: 429).

In our study, such peer groups were powerful in shaping the range of activities, identities and futures that were deemed possible by their members. Their habitus (Bourdieu, 1990: 53) defined 'things to do or not to do': for example, whether it was seen as permissible and proper to attend school, sit examinations, go to college, remain on benefits, use heroin, burgle houses, and so on. Long-term participation by young men in street corner society generated adherence to a particular form of (sub)culturally defined personal identity, values and 'life-style' which became important in circumscribing broader career possibilities at a particularly important life stage. Collison interpreted the narratives of the young male offenders in his study as being imbued with global cultural references and largely detached 'from fast disappearing local cultural traditions and structures' (1996: 441). This may have been true of his subjects, but it was not for ours. Rather, the form of masculine identity they described showed clear, cultural correspondence with longer-standing ways of becoming a working-class man in this place (Crawshaw, 2004).

These local, informal cultures of the street placed great value on becoming/being (seen as) a young man with a particular style of resilient, 'hard' masculinity (Campbell, 1993; Hobbs, 1994; McDowell, 2001). Defining features here were a continued hostility to abstract, academic learning and preference for 'real' manual work (Willis, 1977), a belief in the importance of being able to 'handle yourself' – which spilled out into occasional and sometimes extreme physical aggression against young men who were not members of their peer group (Loader, 1996) – and a (perhaps self-deluding) self-image that proclaimed their ability to get by in hard times through individual, sometimes criminal enterprise.

Kearns and Parkinson (2002: 2106) remark on how young people in poor neighbourhoods seem 'extremely territorial in their behaviour, so that their action spaces or wider neighbourhoods have very limited horizons'. They ask whether this derives from 'the urban problem of fear and anxiety concerning the unknown, or due to the comforting benefits of one's familiar neighbourhood, or simply the result of "knowing one's place"'. We suggest that all their proposed answers are correct to some extent. Our answer would, however, prioritise the progressive, contingent effects of particular combinations of school-to-work, family, crime and leisure career so that, for some 'excluded youth', but not others, social life becomes almost wholly centred on the home neighbourhood (Ball et al., 2000b). Kearns and Parkinson (2002) link their question to a wider discussion of the influence of neighbourhood on social capital and social exclusion; a topic to which we return in chapter 10.

The subject of this chapter has not been the usual fare of the transitions studies that have dominated youth research in Britain over the past twenty years. The subject matter perhaps comes closer to the sub-cultural studies tradition (see chapter 2). The seminal work of the CCCS has been criticised for, among other things, taking a too restricted view of youth culture and ignoring what the mass of young people do most of the time. Yet their most developed statement of sub-culture theory – the introduction to *Resistance through Rituals* (Clarke et al., 1976) – described the importance of understanding how 'loosely defined' and 'unlabelled' youth sub-cultures offer 'solutions' to the immediate, concrete problems that young people encounter.[7]

In re-reading *Resistance through Rituals* we were struck by the correspondences between its depiction of the more generalised and prosaic forms of masculine, working-class, delinquent sub-culture and our own description of the street corner society of 'disengaged' young men in

East Kelby. The CCCS's theorisation of how sub-cultural forms reflect historically and locally specific, class-based problems and possibilities also tallies with our account of how the peer networks and leisure lives of working-class young men in East Kelby reflected, and contributed to, their broader social and economic exclusion.[8] Their peer group associations and leisure pursuits grew out of their experiences of school and neighbourhood and shaped their involvement in crime and drug use. They also articulated with and held consequences for their engagement with the post-sixteen world of work. Whilst more or less committed to the 'delinquent solution', virtually all of these disengaged young men still clung to traditional, working-class values about the importance of work, even if their periods of imprisonment, drug habits and loyalty to street corner society often hindered them in getting and keeping jobs. They shared an understanding of their locality, gained from their personal and family experience, that told them that what was important in terms of 'getting on', for instance in terms of finding a job, was not what you knew (e.g. as evidenced in school qualifications) but who you knew (see chapter 3). Being 'streetwise' and 'one of the lads' connected into the publicly visible, social life of their estates – and the informal tip-offs about job vacancies and informal references to potential employers that came with it – was, they argued, a key, initial element of an effective job search strategy. Being physically capable and ready to work long hours, in hard conditions, for low pay, at short notice was a second requirement (see chapter 6).

In chapter 9 we see how the early criminal careers of some disengaged young men hardened up, often under the pressure of interconnected careers of problematic drug use. Before that, though, we return to a consideration of school-to-work careers and, as part of this, explore how the culturally derived knowledge and strategies of these young men, and of the sample as a whole, articulated with the facts of their local labour market.

5
Paths to Work? Youth Training, New Deal and Further Education

Introduction

Despite moves towards more encompassing analyses, the study of school-to-work careers remains a mainstay of youth research and economic aspects of transition remain crucial to understanding the wider experiences of youth (Roberts, 2000). As described in chapter 2, changes in the 'structures of opportunity' facing school leavers have helped create pathways to adulthood that are more extended, complex and fluid than in previous decades (Coles, 1995; Jones, 2002; Mizen, 2003). Key among these developments has been the proliferation of routes for working-class youth through further education and vocational training programmes. For most young people in Britain, quick-step entry to the labour market of jobs – once typical of working-class youth transitions – has been postponed, subsequent to the completion of courses in the new institutional panoply of post-sixteen 'options'. Chapter 1 showed how dominant British policy analyses present worklessness as the key cause of social exclusion. For young people 'at risk' of social exclusion – like those young men focused on in chapter 4 – the main government effort has been towards engaging them in pre- and post-sixteen training and educational courses, thereby increasing their employability and their likely incorporation into more socially inclusive transitions.

This chapter provides the first part of a discussion of our informants' post-school, labour market careers. It investigates school leaving and those elements of these new transitional arrangements that were most significant in their biographies: post-compulsory, further education (FE); Youth Training schemes (YT); and the New Deal for Young People programme (NDYP). Chapter 6 examines the notional end-point of these encounters: the getting of jobs.

'That's the way it is, isn't it?' gender, class and leaving school

Our questions about interviewees' plans, feelings and decision-making at the time they left school evoked answers reflective of well-known patterns of gender differentiation. Although there was some uncertainty about the *particular* job a person might like to end up in, preferred training, educational or employment options were stubbornly bound to their perceptions of appropriate choices for young women and men (Griffin, 1985). Where young women spoke of wanting to work or train in hairdressing, catering, cleaning, childcare and 'business administration' (i.e. as secretaries or receptionists), young men spoke of becoming builders, mechanics, scaffolders and soldiers (Howieson, 2003). When individuals did switch between courses they tended to remain within gender-typical parameters, for example, swapping a business administration scheme for one in hairdressing. Rebecca (16) aspired to a range of typically 'female' jobs:

I wanted to do like elderly care, or childcare, cleaning or hairdresser — I'd rather do, like, cleaning most...I just like doing it.

For a few, theirs was a long-standing ambition. Kayleigh (16) said she had wanted 'to do hairdressing from when I was little'. Louise (17), on the other hand, opted for 'the first thing that came into me head' (a course in business administration). For most, there was little obvious motivation beyond the apparent enjoyment they derived from (or imagined in) the work itself and the indirect influence of others they knew who had worked in a similar job:

I can't remember choosing my career at all. I don't know why I chose it [hairdressing]...I enjoyed messing around with hair and things like that and then my Auntie was a hairdresser.

(Marge, 23)

Knowing same-sex relatives or friends who were employed in a particular line of work was a widespread influence on the way that young people 'chose' their working futures. Richy told us he wanted to join the Navy because 'most of me family have been in the Forces and I just wanted to carry on'. Paul had wanted to become a car mechanic for a long time: 'My Dad is a mechanic and owns his own garage.'

The dogged persistence of gender stereotyping in the plans and desires of this sample is intriguing. The interviewees gave the same sort

of answers as their predecessors in youth studies from the 1980s and
before (e.g. Griffin, 1985; Cockburn, 1987). These 'occupational choices'
by gender appear, however, to be more narrowly confined than the
employment horizons envisaged in more recent studies (see Ball et al.,
2000a, on post-sixteen choices and pathways in London). This contrast
can be explained in part by the differences in the 'structures of opportunity' facing school-leavers in London and East Kelby; with the former
possessing a greater range and mix of post-sixteen, employment-related
opportunities than this smaller, working-class town. As we described in
chapter 4, social networks of peers and kin also played a powerful role
in shaping the way young people perceived and acted on the choices
open to them. Informal, collective knowledge and rules about the right
way of becoming and being a working-class young adult did much to
govern the shape of school-to-work careers. Unlike their counterparts
in Ball et al.'s study, these young people were embedded in a relatively
stable, 'closed' and mono-cultural, working-class community and their
reaction to the 'options' presented to them were, at least in part, steered
by the values and traditions of the place. The channelling of young
people towards work sharply defined as 'masculine' or 'feminine' reflects
one aspect of this cultural inheritance.

Formal agencies also helped shape 'occupational choice' and statutory
careers advice and guidance served, overall, to confirm the sample's
predominant choice to exit formal education at the earliest opportunity
and their prejudice in favour of gender stereotypical training. As in
Britton et al.'s study (2002), the formal advice and guidance received
about post-sixteen decisions (whether from Careers Teachers or Careers
Officers) was reported as being rushed and superficial. Typically, these
meetings revolved around the career adviser asking young people what
they might like to do and then the provision of standard information
about what steps were needed to achieve this outcome (e.g. where to
enrol for a particular sort of YT scheme), as Matty describes:

> Yeah, they asked me what I'd like to do and I just told him them
> options and he said, 'Yeah, that's fine'. It was only very brief,
> though, that he was talking to me — a ten-minute interview thing.
> 'Cos he had to go round everyone — He just sent me out a print out
> of an action plan, that was it — that's all I got.

Although several people mentioned that they had few definite plans
(beyond an awareness of 'masculine' and 'feminine' options), rarely did
interviews open out into a fuller discussion of the young person's interests

or potential and the range of possibilities that might be open to them. Rather, 'they just asked you what you thought you wanted to do, you told them, they told you what you need and that was that' (Sarah) or, as Lisa put it, 'I think that's what most people do now, innit? Give you information rather than try and talk you through things.' Going by these accounts, our interviewees were not often encouraged to consider further education. Shifting uncertain school leavers onto local training schemes appeared to be the most common practice for careers advisers working with East Kelby young people:

> *Kelly*: Yeah, they just shoved me in 'Futures' [a large YT provider].
> *Kate*: Yeah, they shoved me in 'Community Training' [another large YT provider].
> *Kelly*: 'You have to go and work there.'
> *Kate*: They said, 'Right, you can go, you've got an interview there'. It's like, 'Oh right' —— I just got shoved there, me.
> (Kelly, 25, and Kate, 22, both non-employed mothers)

Describing these young people as forced conscripts onto YT would not, however, be completely accurate. Rather, training schemes were 'the easy option':

> *Fox*: Yeah, it seemed the easy option plus a bit of money in their pocket —— Easy as it was there for them. They could go on and do a YT —— it was a thought put in people's minds.
> *RM*: So who put that thought into their minds?
> *Fox*: I suppose it was some of the careers advisers, they were just several of the options that were around – college, YTs, jobs, whatever you can get into and this one seemed to be open... They didn't really have to prove themselves to do it. It was just a case of going there.
> (Fox, 19, New Deal trainee)

So whilst interviewees did refer to being 'pressured' into 'what they wanted me to do' (Paul, 16) – and understood this as the consequence of careers advisers having to process a large case load of 'clients' quickly and the many YT places that needed filling – there was also a begrudging acceptance that there were few other realistic alternatives. With a general distaste for continued education, limited or non-existent educational qualifications and few decent jobs available, YT was seen as the easy, possibly only, option. Older friends, siblings and other relatives had often been through local schemes and were able to suggest particular ones to approach but, perhaps more importantly in attempting to understand these school-to-work careers, this also reinforced a perception that this was to be their own likely destination too.[1] This is an example of what we mean when we refer to the power of social networks in shaping transitions. The mood of many of these discussions was, thus, one of resignation even when interviewees expressed a strong sense of being directed into low-grade futures. Allan (now 21) had taken steps to join the Navy at sixteen and 'had arranged all that meself'. He failed the required maths test, however, so asked a Careers Adviser to identify courses that he might take to remedy this, but:

> I didn't hear nowt from her. In the end, she was just giving me warehouse jobs to try out and that —— 'Cos I was in a low class [at school], you know what I mean? I'm brainier than half the top classes but that's the way it is, isn't it?

The mixed experience of further education

Not all the sample dispensed with formal education for good at the age of sixteen. By the time of our second round of interviews, just under a quarter of the sample had been enrolled on some form of educational course outside the ambit of YT. Given the modest qualifications gained by the age of sixteen and their generally less than positive experience of school, it is not surprising that few entered full-time, further educational courses as their *first*, post-school destination. Ten of these re-sat GCSE subjects to improve their grades or enrolled on National Vocational Qualification (NVQ) courses. Only one person moved straight to a more academic, A-level course.

Another ten people had experience of educational courses undertaken *later* in their school-to-work careers. As well as GCSE re-sits and NVQ courses, these included short, skills-oriented courses delivered in community centres (e.g. in basic computing and first aid), Access courses run by FE colleges (designed to qualify 'mature students' for university degree programmes), A-level studies and for three people undergraduate courses at the local university. Our term 'further education' therefore covers a broader set of encounters than usually referred to under this heading. As noted in chapter 3, there was, therefore, some evidence of young adults re-engaging with education following earlier, disappointing and sometimes disaffecting experiences and a key aim of our discussion here is to understand young adults' changing motivations towards and mixed experiences of further education.

Reluctant recruits?

Several factors explain these young people's limited and episodic take-up of further educational courses during their late teenage and early twenties. Given their personal and household poverty, financial reasons were given by several people for their earlier choice not to continue in education:

> I thought at the time, getting a wage [in fact, a YT allowance], which was only £30 a week, was better than going to college and getting nothing, so —— I decided to go with Futures [a YT provider] —— If I could go back now, I think I would've went to college.
>
> (Martin, 20, employed)

The Educational Maintenance Allowance (EMA) is designed to encourage higher rates of participation in further education (Ashworth et al., 2001; Legard et al., 2001; Maguire et al., 2001). The allowance is means-tested, can give up to £30 per week and has bonus payments dependent on attendance and attainment. Although Kelby was one of the places in which the EMA was piloted by government, most of our sample had been too old to be eligible. Nevertheless, that EMAs might open up – materially – the possibility of further education was welcomed by a number of interviewees. It would help people contribute to household budgets and sustain leisure life-styles whilst studying at college (see chapter 4). National evaluations suggest that the EMA might lead to increases in post-compulsory education of between 3 and 11 percentage points (Ashworth et al., 2001). In Kelby, there was an apparently dramatic increase of 16 per cent between 1998 and 1999 (www.teesnet, accessed 22 March 2000).[2] The real test of the value of EMAs is whether they encourage individuals like Martin (above) into further education as a way of widening post-sixteen – and possibly post-eighteen[3] – educational participation to socially and materially excluded groups, thereby improving their chances of entering higher-level employment in the longer term. The timing and design of our study – and other evaluations to date – are such that we cannot yet answer that question.[4]

For others, it was disenchantment with secondary-level schooling that led them to avoid 'more of the same' when the chance came at sixteen: 'I don't fancy it, I just think I've had enough of school' (Clare, recent school leaver). Some who did go on to FE college had little belief in the utility of their course of study or much commitment to it. They were reluctant recruits. For them, the classroom atmosphere and academic curricula were too reminiscent of school days. Sam (16 and receiving the EMA) was studying electrical installation:

> I'm actually having second thoughts about going to college at the moment. It's getting me down and I'm thinking about asking our Dad to see if there's any [jobs] going at his place [a removals firm] ... I'd rather have something that's always practical or use my hands instead of, like, sitting down just writing forms out and stuff like that — If I get a job before I leave college then, yeah, when I've got the job I'll leave college but if I don't, then I'll actually stick at it. Plus the fact you get £30 a week through the EMA.

By second interview, however, Sam had decided the more theoretical aspect of his course was not to his liking, had quit college and joined a YT warehousing scheme, which he enjoyed a lot more. Some of those who re-engaged with education had similar experiences. These informants were particularly dismissive of the disruptive, 'childish' behaviour of other students. Susan (22) had returned to college briefly, a couple of years earlier, having spent the years since school looking after her daughter and trying unsuccessfully to get a job:

> But 'cos I've got no GCSEs, no work background — so I thought I may as well get some more certificates ... [but] I mean, college! I'd rather do what I'm doing now [Employment Training].[5] College was all sixteen-year-old kids and they were giggly and, like, you know, sat at the back of the class and I felt a bit out of place. I'd rather come here and actually do something. I mean I'm doing all practical work here, so I'm actually doing summat, not just doing write-ups about things —

Sam and Susan dropped out of college because – in different ways – they felt they did not 'fit' with the route selected or others on it. Tara (22) hints at the same process, but in this case she implies that differences between her and her new peers in respect of previous schooling, academic confidence and cultural capital motivated her departure:

> When I left school I was going to college to do my A levels. I had all these big plans so I went to Ackthorpe College and hated every minute of it! What I found [laughing] was that St. Claire's [her previous secondary school] wasn't that great a school compared to the schools

these other people had gone to. They'd all read Shakespeare and I'd never read a Shakespeare book in my life! . . . I managed through a year, just! —— I sat, like, a mock exam half way, and —— my results were that lousy I said 'Oh, I've got no chance'. So that was the end of that really.

Several interviewees referred to their distaste for more abstract learning as an important source of dissatisfaction with college (despite the fact that the courses on which they had been enrolled were vocational ones).[6] Doing 'practical work' (Susan) was preferred and more likely to be found on YT, ET and NDYP, if not in the form of employment. In Tara's case, she switched from studying A-levels to a YT course in hairdressing: 'The best decision I've ever made.' These same tastes and preferences sometimes generated alternative patterns of post-sixteen educational participation and quite different assessments of college. Andrew stepped quickly from school into YT, abandoning this after four months for an FE course in catering. Although it involved (only) one day per week on work placement, it was this aspect of it – the 'hands-on' learning of the job – in which he took most pride:

I loved every minute of it —— I did a range of jobs [at his hotel place-ment]. I did portering. I did silver service waitering. I did laundry service and also catering —— You had to do all your whites and every-thing and you need to know how to fold them correctly. We used to, like, turn up at half past eight and the chef'd need to see your whites. If they weren't right he'd send you to the spare room to iron them before you came back in the kitchen. So that's how we learnt how to press them neatly, like they do in the Forces!

Accessing Higher Education

Even in places like East Kelby with historically depressed levels of entry to higher education, some young people pursue paths that lead them eventually to university. By the time of our second round of interviews, three female informants had achieved this. Their perceptions of becoming and experiences of being 'non-traditional students' were typical of others like them (Forsyth and Furlong, 2003). They had enrolled for courses at the nearest university, one that prides itself on its systems for 'widening access' to working-class people. One of the most obvious, cultural barriers to fulfilling this mission is the belief, shared by our interviewees, that university is 'not for the likes of them'. Their class-based and gendered self-identities (Reay, 2003) – together with their disappointing experiences of school and life since – made university enrolment seem a very distant possibility. Simple lack of confidence in taking this step was a theme that ran through several interviews.

Having left school with low GCSE grades, Sarah moved between factory jobs, unemployment and unfinished YT and college courses. Her housing career had been particularly chaotic (see chapter 8). When we first met her, aged 23, she was more settled. When she was not caring for her young children as a single parent, she studied a one-year university access course, hoping to make progress in her life. By the time of our second interview, Sarah had become a history student at the local university. She found that at least some of the other students were not too dissimilar to herself: 'It's not what I expected at all. I expected it to be this big, posh university and the people to be mammy's and daddy's girls and boys and they're not.'

Despite enjoying the course, her re-engagement with formal learning was still precarious. Her mother and grandparents were very supportive but her previous circle of friends – other young mothers from the estate – had not been encouraging of Sarah's ambitions to go to university, and the academic work was a challenge:

I have thought about packing it in a couple of times but I can't 'cos of everybody else [her family] —— They'll go mad. They keep saying 'You've got to stick at it. You can't pack it in', but it just seems like a lot of hassle for nothing at the moment —— Our Mam just says, 'Well, it's about time you stuck at something'.

For Sarah and other young mothers who had – or were thinking about – re-engaging with FE and HE courses, locating acceptable quality, affordable childcare was another barrier to be overcome (Webster et al., 2004). Lisa (20) hoped to study nursing at university but this plan was wholly dependent on whether she was allocated a free nursery place by the college where she aimed to enrol on an Access course. Even when subsidised childcare places could be found, the practical realities of combining mothering, full-time study and life on a low income remained.

Overcoming the obstacles that prohibit entry to university could generate new-found feelings of self-worth (Schuller, 2004) beyond the material benefits said to accrue to graduates (Bynner et al., 2002). Having struggled against 'the Orchard Bank attitude' (see chapter 4), Annie (24) was a first-year university student when we initially interviewed her. Like Sarah, Annie's school-to-work career had not been straightforward: frequent truancy, no educational qualifications, a chequered employment history, repeated unemployment. Having overheard a work colleague mention Access courses, she quickly enrolled at college and then university, but found the academic work difficult: 'I was out of school for seven year, so — and like not using my head sort of thing in that much depth. I was like – "I'm never gonna do it" – but I stuck it out and I done it.'

By the time of her second interview, Annie was a volunteer student mentor, working to raise the aspirations of pupils from local, poor neighbourhoods. Passing the first year of her course had filled her with a sense of achievement: 'I'm more confident, brighter and happier.' Previously, she 'used to feel inferior, whereas I don't now'. Nevertheless, other factors meant her commitment to her studies remained insecure. Annie's long-term boyfriend (currently not working and allied to neighbourhood street culture) was beginning to pressure her about starting a family. She was also 'struggling like mad with the money' and could 'understand why people pack in for financial reasons'.

Youth Training: 'didn't do nowt'

The proportion of Britain's school-leavers entering government-sponsored training programmes (such as Youth Training and the more recent 'modern apprenticeships') has declined substantially since the 1980s and 1990s (Learning and Skills Council, 2003). This has partly been the result of more buoyant labour markets (with jobs on offer), the increased emphasis on the importance of further and higher education and long-standing criticisms of the quality of much youth training (see Mizen, 2003). Nevertheless, for this sample of young people, who left school during the 1990s, Youth Training was a quantitatively and qualitatively significant element of their school-to-work careers. National trends can mask local (and class-based) differences as well. In 1998, 27 per cent of sixteen-year-olds from Orchard Bank entered Youth Training compared with just 3 per cent in nearby, middle-class Ackthorpe (Future Steps, 1999). Of our sample of 88, 33 had entered a scheme straight from school (the most common immediate destination) and, overall, 53 had been on YT at some point. Between them they had participated in 72 schemes with 20 different training providers.

Because the contours and details of young people's accounts of YT were so similar to those gathered in earlier studies (e.g. Cockburn, 1987; Finn, 1987; Lee, 1991), we only draw attention to main themes and limit illustrative quotation here. Many interviewees were able to describe the *potential* benefits of participation, such as the opportunity to gain qualifications, the chance to gain valuable, practical work experience and to earn a training allowance. Positive accounts of interviewee's *actual* experiences of YT were much rarer. YT was held in low regard by a substantial majority of the interviewees.

The most common criticism was that schemes were exploitative: trainees were given the least attractive jobs when on work placement, were the first to be blamed by employers when problems arose and the training allowance (£45 per week in the second year) was far lower than acceptable given the work done. That they were doing similar types and amounts of work to employees but receiving much lower 'pay' for it was a common refrain. Low training allowances led some to avoid YT altogether. Those that joined sometimes found it a struggle to cope financially on YT 'wages', were unable to be more financially independent and had, instead, to borrow money from friends and family.

Of course, not all youth training schemes are the same. They are stratified in terms of the quality of resources[7] and training, the allowances provided and their likelihood in providing decent work placements or in leading to jobs (Raffe, 1990; Roberts and Parsell, 1992). Informants showed some awareness of this but, because better schemes select the better qualified trainees, most ended up on schemes that seemed to fall short of official ambitions to provide consistently high-quality training (Kingston, 2003).

A few relished the undemanding, youth club atmosphere of schemes like Community Training. Broderick and Paul enjoyed this scheme more than others did because they 'didn't do nowt' and won days off for being pool champion. Overall, though, complaints about YT as being 'boring' and 'a waste of time' were very frequent. Mandy (18, unemployed) said she 'hated it. It took so long. It could have been done in six months. Training was crap. Placements were crap. Making cups of tea and stuff. Not proper admin work.'

The perceived poor quality of the training was one factor that led to a high proportion of interviewees switching between schemes or abandoning YT altogether. Only 13 per cent of those who entered YT completed the full two years of training. Whilst one or two people acknowledged that their lack of perseverance or career uncertainty accounted for their 'dropping out', other specific explanations were cited more frequently (e.g. pregnancy, illness, sexual harassment from a placement employer). More significant still in explaining the apparently weak attachment of young people to YT was the general perception that it was not likely to deliver their primary goal: getting a job.

For the 53 YT participants in our sample, only four remained in their placements as employees on completion of the scheme (and one of these was made redundant shortly afterwards). Reminiscent of studies from the 1980s and 1990s, interviewees described how YT placements operated with a 'revolving door' whereby employers had a steady stream of low-skilled but cheap, malleable labour (and trainees had a steady stream of fruitless placements). Six months after leaving, only seven of the 53 participants in YT were employed in occupations that bore any relation to their training or newly acquired qualifications. For instance, after finishing his YT in Retail, Malcolm took a job with a roofing company: 'At the end of the day I wanted a job, I wasn't bothered what job it was, as long as I could do it.'

Malcolm's comment reveals the high value placed on having a job by these young people and their scarcity within their structure of opportunities. In this context, YT was a 'second-best' option for those unable or unwilling to continue in education, often uncertain about exactly what sort of employment or career they desired but sure that employment of some sort was the primary goal in the short as well as longer term. Because jobs for relatively unskilled, under-qualified young adults were in short supply, YT – designed to inculcate 'employability' through quality skills training – became, in practice, a holding pen periodically entered and left by young people as they weighed up the possibilities of their immediate post-school years. Because informants knew it provided little labour market dividend (Furlong, 1992), schemes were swapped for what appeared, at that moment, better options (college courses, jobs or other schemes).

Our findings confirm Furlong and Cartmel's conclusion that 'working-class trainees with few qualifications' often get 'trained in contexts where the chance of employment are virtually nil' (1997: 32). Many of our first interviewees were YT trainees. We re-interviewed many of them after they had left YT. Answers to our questions about their current activities became very predictable. Virtually all were unemployed. Billy (18), who had finished his Construction YT six months earlier, summed up his situation with the words 'nothing good is happening at the moment'. He was biding his time until he became eligible for a New Deal programme.

A new deal for youth?

None of the interviewees entered stable, longer-term employment after transiting through YT schemes and/or FE courses. Episodic employment and unemployment became the norm with the next 'official' stop-off point in their labour market transitions sometimes being the New Deal for Young People programme (NDYP). The Labour government introduced this in 1998 as its flagship policy to reduce the social exclusion of 18–25-year-olds. Versions for lone parents, the over-fifties and the long-term unemployed quickly followed (Millar, 2000).[8] A key ambition was to raise the quality of work-based training for young people in the wake of numerous, long-standing criticisms (of schemes like YT). The initial, four-month 'Gateway' period offers a more 'client-centred' approach with personalised advice and counselling to promote 'job-readiness'. Participants, if then unable to find a job, choose from: employment (for which the firm receives a £60 per week subsidy); full-time education or training (leading to an NVQ level 2 qualification); a placement in the Environmental Task Force or voluntary sector; or self-employment. Participants get benefits plus £15 per week.

Whilst we discussed this programme with all interviewees, we concentrate on the accounts of those with direct, personal experience. Its reputation rests, however, not only on first-hand experience. Most interviewees knew of somebody who had participated in NDYP. As with YT, the localised, subjective assessment of the value of a particular scheme – and indeed of New Deal as a whole – became part of the common knowledge that shaped the decisions and steps of young adults.

Twenty interviewees (twelve men and eight women) had joined NDYP (and two of these also had accessed the New Deal for Lone Parents). Beyond age, the only criteria for entry are that Job Seekers' Allowance (JSA) – the main unemployment benefit for over eighteens – has been claimed for at least six months. Participants from this study had been unemployed for up to two years before being picked up by NDYP and were at different stages (e.g. some were in their first 'Gateway' phase and five were on their second programme). Because of this – and because we were unable to re-interview all the original sample – we cannot provide an evaluation of NDYP in respect of its efficacy in moving young people 'from welfare to work'. What we can do is describe the individuals' accounts of NDYP as they were experiencing it (or in retrospect) and discuss how these fit into our broader analysis of their school-to-work careers.

'Bounded agency' and compulsion

Whilst the compulsive nature of NDYP is, in fact, not new (i.e. other government schemes have contained benefit threats to induce involvement), it is also true that this has became one its defining features, chiefly because New Labour highlighted this as an example of the 'rights and responsibilities' discourse that heralded in these programmes (see chapter 1). Those meeting eligibility criteria are likely to be 'invited' to join NDYP by Employment Service staff. This was the case with the majority of our informants; only a few volunteered for it. Refusal is likely to incur reductions in, or complete withdrawal of, JSA. Quite contrary responses to the question of compulsion were given, exemplified here by Richard and Debbie:

> Either you accepted it or you got took off the dole . . . I was all right about it, 'cos I wanted a job. Like the New Deal like helps you find a job and all that.
>
> (Richard, 20, YOI inmate, ex-NDYP participant)

> I feel forced a bit, because I didn't have no choice really. I couldn't say no because they were looking for people 18–24 —— My name come up so I had to do it, and if I didn't do it, they'd stop your benefit.
>
> (Debbie, 19, NDYP participant)

Many *non*-participants chose to emphasise its non-voluntary character in their broader criticisms of the scheme. Here NDYP was an attempt by 'them', the state, the more powerful, to 'run your life' (Broderick) and to 'stitch you up' (Roy). Whilst one might dismiss such comments because they lack the authenticity that comes with direct experience, we need to remember that such views were coloured by the reports of people who *had* participated. Broderick, for instance, claimed that his brother, prior to participation, had been told by Employment Service staff: 'You've been on the dole for so and so, you're bone idle, you're lazy, we're going to put you on this course.'

Appreciative comments about NDYP were, nevertheless, more frequent than those in respect of YT even if they were still overshadowed by more hostile assessments. This different evaluation of NDYP can be understood partly in terms of participants' personal experience of it, in respect not only of its function in shifting people into suitable jobs, but also in terms of it providing training, work experience and job search guidance that was perceived as valuable and geared to personal needs and aspirations. Thus, several interviewees accepted compulsion because they had generally more benign views of the programme's purpose and value. Fox, aged nineteen, provided the most up-beat assessment of

NDYP and the best example of our point. He was enrolled on a programme run by a local university:

> *Fox*: I decided I had to do it. I wanted to do it.
> *RM*: So you weren't too bothered?
> *Fox*: I'd spent too much time on the dole and I realised, 'I've got a chance to do something here'.
> *RM*: In your case, the New Deal was a positive intervention?
> *Fox*: It was. It was very positive. I'm enjoying it...It's nice to be here. It's nice to have the option. Makes me feel that I'm going somewhere.

Contrast this favourable depiction with that given by Michael (21). Articulating New Labour thinking on this question, many of our 'stakeholder' interviewees felt local youth unemployment could be explained by the poor vocational and social skills of young job-seekers; their joblessness resulted from what they lacked (Mizen, 2003). Like others, as part of the Gateway period Michael had been sent on a twelve-week course designed to enhance 'work-readiness' (e.g. by improving communication, numeracy and literacy skills and through advice about punctuality, attendance, dress and personal hygiene). Michael entered NDYP with a cynical view of its likely benefits, a view that was bolstered by his initial encounters:

> They put me onto that course and I didn't like it and they still made me go...Just sat in a room playing games...Well I just told them. I said, 'I don't wanna come in no more'. I said, 'I don't like it' and they said, 'Fair enough, you could have your benefits stopped'. I said, 'Well, I'll have to appeal against it, won't I ?' 'Cos I'm not going on summat that I don't wanna do.

Those that avoided NDYP altogether tended to project their criticisms of earlier encounters with YT onto this programme. Some who did take part found it very similar. Echoing some descriptions of YT, Michael described how much of his time on this 'employability' course was spent 'sitting around' or doing what he felt were pointless exercises. Because he believed he was not improving his job prospects he decided to stop attending and was threatened with the withdrawal of benefits. Subsequently, he was placed with a voluntary agency refurbishing flats for homeless people. He enjoyed this and was keen to become a bricklayer (like his father), but Michael argued that without a proper, lengthy trade apprenticeship his chances were slim: 'I don't feel confident what I'm doing. You can't learn a trade like that in six months, can you? It's gotta be like a couple of year.'

This central criticism – that participation did little to improve their chances of rewarding employment of the type they wanted – was the general theme that framed more particular objections to NDYP. Those that felt that NDYP was 'just another government scheme' designed temporarily to soak up the unemployed were much more likely to find fault with other details of the scheme. Conversely, if interviewees took a general view that the NDYP *was* likely to help them into meaningful jobs, then such people appeared more prepared to accept (what others saw as) more negative aspects of the scheme, such as compulsion. This begs another question. Why did some informants adopt one position and some the other?

These differences had nothing to do with different personal dispositions towards becoming independent of welfare, as suggested by some theories of the socially excluded, underclass. The reverse seemed true. Those that devised ways of avoiding the scheme altogether (Kalra et al., 2001; Gunter, 2004) – such as signing off the benefit register shortly before they became eligible – disavowed its usefulness in the transition to secure employment. Others on the programme dodged interviews that they felt would result in short-term, 'skivvy' work placements or made desperate efforts to locate suitable jobs for themselves. In these cases, NDYP helped meet a primary political aim to reduce the unemployment count – not by making young adults more 'employable', but by operating in ways which alienate potential and actual recruits and thus further energise their search for jobs. Even those who, on the face of it, seemed disinclined to conventional employment complained about its inability to help them into sustained jobs. Curtis (21) had been claiming benefits and doing occasional, undeclared 'fiddly work' at Kelby docks when he 'got put on New Deal'. The reason he was 'gutted' about this was not because of a distaste for legitimate employment but because – he insisted – engagement in this sort of 'fiddly work' and the social networks that distributed it was far more likely than NDYP to lead to a 'proper job' (see chapter 6; MacDonald, 1994).

This general scepticism about the value of the programme was not conjured out of thin air but rooted in their practical experience of restricted school-to-work careers, particularly of YT. Many NDYP participants faced the same 'choices' previously encountered under the umbrella of YT – care, catering, business administration, painting and decorating, and so on – sometimes offered by the very same training agencies. Peter, for example, completed a joinery YT scheme but was unable to get a job in this field. He spent three years unemployed before entering NDYP. By the age of 23, Peter had added two NDYP placements in building maintenance and kitchen fitting to his CV but returned again to the dole queue. Experiences like his conjure up a 'nightmare vision of the learning society: excluded groups confined to segregated settings undergoing continuous training as a form of warehousing' (Riddell et al., 1999, cited in Coffield, 2000: 30).

Our interviewees suggested that the ambition of the Employment Service on Teesside that 'New Deal must not become a revolving door to unemployment' (1997: 46) has not been met. For them, the revolving door of YT has been replaced with that of NDYP, leading some to conclude that employers actually substituted NDYP work placements for jobs in order to reduce labour costs ('getting work for nowt', as Amy put it). If true, the programme has *added* to the social exclusion of young adults (Byrne, 1999). One national government study found that 52 per cent of the 3,209 companies surveyed admitted that their main motive in participating in the NDYP was to reduce their labour costs (Tees Valley TEC, December 2000).

The cumulative experience of school-to-work careers do much, we argue, to shape different individual's responses to NDYP and can confirm (or confound) more deeply held personal perspectives on the 'bound-edness' of individual agency (Evans et al., 2001). In chapter 7 we discuss this idea in relationship to young parenthood. We note that many people responded to our numerous areas of questioning in a manner that implicitly positioned their lives as being subject to constraints over which they had little room for personal choice or control. This did *not*, however, lead in the majority of cases to world views that explicitly blamed external social forces for individual circumstances. When 'failure' was theorised (and these interviews sometimes appeared to be the first instance of this sort of active reflection), it was usually interpreted as a personal problem (Furlong and Cartmel, 1997). When pushed, most claimed that they were the authors of their own destinies, even if their graphic descriptions of their lives told *us* the opposite story. Descriptions of NDYP gave the same sense of people struggling to make individual progress in conditions of limited choice and struggling to comprehend such progress – or the lack of it – in largely individualist terms. Fox gives a particularly pure version of this individualist frame of reference. For him, the status derived from attending a NDYP course located at a university, together with the close attention of a particularly supportive Personal Adviser, helped to confirm his benign outlook:

> *Fox*: She [Personal Adviser] was talking positively about my future. 'Would you like to do this? Would you like to do that?' It wasn't a case of before: go in, sign on, leave. 'We can do this. Let's get your CV sorted. Let's get this sorted.' I'd already had most of it sorted but she like checked over things and told me the options. Someone actually telling me I *had* options. It was a big step but a good one —
> *RM*: So would you have any criticisms of New Deal?
> *Fox*: At the moment, no ... So far it's been a shining light for me. Everything's gone really well. I'm here doing something I want.
> *RM*: If the course has finished and you're back on the dole, will that make you more critical of New Deal?
> *Fox*: No, that'll make me more critical of myself. New Deal's given me the opportunity to have more options open to me. I'm on a university course. I'm now a university student. I have the options of possibly going into a job or going onto a degree course and it's my choice. If I decide to go and do nothing and go on the dole, then I can't say that New Deal didn't give me those options ... It's up to me now. I will get through this course — if it doesn't get me a job, it's my own doing so really. When I'm on the placement, if I impress them I should get offered a job.

Here we see the importance to the success of NDYP, in some participants' eyes, of the *details* of the support they receive. This could reinforce 'positive' or 'negative' viewpoints. Although, as one Personal Adviser told us, 'the employment option would be the most popular if the opportunities were there', the limitations of the local labour market meant that most participants were allocated second-choice placements in the training or Environmental Task Force routes. Another Adviser said that 'the main push is getting them into options', even if suitable placements were not obvious. Allan (21) had already experienced a succession of YT and ET schemes and was now on his second round of NDYP (and facing further 'training'). He was dismayed about the prospect of again 'just getting put on something' and being 'palmed off' with a placement that he did not want to do 'in one of these places where you're just gonna be grafting. I've done enough work like that already.' Martin (20) worked in an enterprise agency that helped people start up in business through NDYP. He was frank about the pressure to meet targets and what this meant for young people's ambitions:

> If a person says, 'Well, I'm interested in doing so and so', what we do is find something *remotely* related to that and stick 'em on it... They get paid for outcomes, where I work. If somebody goes self-employed, I get, we get paid.

Consequently, several interviewees felt rushed into making and revising their 'choices'. Alex (23) had abandoned her first option of an employment placement in care work after her Adviser had been unable to locate a position for her: 'So I said to her, "Well, look for Business Admin. stuff for me then". There was nowt there for that neither. They all wanted experience and I hadn't done it for about four years.' As we saw in Fox's commentary, the dedication and support of New Deal Advisers was also sometimes significant in making NDYP attractive (Millar, 2000). Adam's (21) first Adviser was helpful and interested in his voluntary work. The second was 'a real annoying dickhead. He thinks he's like — "I'm in a higher place and you're just a little person". He doesn't care about nothing, so long as you're getting out there working.'

Welfare to work?

Of the twelve interviewees who had completed NDYP, six (including Fox) were in employment two months afterwards (with the other half being unemployed). Fox was the only one whose job – as an office administrator – bore any relation to the training and work experience he had undertaken.

Predictably, there has been considerable debate about the success of NDYP (Coles, 2000a; Millar, 2000). The New Labour government has been keen to present it as having played a large part in meeting its 1997 election manifesto pledge to reduce youth unemployment by 250,000. Undoubtedly the number of unemployed under-25s fell dramatically after the programme's inception, but this may have been the result of the concurrent improvement in the national economy. As Mizen (2003) points out, many of those no longer unemployed may have become so regardless of participation. The government's National Audit Office (2002) has deflated more bullish claims of success by suggesting that it has possibly created jobs for only between 8,000 and 20,000 people. National statistics can also mask continuing problems at regional or local level. Obviously, moving the unemployed into jobs is much less of a challenge in buoyant local economies than in those with persistent, structural worklessness, like Teesside. Wicks reports that 'six months after leaving the New Deal for a job, as few as ten per cent of people are still employed in the least advantaged areas' (2004: 51) and the north-east of England is said to be the region with the lowest rate of participants finding lasting employment (*Northern Echo*, 20 June 2000).

Furthermore, using bare statistics about the movement into jobs (measured at a point three months post-NDYP) is, for us, short-sighted. Under government rubrics, employment at any one moment – regardless of its duration, quality or pay – signifies success and social inclusion (see chapter 1). In chapter 10 we show how this approach is flawed and how rigid policy categories such as 'the unemployed' and 'the excluded' fail to grapple with fluidity and insecurity of school-to-work careers of the type we describe.

Summary and conclusion

Young people in East Kelby are no different from their counterparts in other parts of the UK in that their immediate post-school world of work is now comprised predominantly of encounters with training and educational courses that have sprung up to fill the void left by the virtual collapse of the youth labour market. For working-class school leavers, however, vocationally-oriented training and educational courses are particularly important. For virtually all our interviewees, A-levels – the more academic post-sixteen route historically typical of middle-class youth transitions – fell outside their radar screen of possibilities. Predominantly, the early phases of school-to-work careers were mapped out through choices and steps taken in relation to YT and FE. In turn, experiences of them did much to set the range of subsequent possibilities and to colour their encounters with them (just as earlier experiences of school had decided most against continued education). The NDYP often represented the next significant stopping-off point in the circuitous school-to-work careers of a group who struggled to carve out more progressive pathways to economic security and independence. Only eleven of the 88 interviewees had not participated in some form of government training programme.

What do these accounts of FE, YT and NDYP tell us about the school-to-work careers of 'socially excluded' youth? Overall, we were struck by the similarities in what was said in respect of each of them or, more precisely, how their combined, cumulative experience generated transitions that had a great deal in common; the overriding motif of which was one of flux. Rapidity, inconstancy and change marked the pattern of young people's enrolment and departure in respect of the different options available in the post-sixteen marketplace of courses and schemes. Careers were distinguished by multiple 'relocations' (Fergusson et al., 2000). Another study of the post-school transitions of disadvantaged young people in the north-east of England has even clutched at chaos theory in an attempt to understand them (Meagre, 2001). Rarely was a YT or college course completed. Less than half had achieved qualifications as a result of their post-sixteen education (although some were still studying). According to our informants, this was in part because of the poor quality of post-sixteen provision. The litany of complaints about YT in particular was vociferous, depressing and familiar (Finn, 1987; Lee, 1991).

Raffe (2003: 2) says that experiences of status zer0 – of falling out of employment, education and training – can be understood either as evidence of 'young people's willingness to sample jobs and courses and to experiment with less conventional itineraries after school' or as a 'product of constraint or lack of opportunity'. The former is less of a concern for policy and might be evidence of the individualisation thesis (chapter 2), but the latter interpretation matches our findings best. The apparent lack of 'fit' between young people's aspirations and aptitudes and the vocational courses and schemes available partly explains why individuals typically grabbed at jobs that had little apparent connection to previous training or qualifications.

For some, the fluidity of post-school careers also reflected the absence of firm objectives in terms of the specifics of a job (or training for one), even though they had clear ideas about what was suitable and possible for young working-class women and men. They felt ill-prepared and undecided and reported that the main role of Careers Advisers had been to steer them towards YT schemes that roughly fitted with young people's own gendered and class cultural knowledge of where people like them might end up.

Because they had made little in the way of a solid decision to pursue a particular course or scheme (or if they did it was often unavailable to them for one reason or another), they felt little loyalty towards such 'choices'. Sticking with their first options, rather than switching among YT schemes or between them and FE courses, became all the harder when the actual experience of them gave plenty of reasons to try elsewhere. Underneath all the finer details of disappointments about a particular scheme, course or tutor lay an implicit feeling – sometimes explicitly voiced – that this was not where they wanted to be, nor was it likely to get them there. And whilst NDYP fared better than YT in informants' evaluations, the majority remained critical. Those who avoided it agreed with most of those who participated in it. Rather than being 'new', its similarities to other, previously encountered government programmes – and their failings – were a constant reference. They argued that NDYP would not lift them up and away from the dispiriting dead-ends of their school-to-work careers to date. One might ask, then, what it is that young people like this want. The answer, though counter to the weighty claims of underclass theory, is straightforward and forms the basis of chapter 6, where we consider more directly the world of work for young people in poor neighbourhoods.

6
Getting Jobs: The Status of Work in Poor Neighbourhoods

What if work, hard, demanding, important work, does not liberate people from poverty at all? 'Work for those who can, welfare for those who can't', 'A hand up, not a hand out', 'work is the best welfare' – these were Labour's mantras and they chimed with the spirit of the times. But what if they disguise the awkward fact that work pays so little that those on the minimum wage are still excluded, marginalised, locked out?

(Toynbee, 2003: 3)

No, I don't wanna go to college. Me Mam wants me to go and do a drama course, but I love where I am. I know it's a rubbish wage, but I enjoy what I'm doing. I enjoy getting my weekly wage and being able to go out drinking and buying clothes on a Friday after I've been paid on a Thursday. If I lost that [wage] I'd be lost.

(Alison, 18, factory worker)

Introduction

Thus far we have described the cyclical, non-progressive and fluid school-to-work careers followed by young people in these poor neighbourhoods. We have hinted that we can make sense of these complicated twists and turns through post-sixteen college courses and government programmes only by reference to the significance of employment for this group. Whilst in sympathy with those that decry New Labour's narrow fixation with regular employment as the route to becoming/being 'socially included' (e.g. Levitas, 1998), the imperative to work was highly resonant with these informants' lived experiences and motives as they struggled to make headway in their post-school transitions. The value interviewees placed upon getting jobs – even where they fell short of what they hoped for – speeded their disengagement from further education, shaped their affective assessments of YT and NDYP and drove their day-to-day decision-making about the next steps to be taken. In this chapter, we attempt to understand interviewees' relationship with employment, in terms of their subjective engagement with it and the structured opportunities that prevail for young people in this context.

Employment and unemployment in youth transitions

A scan of the work histories of the sample reveals how unemployment *and*, to a lesser extent, employment were common experiences, demonstrating again the fluctuating, multiple economic statuses that made up these post-school careers. Thirty-four of the sample of 88 had never held a full-time job (but this included twelve recent school-leavers on YT or FE courses, twelve mothers primarily engaged in caring for children and five with substantial records of imprisonment). In other words, the majority of those who were able and willing to look for employment had found it at some point. This is not to underestimate the extent of unemployment: only nine people had never been unemployed (and all but one of these was just at the point of school leaving). Our count of 'unemployment' is based on self-descriptions (not whether a person was in receipt of or was eligible for unemployment benefits). They reported periods – and we counted only those of over two months – when they had been available for and wanted employment but had been unable to find it. In short, despite the problems of joblessness in East Kelby, work has not disappeared (Wilson, 1996). This finding will take on more significance as we unravel the detail of their encounters with employment and unemployment and relate these to broader debates about social exclusion and inclusion (in chapter 10).

Searching for jobs

Interviewees' job search repertoires combined formal and informal strategies. The latter were overwhelmingly seen to be the most effective. When asked about how they had accessed a particular job, the typical response described the role of personal networks for information, advice and recommendation. Knowing (or knowing of) others who worked, or had worked, in a particular firm gave access to information about current and future vacancies and allowed for personal recommendations by intermediaries on the young person's behalf. Siblings, partners, parents, extended family, neighbours and friends were variously mentioned as the key players that had helped them secure a particular job and, on a rough count, over two-thirds of all jobs had been got this way:

> There's this part-time job at the turkey factory. They're looking for people. I've asked this lad – 'cos his uncle works there – to see if they want any more.
>
> (Lindsay, 17, YT trainee)

> My Dad said, 'Tell Louise' – that's my girlfriend – 'to give us the number of her gaffer'. So he rang him and he said 'Oh, you [Malcolm] can start so and so a time'.
>
> (Malcolm, 21, NDYP participant)

> One job was through a friend of mine who gave me the number of an agency and they got back in touch with me and, well, the second one was an ex-girlfriend, her uncle was the manager. All my jobs have been through people I know. I've never had any luck with Job Centres or nothing. They're pathetic.
>
> (Anthony, 23, part-time college student)

Being tied into locally embedded, informal social networks appeared crucial to job search for these informants. Broderick, who had secured his last job as a scaffolder through his girlfriend's father, echoed the common refrain: 'It's like not what you know, it's the people you know these days', or, in Richy's words, 'If you know the right people, you're sorted, aren't you?'[1] One consequence of reliance on such networks was that the search for jobs became proximate with the geographic spread of such networks (see chapter 10). Although some did – on a few occasions – work in other parts of the region on a daily basis or move to other parts of the country for employment, the predominant pattern was of individuals seeking jobs close to home (a practice compounded by very limited car ownership, poor public transport systems and the financial costs of travel to jobs that paid little). Indeed, part of the explanation for not uprooting to towns and cities where jobs might be more plentiful was that this would bring isolation from social networks and tried-and-tested methods for getting jobs (see chapter 8).

In comparison, the methods practised by Job Centres, Job Clubs and New Deal programmes were seen as largely ineffective. One tactic encouraged in the job search sessions of the latter two is the sending of numerous, speculative application letters to local employers (with addresses scoured from telephone directories), regardless of whether they were currently advertising vacancies or not. Continued eligibility for 'Job Seekers Allowance' requires recurrent evidence of job applications. By the time informants entered the job-search sessions on NDYP, for instance, they had usually encountered this strategy several times on other programmes. Because their CVs and standard application letters were by now as polished as they were ever going to be – and because they (and perhaps tutors) recognised this strategy to be ineffectual – participants were 'just left in the canteen all day' (Allan, 21) or asked 'to sit looking through the papers and there's no way you can do that for three hours, so we end up just sitting there bored' (Elizabeth, 19).

Others reported pursuing this 'totally stupid' strategy assiduously, but rarely receiving any response. Not one of them reported receiving a job offer as a result, despite having fired off several hundred if not thousands of such letters in total. Andrew provides an extreme case. During one year-long spell of unemployment he sent 'a hundred plus letters a week through the Job Club, constantly without getting replies'. He wanted to become a chef and was encouraged to undertake various 'work trials' in the hope that those he worked for might take him on: 'I spent days and days as a chef in kitchens, not getting the jobs and not getting paid'. On the rare occasions when young people were treated to the courtesy of a rejection letter, employers pointed to what these young hopefuls lacked: no references from previous jobs, inadequate qualifications, slim work experience, no driving licence,[2] too young, too old, etc. Adam (21) was one of those frustrated by the lack of opportunity to prove his worth: 'It's just what's on that piece of paper [the application form] and they look at it and they say "do we want him or don't we want him?" That piece of paper holds me back.' The 'future blocking' potential of the CV was most pronounced for those with criminal records. In a tight labour market like this, ex-offenders stand towards the back of the job queue. As a consequence, fake work histories were concocted: 'That's how I've got most of me jobs, through lying' (Richard, 20). For some, this regular pattern of 'sending stuff all the time and not hearing' (Leo, 22) and occasional outright rejection was experienced as a demotivating series of personal knock-backs that undermined confidence:

I've got no brains. I'm not very good at maths and things like that, so I thought well, after everything, 'maybes I can't do a job'. About the only type of work I could do really was, maybes, cleaning and things like that.

(Susan, 22, ET trainee)

The composition of the labour market for young adults

Listing the actual full-time or part-time jobs ever undertaken (or the type or place of work, if the job title was imprecise) helps describe the composition of the labour market as encountered by these young adults. Also noted here are the total numbers of people who had ever done this sort of work:

> factory-based food processing, fifteen (eleven males, four females);
> factory-based textiles/knitwear production, six (all female);
> sales assistants and shelf-stackers, six (all female);
> bar work, five (three females, two males);
> care assistants, five (four females, one male);
> clerical/administrative work, five (three females, two males);
> cleaners, four (two females, two males);
> fast food outlets, four (three females, one male);
> labouring/unskilled construction work, four (all male);
> warehouse work, three (all male);
> scaffolders, three (all male);
> hairdressers, thee (all female);
> Armed Forces, two (both male);
> car and bicycle repairs, two (both male);
> chefs, two (one male, one female);
> security guard, one (male);
> janitor, one (male);
> petrol pump attendant, one (male);
> telesales, one (male).

There are several things that are noteworthy here. Obviously – as with the training schemes entered – young people's employment remains strongly gendered (Furlong and Cartmel, 1997). More notable is the dearth of semi-skilled or skilled jobs of the type that underpinned the historic development of Teesside, let alone managerial or professional employment. These 'entry-level' jobs in the lower reaches of the service industries and routinised, factory production were not confined to school leavers and there was little indication that people worked their way through these sorts of job before accessing higher positions. They were the jobs that individuals laboured at when they were sixteen and when they were 26 (also a key finding of Webster et al.'s (2004) study, which followed up the fortunes of some of this sample as they reached their mid- to late twenties). We are not, then, describing the details of a separate *youth* labour market (Ashton and Maguire, 1986; Lee, 1991) but a secondary labour market (Beynon, 1997) marked by the poorest conditions of work and pervasive unemployment and underemployment, to which many working-class people are now confined, regardless of age:

> Low pay is also fair enough if these jobs can be labelled 'entry-level', just a first step on a ladder. But it is now clear that very few of those in low-paid jobs can ever move far...few make it to the next step. They inhabit a cycle of no-pay/low-pay job insecurity. This indeed is the end of social progress. (Toynbee, 2003: 5–6)

The evidence from interviewees' work histories, from what they told us about the working lives of their friends and family and from 'stakeholder' interviews, suggests that these types of low-paid, insecure employment were typically the sort gained by people in East Kelby and places like it.

On the fiddle

Despite popular stereotypes to the contrary in the local press – and despite the fact the interviewees often claimed that 'loads of people do it' – more informal economic activity did not appear to be widespread. Twenty people reported being currently or previously involved in such work: and our definition here includes a handful who engaged in voluntary work (MacDonald, 1996) as well as more illicit, 'fiddly work'.[3] This is the local term for cash-in-hand jobs done to augment benefit income that is undeclared to benefit or tax authorities. Because our findings *exactly* match those of a previous study in the locality (MacDonald, 1994), our commentary will be brief.[4] Since being unemployed, Adam (21) had done scraps of fiddly work:

> Painting and decorating, car valeting, fixing people's bikes, stuff like that. Just odd jobs. For a week, or a couple of weeks that's about it — just through friends, from people. It's not really worth signing off the dole.

When it was done, fiddly work was typically: very short-lived (from a day to a few weeks); informally organised (via the same social networks that distributed offers of 'legitimate' jobs); insecure (because work was so unpredictable and sporadic it did not make logistic sense to de-register – and then re-register – with the cumbersome bureaucracy of the benefit system); and low paid (i.e. income could only realistically be perceived as a 'top-up' to, rather than in place of, benefits). Helpfully, Lisa, a young mother, summed up the general picture in commenting on her recent work as a barmaid:

They probably pay you a bit less than they would have 'cos you're on
the dole — but we were glad for the money. Just to make ends meet.
Pay the electricity bill. Irregular. Every now and again. It's just word
of mouth. Not what you know, it's who you know.

As Lisa implies, there was some evidence that employers colluded in creating and/or sustaining 'fiddly work' and Beynon et al. (1994) describe how,
for example, an increased use of subcontracting by Teesside employers
encourages, and in some cases may be dependent on, 'fiddly work'. One
interviewee told of how he had been 'sweeping up' at a chemical plant on
a temporary contract and was allowed by his employer to take every other
Wednesday afternoon off so that he could 'sign on'. Another reported
that her brother had worked briefly as a security guard 'on the fiddle'
for £1.75 per hour (rather than the usual £3.60) because the employer
knew he was simultaneously claiming benefits. In these ways the so-called
'underground economy' overlapped with and mirrored the formal economy of jobs as accessed by these young adults (Harding and Jenkins,
1989). The sorts of jobs they did – and the conditions under which they
did them – were much the same as those in the 'legitimate' labour market.
This meant that some people had difficulty in saying definitively whether
a particular work episode was part of one or the other and is one reason
why some people overestimated the extent of 'fiddly work' locally
(Hakim, 1992).

Informants distinguished between fiddly work that was motivated by
'need' and that motivated by 'greed'. Because benefit dependence was
understood to confine people to poverty ('bend the rules – you've got
to in this world cause of the pittance you get off the government'), and
because doing fiddly work indicated a commitment to self-reliance ('at
least they're working'), it was widely condoned. If fiddly work went
beyond irregular, incremental additions to household income it was
widely condemned: 'if you've got a really good job and, like, earning
loads of money off that and claiming, I think that is disgraceful'
(Leanne, 16).

Engaging in fiddly work was risky. A handful of informants knew of
people who had been caught by the benefit authorities and the fear of
the financial consequences acted as a clear deterrent. Kayleigh's brother
was still paying off a fine he incurred two years earlier for undeclared
working. Susan talked about a friend – another young mother – who
had been caught doing fiddly work at a nearby theme park, had lost all
benefits for a period and was now working very long hours to pay the
subsequent fine (and to provide a family income).

Pay at the bottom of the labour market

The types of employment these people had are ones that are notoriously low paid, but it was difficult to get reliable estimates of pay. Interviewees variously cited hourly, weekly or monthly rates and pay could vary week by week, depending on overtime, bonuses and tips. People working in similar jobs for the same employer occasionally quoted quite different rates of pay. Some cited pay they had received prior to the introduction of the National Minimum Wage. At the time of the study this was £3.60 per hour for those aged over 21, and £3 per hour for those aged 18–21; under-18s were excluded from the National Minimum Wage (McKnight, 2002). Others insisted that the low wage they reported was current, even though it fell well short of that agreed in law. Once or twice individuals confused training allowances with wages (McAlister, 2003). Notwithstanding these caveats, the overwhelming story was one of low pay. Some worked part-time (often legitimately) to supplement benefits. Some were working full-time for amounts similar to benefit levels. A few examples follow. The one interviewee who was a security guard received £3.20 per hour. Reportedly, his employer recognised that this might not be sufficient to live on and expected employees to work twelve-hour shifts (on their own) so that they could accrue enough to make ends meet. One of our care assistants received £22.50 for two night shifts working unsupervised in a residential home for the elderly. Another care assistant quoted the going rate as £2 per hour in this line of work (which was the same as the pay received by two informants who served in bars). Two of those who worked in clerical jobs reported a weekly wage of around £60. The highest reported pay came to two men when they had been in the armed forces (around £1,000 per month). Only three – who worked in tele-sales, youth work and in a business start-up agency – quoted their pay in terms of an annual salary (of around £10,000–£12,000 p.a.).

'Poor work': the turkey factory

In seeking to understand the apparent appeal of employment in young people's post-school careers, we need to dig deeper into their experiences of jobs, especially given the low-skilled and low-paid work that they were able to access.

Over the past twenty years, a combination of weakened trade unions and government-sponsored, labour market deregulation has aided employers' attempts to promote more 'flexible' ways of working (e.g. 'numerical flexibility' refers to the reduction of labour costs by the employment of staff only as and when needed). As employers seek to enhance profits by a more 'flexible' use of labour, temporary and short-term jobs replace the standard 'full-time, permanent, open-ended and secure' jobs and careers regarded as the norm in the mid-twentieth century (Rifkin, 1995; White and Forth, 1998; Felstead and Jewson, 1999: 1). Pay 'flexibility' is a feature of these new managerial practices, as is the search for more 'functional flexibility' (i.e. increasing the number and range of tasks assigned to specific jobs) (Atkinson, 1984; Fevre, 1991; Grint, 1991). In the lower reaches of the labour market 'flexibilisation' slides into casualisation and, according to Beynon et al. (1994), it is exactly this process that characterises employment in the newer manufacturing and service industries on Teesside. Permanent contracts (underpinned by collectively agreed pay and conditions of employment) give way to more contingent arrangements often agreed informally, individually and – in many of our cases – without written contracts.

As Felstead and Jewson (1999: 3) describe, 'the surge of non-standard work' in Britain in the latter part of the twentieth century 'is associated with rock-bottom wages, coercive management, intensified labour processes, unsocial hours and high rates of job turnover'. This neatly encapsulates the casualised, 'poor work' that defined the labour market experiences of our sample. Casualisation also extended to the processes whereby they were hired (as indicated in the apparent effectiveness of young people's informal, word of mouth, job-search strategies) and fired (as we will show shortly). Although some commentators celebrate the shift to more flexible working practices as indicative of post-Fordist employment that better suits the needs of workers and management, Beynon et al. prefer to see 'the intensification of work, deteriorating working conditions and...cuts in wages' that it often entails as 'a return to undesirable past practices' characteristic of previous periods of capitalist development (1994: 160).

Jobs at the 'turkey factory' have a quantitative and qualitative significance for our discussion. More of our sample had worked at this place than for any other, single employer. Descriptions of its casualised working practices also provide for a useful, brief case study of the sort of employment experiences that extended across the sample.

Fifteen people had worked in factory-based food processing industry. Referring to a local factory that makes potato crisps, Beynon et al. note that 'the main recruitment criteria for such unskilled workers related to a person's physique, manual dexterity and personal hygiene' (1994: 143). For the young men who worked at the turkey factory, similar rules applied. According to our interviewees, it was the sort of place where 'there's always work going', where the employer paid little attention to the educational qualifications, work histories, criminal records or formal references that potential recruits might offer and where a recommendation from a current employee carried more weight. Although tasks differed, the work interviewees did was all described as dirty, unpleasant and dull. Some packed the product on an assembly line; others stocked the freezers. One or two had cleaned the section where the poultry were slaughtered. All the work was unskilled and, in practice, short-term. Broderick got a job there straight from school:

> I was in like a big freezer, freeze your bollocks off. The money was quite good. I'd come out with about £700 per month. I don't like work like that. It was boring, dead-end, innit? Just doing the same thing. I asked this bloke how long he'd been there and he said 'fourteen year, man'. It wasn't for me.

Broderick reported receiving higher wages from this factory than any of the other interviewees. Even though this was a beguiling wage for a school leaver it was not enough to buy his continued loyalty to the firm. Others typically reported receiving about £130 a week, but Curtis, who described the job he did for just two weeks as 'dirty, horrible, cruel', quoted a much lower figure:[5] 'I started 5 o'clock in the morning until 8 o'clock at night, every night, for seven days one week and they paid us £30 I thought, sort of, "no way!"'

As a result of the low-grade work, poor pay, nil career prospects and unsociable hours all those from our sample who accessed jobs at the turkey factory soon left (after a few months at the longest, a few days at the shortest). Employees knew that jobs here were unlikely to last long but members of the youthful – and older[6] – cohorts of East Kelby returned month after month, year after year to take what they could from the jobs at the turkey factory. The locale supplied a constant flow of casual workers to undertake this employment of last resort. Although we cannot know his or her mind, judging by the consistency of young people's accounts the employer seemed content to take on a steady string of highly replaceable, physically able, cheap workers to undertake the 'poor work' on offer.[7] This was a most debased form of work 'flexibility' in action.

'Poor work' (Brown and Scase, 1991) was not restricted to the turkey factory. Elizabeth and Ellie had undertaken many of the types of job reported by the sample as a whole. By the time she was nineteen, Elizabeth had been through YT, various part-time and short-term jobs, night classes at college to raise her qualifications, spells of unemployment and the NDYP, following which she 'went back on the dole'. She bided her time hoping that work with special needs adults might come up (the area of Elizabeth's training and qualifications), but after two frustrating months on benefits she took, instead, a job as a care assistant at a nursing home for the elderly. To her surprise, when she arrived for her first night shift she found all the residents asleep and no other member of staff present. The same happened the following night and she resigned, still not having met another member of staff or having had any induction into the job. She had to pester her employer – by letter – to receive her due wages (of £22.50 for the two night shifts). Elizabeth lost confidence in working as a care assistant. She started to look for 'any job', chiefly via the local free newspaper:

> I was desperate to work anywhere. Nothing was gonna come up so I went for a job in the wool factory. I'm working in a knitwear factory at a really crappy job for £3.17 per hour, nine hours a day.

Elizabeth found this work simultaneously stressful and boring. The training period was brief and the promised pay rise never materialised:

> The employers lied at the interview. They said that our money would go up after training and every four weeks but I've been there six weeks and passed my training and it's not moved.

Ellie (26) had not worked in factories but had undertaken a series of 'crap jobs', as she termed them, serving in bars, fast food restaurants and betting shops:

> 'Burger Delight' was the hardest job I've ever had. An absolute night-mare. Horrendous. They had me doing absolutely everything. They tried to get me into the skip outside where all the waste goes, to clean it out... I was getting £1.85 an hour when I started and £2.50 when I left. They've all been pretty crap. There's only so much that you can do [to make them more interesting]. You get to a point where you're doing it to the best of your ability and then that's it. Occasionally I've been moved up to a relief stewardess [in the social club] or to second settler [in the betting shop]. It's just a means to an end. It's certainly become that now with the job I'm doing 'cos I just can't stand it. I'm just so bored with the job. It bores me to death.

At times, these jobs had been her main activity. At others, they were secondary and supportive of her ambition to progress through further and higher education. When interviewed, she was a final-year university student and gave all her maintenance grant to her parents (she lived on the wages she earned from jobs). Ellie tended to persevere with a particular job until she had exhausted all her strategies to make it more interesting.[8] Typically, she left them after a year or two (and even persisted with 'Burger Delight' for eighteen months).

Losing jobs

Boredom, however, was only rarely given as the reason for leaving a job. Instead, informants described being 'laid off', 'cancelled', 'sacked' or 'made redundant' and used these terms interchangeably and, from what we can discern, often wrongly to describe the loss of their jobs. Their inaccurate terminology stood in place of a more developed consciousness and language to describe the casualisation of employment. Certainly some reached the end of a temporary contract of employment and were duly 'laid off', but others picked words like 'redundancy' even though the firm in question continued to recruit workers just like them for the same jobs (the turkey factory was a case in point). For most, the job was simply not there for them any longer and they were not really sure why this was the case.

Half a dozen people described instances of what seemed to be unfair dismissal, but rarely used this phrase directly. Examples included dismissal following one day of medically certificated sick leave, sacking after becoming pregnant and the reallocation of a job to a relative of the employer. Only Ellie had sought legal or trade union advice regarding 'unfair dismissal' (she explained this with reference to the fact that her father had been a union shop steward). It tended to be the interviewers, not the interviewees, who sought to dwell on the circumstances and apparent injustices involved. There was an implicit acceptance that most jobs would be like this.

Interestingly, the predominant answers given stressed the decisions of others to terminate work, rather than the decisions of young people themselves. Of course, some chose to leave jobs, citing factors such as the lack of adequate training or supervision, the unrewarding nature of the work and the under- or non-payment of wages. Some analyses of this sort of labour market 'turbulence' – the rapid movement of individuals in and out of job positions – stress the weak employment attachment of young people (e.g. Carter, 1966; Murray, 1990). They lack 'job-readiness' and their commitment to employment is said to be fickle. They are claimed to be unprepared to work 'flexibly' across unsociable and/or long hours, to insist on unrealistic rates of pay[9] and to be uninterested in jobs that are not close to home. Interestingly, only three of our interviewees ever cited these reasons for quitting a job.

Of course, we are only reporting here the explanations given by the young people. Interviewees might be expected to proffer accounts that played down, for example, their lack of commitment, ability or appropriate conduct at work. Employers might give quite different reasons why the individuals in question were no longer in their employ. Nevertheless, the nature and details of the accounts given to us were so overwhelmingly consistent in their description of the casualisation of employment (in this case, the circumstances that surrounded the end of a job) that it is difficult to dismiss them as baseless rhetoric of self-interest. We read the fact that virtually all presented their accounts of exploitation (our words, not theirs) in such a matter-of-fact, taken-for-granted tone as further evidence that these sorts of practices were widespread, common and 'the way of the world' (as one young man put it). Finally, Furlong and Cartmel's study of the longer-term economic fortunes of disadvantaged young men in Scotland reached conclusions that are virtually identical to ours here:

> their main problem was not finding work, but keeping it. This employment insecurity tended not to reflect negative attitudes on the part of the young men or necessarily a lack of skills; it was almost entirely a consequence of the 'flexible' nature of low-skilled employment in modern Britain. (2004: 27)

The appeal of work and the shadow of unemployment

What was it, then, about employment that appealed? Why did 'poor work' like this command such a hold over the transitions of this group? Part of the answer lies in the determined connection of all but a few to conventional social goals and values, mediated through the not-so-distant memories and traditions of working-class culture. As we sketched in chapter 2, Teesside is a working-class place, shaped by the needs of heavy industry and in which the commonplace route to adult, working life – albeit predominantly for young men – came via apprenticeships and 'entry-level' jobs for school leavers that led to reasonably well-paid, reasonably skilled manual jobs. The restructuring of the local economy over the past thirty years has increased employment opportunities for young women in an expanded service sector (and reduced the number of 'masculine' jobs). In chapter 7 we show how the young women of East Kelby held views of their futures in which parenting was – in the best of worlds – to be postponed subsequent to more extended engagement with the labour market than was typical of women of their mothers' or grandmothers' generations. That these scenarios did not play out in practice for some (with motherhood 'happening' earlier than desired) does not diminish the fact that young women here – like their male counterparts – saw themselves as leading lives in which jobs had an important place. Both imagined adulthood in terms of self-reliance, most obviously symbolised and bought by a wage. The historic and cultural legacy of the locality – and more recent changes to its labour market – can, however, only partly explain the way young people oriented themselves towards employment.

Their feelings about work were also deeply coloured by their practical knowledge of jobs – encountered first whilst at school (on a part-time basis and through spells of work experience) and in the years since leaving – and of the various alternatives to being in them. Work, if not the actual jobs they did, was valued highly by most informants. Probing for explanations to our question produced answers that usually described employment in terms of its *potential* material and social-psychological rewards. It also compared favourably with their negative experience of unemployment and, in their view, the lack of obvious rewards to be gained from further education or training. The material imperatives of employment for young adults should not be underestimated, even under conditions of severely low pay (see Alison's comment, which we quote at the start of the chapter). Getting a wage underwrote the consumption of youth leisure which, whilst often modest in scope, was typically denied to those who remained out of jobs in their late teens. For Leo and Louise, their current unemployment led them to stress the more mundane, immediate needs that a wage might fulfil for poor young people:

> Why don't I think about going to college? Well, you can get qualifications but they are not going to pay the bills, are they? Money's more important than the qualifications are. You can't live on qualifications.
>
> (Louise, 17)

> Getting a job is the main object, isn't it? You need that job first, then you can get, like the next one is a car. So you can get there [to work] and get back home. There's money for clothes and so on. Holidays and saving up and that. That's the main thing, a job. Without a job, you're stuck. Nowhere to go. You're stuck in a dead end, aren't you? That's how I feel now.
>
> (Leo, 18)

Work gives more than a wage, as social psychologists have long pointed out. Jahoda (1982) argues that the personal psychological decline that typically comes with worklessness is understandable in terms of the 'latent functions' that work (most often as employment) fulfils. From this perspective, as well as providing the material means for subsistence, employment enforces individual activity, structures time, assigns social identity, provides social contacts and attaches the individual to broader goals and purposes in life. Even 'poor work' that ascribes low status, demands unsociable hours, enforces unpleasant activities, brings limited or hostile social contacts and has undesirable goals and purposes can contribute to social-psychological well-being. Unemployment typically strips away these categories of experience with deleterious psychological consequences for most people (Fryer, 1992). Although one or two individuals in our study and elsewhere (Wilson, 1996; Donnison, 1998; Simpson, 2004) described the work-like character of their criminal endeavours, especially when it took on the urgency of heroin-driven offending, research shows that most people are unable to maintain continuous, regular work outside of formal employment (Fryer and Payne, 1984).

We think this helps explain why informants could talk positively about the most menial of jobs. Lucy, aged sixteen, had just got her first job as a cleaner at the local football stadium. Although she described it as 'back-breaking and boring', she enjoyed it because 'it's nice to be earning some money and to make some new friends and that'. Alison, aged eighteen, made sandwiches on a factory production line from early in the morning. She said, 'There's three of us in there — I love it. We have a good laugh. Everyone's dead friendly. The atmosphere. No one's the bosses. They don't shout at you. They're nice to you.'[10]

The following conversation between Andrew (23, employed), Linda (23, unemployed) and Stuart (26, employed) provides some confirmation of Jahoda's thesis (and even draws upon the same terminology at times). For them, the appeal of employment rests in the sense of social purpose and personal worth that can be derived from it, especially when compared with the continued social stigma that attaches to 'the unemployed':

JM: What would you say is the benefit of working, then?
Andrew: It gives you a sense of well-being.
Linda: Enjoyment, innit?
Stuart: It gives you a sense of achievement.
Andrew: It gave me a purpose in life, something to do. Like Stuart said, it's an achievement. You get recognised. I go out and get respected more as working. On the dole people would just say 'Oh!', turn their

shoulder. Whereas if you're working you get more respect... I get on with them brilliantly [the elderly people he cares for in his job]. I love them, me. The stories you hear from them. It just fascinates me... it gives me a sense of purpose in life.

JM: Do you think you get job satisfaction whatever you're doing, or do you think there's some jobs where you'd rather be on the dole?

Stuart: It depends on the gratifaction [*sic*] you get back off the people you're doing the job for. If you were doing a job every hour God sends but you were getting no respect, then you might say, 'Sod you, I'm not doing it' — If you're getting respect you're actually putting your foot on the ladder to go up. You can actually work your way to a higher status than what you started off.

One might expect Jahoda's thesis to have less purchase in a context of prolonged, widespread unemployment. Where work opportunities are minimal over decades, individual and collective social-psychological coping strategies might be expected to emerge out of necessity. Unemployment might become – and be seen to be – more acceptable. We found little evidence of this. Scanning the whole set of interviews for descriptions of the experience of unemployment which were in any way 'positive', produced four brief comments which all referred to very short episodes. Kayleigh, for example, said 'It was OK, it didn't bother me. It was only for two weeks during the summer.' Longer periods of unemployment were *uniformly* described in unfavourable terms: 'awful', 'boring' 'horrible', 'grim', 'doom and gloom'. A few reported more extreme responses and had sought medical treatment for depression as a consequence.[11] Most common, though, were accounts that portrayed the general tedium, aimlessness, isolation and limited life of the young unemployed (Kelvin and Jarrett, 1985). Money was short and friends were occupied on schemes, at college or in jobs. Unemployed days were intensely boring, mainly solitary affairs that typically consisted of a humdrum routine of daytime television, mooching round the house, walks around the neighbourhood and occasional visits to the Job Centre. Alex, aged 23, summed up the experience of many:

I used to get up at about half-ten. Go downstairs have a cup of tea. Sit about for a bit. Clean up. When I'd done that, I'd go upstairs, go in the bath. Get ready to go round to me mates or summat. Just boring. Every day, that's what I used to do. Have the radio on, watch a bit of telly. It done me head in.

Dependency culture?

Remarkably – given the claims of underclass theory and the weight of experience of 'poor work' – the interviews contained numerous expositions on the social and moral value of working for a living. Some of these came from unlikely quarters. Malcolm (19) was brought up without his father around. He had been a frequent truant and school excludee, was wholly unqualified, regularly unemployed, an occasional house burglar and drug user, and father of an 'illegitimate' child. Was he the living embodiment of Murray's immoral, 'benefit-dependent' underclass?

> I [would] hate being on the dole and having to go to the dole office once a fortnight. I won't do it. It's embarrassing going to the Post Office with your giro. You just become lazy, have a lazy life. I just don't like it. *I just don't wanna sign on the dole.* I wanna work —— it's a weekly wage for a start. So instead of a daft £78 per fortnight, it's a weekly wage. It's just part of life really, innit? To have a job and support your family and stuff. So instead of 'im [his son] growing up and when his friends' Mams or teachers say, 'Oh. what does your Dad do?' 'Oh, he's on the dole'. I don't want none of that. I want him to grow up and say, 'Oh, like our Dad's working at summat', so he can feel proud and have nice things when he gets older. Buy him nice things.

As well as being opposed to claiming benefits, Malcolm was not interested in NDYP because that would mean signing on and visiting the Job Centre, associating with other unemployed people and risking the ascribed identity of a 'dole wallah' (as a consequence, his family survived on the £50 a week benefit claimed by his girlfriend, Gail). Although Malcolm was one of only a handful that completely resisted claiming unemployment-related benefits, opposition to 'dependency culture' was not uncommon. Like Malcolm, a number of young fathers, in particular, voiced their concerns about the potential negative 'role model' they might present to their children if they remained unemployed. Several mentioned spontaneously the connection between a family background in which 'benefit dependency' was prevalent and their own strong commitment to employment. In doing so, they turned on its head one of the key tenets of underclass theory. Rather than the cultural inheritance of a personal taste for welfare dependency, they proposed a 'reverse role model' effect in which family experience of unemployment, together with their own depressing encounters with it, invigorated the impulse to work. Chrissie (21) had been unemployed for two years, before joining NDYP in the hope of getting a job:

> You go to sign on, you come home, and on the Friday you go up and get your money, do shopping, pay bills, come home and nowt on the telly . . . I felt it was running in the family, being on the dole, and I didn't want to —— my Dad and my uncle and my brother are on the dole —— I like it now [at the NDYP]. I enjoy working now. It's something to do and you meet lots of people. I used to be shy, but I'm not now. Meeting new people and talking has brought me out of my shell.

In such accounts we hear deeply felt, moral orientations to work (and surrogate work in Chrissie's comments about NDYP), meshed with direct personal encounters with the social psychological experience of employment and unemployment. Informants' valorisation of employment was shored up not only by an appreciation of what was to be gained materially, socially and psychologically, but also by an understanding of how others viewed the unemployed. Even in a place like this where unemployment has been a fact of community life for decades, negative rhetoric about 'the unemployed' was prominent in the interviews. Stigma still stuck to 'the unemployed' despite the fact the vast majority who rehearsed such rhetoric were, or had been, unemployed themselves.

Conclusion: on not being a 'dole wallah'

This chapter has described young adults' encounters with employment in deprived neighbourhoods and has attempted to understand their remarkably durable, emotional attachment to 'poor work'. As we noted in chapter 1, underclass theses present the long-term or regularly unemployed as prime candidates for underclass membership. Those that favour the terminology of 'social exclusion' also posit economic exclusion as a prominent feature of this condition. Near-permanent, structural excision from the labour market and, for some theorists, accompanying cultural preferences for 'benefit dependency' are the defining features of the excluded underclass. We return to this question in chapter 10, but note, for the time being, the glaring lack of fit between the experiences and views reported to us in a prime 'underclass' locale and, to give one example here, Wilson's influential analysis of the American ghetto poor. Unlike in Wilson's study, work here has *not* disappeared (1996: 52–3). He documents how in that context young people, in particular, can lose their feeling of connectedness to work in the formal economy... they may grow up in an environment that lacks the idea of work as a central experience of adult life – they have little or no labor force attachment... [those] who maintain a connection with the formal labour market – that is, those who continue to be employed mostly in low-wage jobs – are, in effect, working against all odds.

Conversely, this chapter has offered evidence of a deeply held and widespread emotional and moral attachment to work as a way of signifying, and providing for, adult independence (perhaps demonstrated most dramatically by those who refused to claim unemployment benefits despite the poverty that ensued). These individuals wanted jobs (Raffe, 2003) – and they often got them.

Talking about the casualisation of employment on Teesside, Beynon et al. (1994: 124) conclude that 'contacts and reputation become almost as important as qualifications and experience, at least in some segments of the labour market'. We would go further and argue that for our interviewees the informal practices and networks they used in finding jobs were *more* important (than qualifications, at least). These practices were rooted in the cultural history and contemporary conditions of the place and seemed to 'work' (better than those encouraged by Job Centres and government training programmes). Reliance on informal, social networks potentially has negative longer-term consequences, a point we return to in chapter 10. Because those they used to help in finding jobs (i.e. extended family networks and friends) were also typically confined to the same sectors of the labour market, our interviewees remained tied to what Beynon (1997) describes as hyphenated jobs (low-paid, low-skilled, short-term); 'poor work' at the bottom of the labour market that offered little chance of personal progression (Lakey et al., 2001; Webster et al., 2004). Because the work they get usually offers no training, little prospect for internal promotion or increased security and few bridges to more permanent, rewarding employment, individuals become trapped in insecure, poor work and are unable to escape the churning of cyclical labour market careers (White and Forth, 1998; Raffe, 2003). As time passes, they become even less attractive to those with better employment to offer (Furlong and Cartmel, 2004).

That the majority stuck with this sort of working life – moving in and out of casualised employment over the post-school years – is further evidence, we think, of their negative assessment of other possibilities (training schemes, further education), the dearth of more rewarding jobs for underqualified young adults and what we might describe as a *hyper-conventional* attitude to work in which the getting and keeping of jobs, irrespective of pay and conditions, was the driving force behind youth transitions. Murad finds this same class-based 'work ethic and enthusiasm for work' among excluded groups in continental Europe, describing its 'persistence in current times' as 'remarkable' (2002b: 98).

As with other surveys of the goals of disadvantaged, working-class young people in general (Jones, 2002) – and particularly excluded sections of them, such as the young homeless (Carlen, 1996) and offenders (Smith and Stewart, 1998) – our informants professed commonplace and obvious longer-term ambitions: a loving relationship with a partner, their own house, children when the time was right, a car and – as a conduit to much of this – a decent job. What is more interesting about this well-established fact is that many young people resident in poor neighbourhoods – and some commentaries about such social groups – deny it. Paradoxically, whilst these young adults described graphically their *own* depressing episodes of worklessness and convinced us of their own attachment to employment, they were often quick to suppose that *others* had quite different feelings about these things. The harshest critics of 'dole wallahs' (a derogatory, colloquial term for the unemployed) were themselves unemployed. Although some posited more structural explanations for local unemployment,[12] most preferred victim-blaming, cultural theories in which personal predilections were given centre-stage.

This strong, grounded support among communities of the 'deserving poor' for the idea that among them lived 'a different kind of poor people' distinguished by their affinity for idleness became the key 'evidence' for Murray's underclass thesis (1990; 1994). Like him, we uncovered exactly this sort of grass-roots, moral survey of the 'good' and 'bad' unemployed. We would explain it, however, not as a direct reflection of locally differentiated, cultural orientations to work, but as an outcome of the stigma that continues to attach to poor neighbourhoods and households. Classic social psychology (Allport, 1979) tells us that individuals usually seek to distance themselves from membership of groups understood to carry negative status: 'I' am not like 'them'. Malcolm, for instance, resisted claiming benefits because it would necessitate him adopting the identity, activities and associations of the unemployed. Kelvin and Jarrett (1985: 123), summarising psychological research on this question, could be describing Malcolm in the following observation:

> he feels tainted by association, he believes others associate him with these 'inadequates', as indeed they often do ... he may have more need than many for social comparisons which enhance his

self-esteem...to feel that he is better than others who are in the same position.

As Lister (2004) points out, unlike many other oppressed, powerless groups there is no political or cultural capital to be gained – and no positive self-esteem accrues – from membership of a social group held by many to be useless and unworthy: 'the unemployed thus constitute a virtually unique reference group. Its members, almost to a man and woman, do not want to belong to it' (Kelvin and Jarrett, 1985: 125).

Few interviewees had anything more than a fragile, inchoate understanding of the structural, economic changes that have shaped the contemporary Teesside labour market. In seeking explanations for persistent, high unemployment, interviewees clutched at answers that reiterated easy, populist and vague stories of 'lazy bums', 'scroungers' and 'the bone idle'. Differentiating oneself from what is imagined – wrongly – to be the typical experience of unemployment offers a buffer against the potential social and psychological damage of negative labelling. Exactly the same processes could be observed in descriptions of illicit, 'fiddly work' (MacDonald, 1994), of 'bad mothers' (see chapter 7) and 'dirty smack-heads' (chapter 9). We understand these as part of a complicated local mythology that sought to defend individual and family reputations against widely held, often heard tirades – against other benefit claimants, fiddly workers or young mothers – by demonising others in the same objective situation. Insecure personal and family 'respectability' is shored up by castigating others to whom they feel these negative labels might apply (see Skeggs, 1997; Mitchell and Green, 2002). In so doing, these powerless groups provide social commentators – who deign not to delve deeper – with 'evidence' further to fuel diatribes against 'the undeserving poor'.

7
Becoming and Being a Young Parent: Family Careers in Poor Neighbourhoods

> I think it's disgraceful — Girls go to school and aged sixteen don't do no exams, think 'I'll open me legs, get a sprog and then I'm set for life'.
>
> (Stuart, 26, married father, part-time employed)

Introduction

Processes of family formation hold a particularly important, contested place in debates about the underclass and policies on social exclusion (Murray, 1994, 2000; Social Exclusion Unit, 1998b; Duncan and Edwards, 1999). Whilst underclass perspectives point to the alleged cultural reproduction of troublesome, benefit-dependent families, government policy targeting of, for instance, teenage mothers emphasises the social inequalities said to accrue to them and, later, to their offspring (Hobcraft,1998; Hobcraft and Kiernan, 1999; Arai, 2003; ISER, 2004).

We begin our examination of the family careers of our informants by interrogating their views on, and experiences of, *becoming* a young parent, setting these against the claims of underclass theory and some other recent research. This section of the chapter hinges on an apparent paradox between interviewees' highly conventional, normative perspectives on parenthood and, on the other hand, objective indicators which seem to confirm this place as one in which Murray's illegitimate, underclass families might be found. The experience of *being* a young parent is then described, with particularly reference to young mothers. We conclude that the lived, day-to-day experience of young motherhood in poor neighbourhoods meshes with notions of social exclusion and, moreover, that the personal identities and social networks associated with being a young mother can compound this condition.

Becoming a young parent: mainstream views from the margin

Twenty-seven young people (in our sample of 88) were parents or expectant parents at the time of interview (sixteen mothers and eleven fathers).[1] These interviewees ranged in age from 17 to 27 years (by the time of the second interview) and had become parents between the ages of 15 and 22. Two-thirds of the parents were in a continuing relationship with the other natural parent of their child (in a few cases both parents were interviewed), with the majority of these living at the same address (either officially or unofficially). The remainder were women who no longer lived with the other parent (if they ever had) and, in all but one case, had no continuing, regular relationship with the other parent. These nine women could be described as 'lone parents', but later we will argue that the complexities of their changing partnerships and housing situations makes such categorisations difficult.

At the right time

All but a handful of interviewees – parents and non-parents – said that they wanted to have children at some time in their lives with some embracing the prospect eagerly. For Andrew, aged 23, fatherhood was his 'biggest ambition'. Richard (20) wanted to repair the damage to his relationship with his mother caused by his destructive drug and criminal career (see chapter 9). He saw fatherhood as a way of 'pleasing her with it —— me Mam always wanted a grandkid off me. Just go up to her one day and say "You're a grandma" —— she'll be buzzing.'

Whatever their particular motivations, those who were *not* parents usually said the mid- to late twenties would be the 'ideal time to start a family'. 'Living my life to the max.!' (Sam) and 'partying first' (Billy) meant putting off the responsibilities of parenthood:

> I don't want a kid until I'm about 25, 27 —— I dunno there's people go round saying, 'I want a kid' and all that, what's the point when you've got all your nightlife to go! I'd rather go out and all that before I have a kid and that.[2]
>
> (Darren, 16, unemployed)

Those who were *already* parents gave more complicated answers. A few agreed that the mid- to late twenties would have been a better age at which to have children. Here Kelly (25) and Kate (22), who became parents at 16 and 20 years respectively, talk about how they wished they had not had their children so young:

> *Kelly*: I'd have liked to have got an education and did things that I can't do, like, I dunno, go out and enjoy myself a bit, have a job, have some money behind me, before I have the kids because ——
> *Kate*: Give them a better life, can't you?
> *Kelly*: Yeah, it's a struggle to bring the kids up.

Contrary to the general view, two interviewees – both men – described how they had aspired from an early age to become parents. Curtis, who had one child and was (possibly) expecting another, was delighted when his girlfriend of one month became pregnant:

> I was over the moon...I've wanted a little baby boy since I was sixteen...People will say how much I care about him and what I've done for him. People say that they don't understand why I'm like that when I'm only 21. I wanted a baby that much, but I don't —— how I see it, I'm 21, I've wanted this baby for like five year and now I've got him, I'm not going to spoil my chances of losing him, I'm gonna keep him. I'm gonna enjoy it with him —— I can't wait until he's talking more and walking and everything.
>
> (Curtis, 21, unemployed)

Although the strong, positive feelings expressed here throw into question some popular views about young men's commitment to fathering (as we discuss later) they were by no means universal. Others (like Lewis, 16, unemployed) expressed equally strong *negative* views about the prospect of having children: 'I'd be devoed [devastated] really, 'cos I'm only sixteen —— 'cos you haven't got a job or fuck all or a house or owt like that'.

In the right way

The vast majority of our interviewees – men and women alike – spoke about forming relationships and raising a family in very conventional terms. It was important to have in place the foundations of stable employment, financial security and a home before having children:

> I'd like a nice house, all the money, a nice job. Don't have kids until after you've got a job —— something you can actually keep doing. Something you like and you're not going to quit after a couple of

years after you've already had a kid…You don't want to end up skint with a kid, do you? You have to make sure you've got everything for it.

(Leigh, 17, Youth Trainee)

Providing for the basic needs of children, through wages, was emphasised by all interviewees. The perceived financial costs of parenthood, coupled with temptations of youthful leisure lives, meant that many wanted to delay becoming a parent. Even some of those in jobs and settled partnerships still felt the time was not right. Martin, who had married and rented a house with his wife by the time of the second interview, had already discussed the issue of starting a family:

I wouldn't wanna have a family now, 'cos I don't think I could afford [it]…I want what every parent wants; to give the best upbringing they can. My feeling is that you have to have a bit of money behind you before you can start a family, so — I – we – do wanna have kids. We've discussed it, but not at this stage.

(Martin, 20, employed)

Although marriage was not seen as a crucial precursor to parenthood, being in a strong, loving and supportive partnership was. Perhaps surprisingly, it was young men who were most vocal about this: 'You've gotta be really in love with someone to have a kid. Really trust 'em and that, you know?…There's no point getting yourself boxed with a kid when you don't even know the mother. I think a kid needs two parents' (Allan, 21, unemployed, no children). Most agreed with Allan and – consistent with our other findings – had conservative views on lone parenthood.[3] The 'traditional' family unit of natural mother and father constituted the ideal circumstances in which to raise a child. Their explanations ranged from practical ones (e.g. the hard work and costs of parenting were more easily borne by two adults) to ones that stressed the different parental roles typically taken by men and women: 'I mean if the dad's there, it's better, isn't it? It's their dad, it's their parent — the strictness of a man's authority, a man's voice, they need it. I think they need sometimes, fatherly things' (Susan, 22, mother).

A paradox of subjective viewpoints and objective outcomes

There is nothing here that marks out these young people's narratives about parenthood as especially noteworthy or significant. Yet the key reason that Murray (1994) named 'Kelby' in support of his underclass

theory was because of the allegedly unconventional, morally repre-
hensible practices of its residents in respect of family formation revealed
(to him) by the high rate of 'illegitimate' births in the town. In 1994,
he was able to cite a rate of 45 per cent. By 2001, 53 per cent of all
births in Kelby were 'illegitimate', compared to 40 per cent in England
and Wales.[4] Other local statistics seem to support his allegations about
the connections between 'illegitimacy', benefit dependency, irresponsible parenting and the reproduction of underclass culture in these
poor neighbourhoods. For example, officially in some East Kelby
wards over half of all families with dependent children are headed by
a lone parent, compared with 19 per cent nationally and only 4 per cent
in Ackthorpe (a more affluent ward a few miles away). In one ward 58
per cent of children live in households claiming income support,
compared with 18 per cent nationally (and 3 per cent in Ackthorpe).
Finally, East Kelby has high rates of teenage pregnancy even compared with the town of Kelby as a whole, which has the ninth highest
rate of conceptions to under-eighteen year olds nationally (SEU,
1999b: 20).

Thus, according to available objective measures there seems – at least
superficially – to be support for the conservative, cultural underclass
theory that Murray proposes. These are neighbourhoods that – when
compared with national figures, with the town as a whole and even
with some nearby wards – show dramatically higher rates of illegitimate births, of lone parent households, of teenage parenthood and
of families being dependent on state welfare. How can we explain the
discrepancy between young people's mainstream views about parenthood and what prevailing theories predict and statistical records suggest
to be the case?

'Perverse incentives' and the pursuit of the 'mothering option'?

Murray (1994) claims that 'illegitimate' births to benefit-dependent
young women in poor areas results from the 'seductive temptations'
and 'perverse incentives' of a social security system that has removed
the 'economic penalties' on single motherhood. We put this theory to
our interviewees. It received plenty of support. Many agreed that immorality, irresponsibility and a rational, calculative assessment of potential
welfare benefits helped explain local parenting patterns. Stuart, quoted
at the start of this chapter, gave a particularly brutal assessment of the
attitude of young mothers in East Kelby.

Us and them: respectable families and 'underclass' mothers

Few felt, however, that such a theory could be applied to their own situations, to those of friends or family or, indeed, to any cases that they actually knew well.[5] This is puzzling. Either we have a strangely skewed sample (and failed to contact the numerous local people said to subscribe personally to underclass values in respect of parenthood) or we are again accessing the rhetorical efforts of the poor and powerless to preserve personal and family respectability by castigating others in apparently similar situations. In chapter 6 we described very similar processes in respect of individual's efforts to differentiate themselves morally from other unemployed people in their neighbourhoods. For instance, Alison compared her sister's situation (and 'good attitude') with that of another local woman:

> Our Jane [sister], she doesn't even want this benefit. She wants to go back to college and earn her own money. Like she says, 'Seventy quid's no good, I want a job, I wanna do things.' Our Jane's got a good attitude but other people are like thinking, 'Right, I'll lay back'. It's like a lass up the road, she's got like two kids to two different fellas. I mean, our Jane has [as well], but this lass is a slag and our Jane hates the fact that she's got two kids to different fathers when she's [i.e. Jane has] only slept with three fellas and she's not a slag. She's [i.e. the 'lass up the road'] slept with lads after lads after lads. She's had about five abortions. She's got two kids now and she's pregnant again. She's married now and she's only 20 and she's just sat in the house, just —— I think they've all got that attitude of getting money and stuff like that.
>
> (Alison, 18, employed, no children)

In other words, *they* are like that, but *we* are not. In our sample, Claire (20, a non-employed mother) provided the only self-report that seemed to match this 'other' category; a narrative that admitted to becoming pregnant purposefully in order to claim benefits and gain access to social housing. Here she explains her actions:

> *Claire*: I got pregnant on purpose —— I was only eighteen and I was in a dead-end job I hated. I was in a flat I hated. I'd get a house, get on benefits and I just didn't look ahead. I was daft, I was young and stupid...I used to go bootlegging for money in Dover [smuggling contraband cigarettes and alcohol from France] because I was always skint. I got sick of that, I hated it. 'I'm having a baby and I'm gonna

get a house and be on benefits', yeah . . . I thought, 'If I get pregnant, he'll go out to work and I'll be sat at home with the baby', you know what I mean?
RM: And did he go out to work?
Claire: No, did he hell — he's got a job now but he didn't work for a year and a half.
RM: And what did you think that [motherhood] would be like then?
Claire: Ah, it'd be brilliant, a little baby in a pram, dead quiet and me own house and I thought it'd be brilliant. I was just — I was so immature.

Feeling trapped in a depressing flat and job and supplementing income through illegal activity, Claire tried to change her life for the better by becoming a mother (without telling her partner, she stopped taking the contraceptive pill). The reality of young motherhood was not as she had envisaged. Claire's longer-term ambition to become a legal secretary after studying at college and maybe university were put on hold until her toddler was old enough to attend nursery. Constrained by the demands of motherhood, she described her earlier dreams about 'the mothering option' (Craine, 1997) as 'immature'.

Safety nets and scroungers

Unlike Claire, the other parents we interviewed did not deliberately enter into parenthood *in order* to claim the associated welfare benefits or to gain access to social housing. Pregnancies were often unplanned. When people found themselves in situations where they had children to support, however, most were not opposed to claiming government benefits in order to help with the costs of running a family. The following exchange with seventeen-year-old mother Gail is illustrative:

JM: OK, what do you think when people call unemployed people — they just say they're scroungers?
Gail: I'm not a scrounger! I'm not a scrounger! No, not really, because some people can't work. Some people have, like, don't wanna leave their kids, you know what I mean? So — scroungers! [indignant laughing]
JM: They do though, don't they? I mean you hear it a lot, in newspapers and politicians saying things —
Gail: Some people do but — everybody needs money to survive, that's what it's there for, to give to you, you know what I mean? Or they wouldn't have invented the Social and the dole and that. That's

what it's there [for] —— You can't survive without it, if there's no jobs about and you need the money —— and you've just had a baby, you know what I mean? They should provide for you, yeah, until you get back on your feet at least. They shouldn't have brought it in if they didn't want it ——

Most interviewees agreed – in respect of their *own* circumstances – that 'if there's no jobs about' or they left the labour market to look after their children, claiming benefits provided an acceptable, temporary, alternative way of getting by.

Resisting welfare, surviving on welfare

A few individuals in our study refused, however, to avail themselves of their welfare state entitlements. These were cases where young parents despised the fact that they had to claim benefits in order to support themselves and their children. In chapter 5 we described how Malcolm, Gail's partner, was so opposed to claiming benefits that he refused to 'sign on' for Job Seekers Allowance resulting in them being far worse off over a period of several months. Gail gave some further explanation:

I know Joe's only a baby, but Malcolm says he doesn't want Joe growing up knowing that all you have to do is sit on your arse, you know what I mean? Just sit there and wait for your giro to come every fortnight, he doesn't want him to do that. He wants him to go out and work and do something with his life... at least then we know we're not gonna have a son, well, probably not, who's, like, gonna just sit around and wait for each giro.

Similarly, Tara (22, an employed mother) described how her husband had been determined that he would support his family without the help of government benefits:

Pete's like that now, you know? He sort of —— he doesn't even like claiming Family Credit because 'it's sponging', he said. I had to fight with him to do that. He's very —— because a lot of his family are unemployed and live in council houses, he just didn't wanna be like that. So I must admit his upbringing's had an effect on him! [*laughing*]

Although claiming benefits was not often as strongly resisted as in these cases, it certainly was not a favoured or easy strategy. It was simply a way of getting by in a place like East Kelby. Life on meagre welfare benefits was a struggle and young mothers told us how they were restricted in the types of stores in which they could shop and the types of food they could buy:

JM: Where do you shop, Kelly?
Kate and Kelly: Netto [together].
Kelly: 'Cos it's the cheapest place we can go. Or Kwiksave or the freezer shop because like Morrison's —— you've gotta be a millionaire to go in there!
JM: But do you think there's certain shops and there's certain foods the kids miss out on 'cos you can't afford them?
Kelly: Yeah, a lot of like fruit and veg and ——
Kate: And yoghurt and things like that.
Kelly: Yoghurts, yeah —— we buy yoghurts, but only in Netto 'cos they're cheaper. Maybe once a week. She'll have veg and that's on a Sunday when we do a Sunday dinner.

> (Kelly, 25, non-employed mother, and Kate, 22,
> non-employed mother)

These parents' experience of poverty meant that they found laughable claims that young women would choose positively to raise a family on government benefits (Phoenix, 1991; Social Exclusion Unit, 1999b): 'By Thursday you're skint. You've got to like miss one bill to pay another. You're like, 'Oh no, here we go again'... it is a nightmare, but like all these old people think one-parent families get everything!' (Kelly). For Leila (18, non-employed), her resourcefulness in making a small income stretch and her success in raising children in adverse circumstances added to her sense of resilience and self-esteem: 'I like living on the Social and struggling, you know? Fighting for myself to kind of prove that I know what I'm doing and I can do it and I have done it.' Thus, those with more direct experience of the struggles of parenthood on benefits (Leila, Gail, Kelly and Kate) rejected wholesale the idea – popular among other interviewees – that such benefits acted as an incentive to pursue the 'mothering option'. Like other studies (Phoenix, 1991; Social Exclusion Unit, 1999b), our findings thus far contradict this aspect of underclass theory. Not only did welfare income barely cover family subsistence, the possibility of subsidised, local authority accommodation played little role in young people's 'decisions' to become parents (as we show in chapter 8).

Becoming a lone parent: single mothers and absent fathers?

Most of the sample regarded two-parent families as the best context in which to bring up children. Given this, how do we explain the predominance of *lone* parenthood in East Kelby and places like it? Here we focus on the narrative accounts of those interviewees we might class as 'lone mothers'; that is, that sector of the alleged underclass on whom has been heaped the most moral blame and among whom, therefore, one might expect to find strongest evidence in support of underclass theory.

'He was the perfect bloke...'

It is difficult to apply apparently common-sense labels, such as 'lone mother', to individuals with complicated biographies and changing circumstances. All but one of the nine young women possibly fitting this category had sole responsibility for their child/ren when we first met them.[6] Only one was in a relationship with the father of her child and most had no contact with their children's fathers (e.g. Kate's partner had 'miraculously vanished' soon after their child was born). By the time of the second interview, however, five 'lone mothers' had new partners, some of whom took some role in parenting. We begin to see that even *describing* the extent of lone motherhood is not as simple a task as is inferred in many policy or academic accounts.

The picture is complicated further by the practice of concealed 'semi-cohabitation' (Phoenix, 1991: 119); concealed because declaring co-residence with a male partner might jeopardise eligibility for single-parent family benefit. We *think* we collected generally reliable accounts of the living arrangements of the parents in the study. Fear of losing (illicit) benefits may, however, have led some to hide the fact that they shared accommodation – and possibly parenting – with male partners. For these reasons, published indicators of 'lone parenthood' may overestimate the extent to which women in poor neighbourhoods raise children independently. Kelly and Kate provided an insight into these issues. They claimed that some streets in East Kelby were notorious for this practice. They also argued that fraudulent access to such benefits only marginally relieved the poverty experienced by lone mothers and stressed the risks involved, given the payment of cash for information about proven fraud. Such 'grassing' was generally frowned on. Those who did it were said to be motivated by financial gain and envy (that others might be getting higher benefit payments).

Kelly had lost her benefits temporarily after being accused of concealed cohabitation:

> After we lost the baby [a miscarriage], Scott [her boyfriend] stayed
> with me for a long time afterwards, 'cos I just couldn't cope at all. He
> stayed, like, while I was in hospital. He stayed at my house to look
> after the kids and after I come out of hospital. Didn't I get the Social
> at my door? ... I said 'But he was only here to support me'. They took
> my [benefits] book off me!

Subsequently, Kelly would not risk Scott living with her because of her
fear – and experience – of being 'grassed' by neighbours. Her boyfriend
had proved to be an important source of emotional and practical support
for her and her children. In her view, though, benefit levels and the regu-
lations that governed it disallowed him moving in to her home and taking a more visible role in parenting.

That said, several women appreciated the freedom that lone parenthood
brought in comparison with previous abusive and controlling relationships with men. Lisa (24) and Emma (25) had both been subjected to
violence and intimidation from their partners and had escaped, at times,
to women's refuges. At first the father of Lisa's children had appeared to
be 'the perfect bloke'. Now she described him as a 'druggie, criminal,
paranoid schizophrenic —— a nutter'. Emma now looked forward to
meeting 'a man who treats you like a human being, not a punch bag'.

'Bang, bang – I'm gone'?

Linda: Not many lads stay with their girlfriends though, do they?
They think, 'Oh God, a baby's coming'.
Stuart: That's it – bang, bang – I'm gone.
JM: Why do you think that is?
Linda: Scared, terrified.
Stuart: They've had their fun but they can't take the responsibility.
Where I think they should be made to pay for the responsibility.
They've had the kids, they've had the fun.
                    (Linda, 23, non-employed, married mother, and Stuart, 26,
                                      part-time employed, married father)

As with negative stereotypes of young, lone mothers, popular views of
young 'absent fathers' as fearful of the adult responsibilities of parenthood were common among the sample as a whole (and are summed
up by Linda and Stuart). The experience of the majority of our 'lone

mothers' – who had no contact with the fathers of their children – suggests that such views are far from ungrounded. Nevertheless the interviews with the four people we might class as 'absent fathers' provided for a different, more complicated perspective on why, and the extent to which, some fathers are absent. We present two of them – not as representative, but as illustrative of the constraints on choice experienced by some fathers.

Curtis (21 and on NDYP) had regular, weekly contact with his child. Soon after the birth, his girlfriend ended their relationship:

> I used to see Daniel [son] every single day and now it's like —— do you know what I mean? —— twice a week and it kills you! It just doesn't work anymore. I'm used to seeing him every single day. It's like, if I see Daniel's Mam walking down the road with him, I have to, like, shout so that I can run over and see him, you know what I mean?

After he threatened court action, his ex-girlfriend let Daniel stay overnight with Curtis twice a week. As he was currently homeless, Curtis relied on the generosity of his sister, who opened up her home (already overcrowded with three children and herself in two bedrooms) so that he could have his child to stay. Despite the difficulties of negotiating access rights, Curtis continued to have a casual, sexual relationship with his ex-girlfriend in the hope that they might be reunited. However, she began a relationship with another man and became pregnant and, at the time of interview, Curtis was in turmoil over whether this unborn child was his or not. He hoped to have a paternity test so that he could show that he was now the father of two children. Whilst the briefest of cameos, Curtis's interview convinced us of his commitment to developing fatherly relationships with his son in very difficult circumstances.

Unlike Curtis, Matthew (19) had no contact with his child. Even here, though, we believe we can observe attitudes to fatherhood that do not chime with popular refrains. Matthew had been a father for three years but for the last four had been heavily engaged in acquisitive crime to support his heroin habit. He was serving a prison sentence when he was interviewed. A well-established criminal career and chaotic life-style had led to episodic imprisonment, thus preventing any sustained, close fathering role:[7]

> To tell you the truth, miss, he's three-year-old, right, must have seen us about three or four times... he's had that many lads [other men] round 'im, you know what I mean? I think when I seen him the last

time he didn't even have a clue who I was —— I think he still remembers my name, you know, 'cos when he was younger and that, miss, his Mam used to say, 'Oh where's your Dad, Matto? Matto this, Matto that'. The lads who go round their house —— well, there's only one Matto and that's me! When I knocked at the door when I got out last time and she said 'Who is it?' and I shouted through the letterbox 'It's Matto,' and he [his son] come running down the stairs and he stood there at the stairs, you know, so I could see 'im and he just started smiling and he come running to the door and he opened the door for us and I walked in and he just started grabbing my legs and, like, I give him a cuddle and whatever, miss. So I think he still remembers my name but he doesn't know what I look like, if you know what I mean.

The lack of contact with his child deeply troubled Matthew. Like many of the other young men we interviewed with long-term, drug crime careers, positive future plans were predicated on a dream of leaving the immediate locale (see chapter 9). Going straight – in this case, getting back with his girlfriend and becoming a father to his child – meant getting out of the neighbourhood he knew and in which he was known:

I've thought about that any amount of times, miss. She wants to stay near her Mam's —— but if she moves somewhere like Deighton [a nearby town] or places what I know what's all right, do you know what I mean, where people can't cause trouble between us three . . . I'd say further out the town, where there's no smack-heads, there's nowt, no little close areas, you know what I mean? Where there's no gob-shites [trouble-making gossips] causing shite between me and her, what'll make us argue and that. I've told her, let her get a place in [another part of] Kelby somewhere, 'Anywhere you want. I'll look after you and the baby all day long. I'm not bothered where, what time of day or what time of night it is, I'll look after you all day long.'

Of course, it is not our intention to paint Matthew as a perfect father. He has barely been a father to his child at all.[8] Unlike Curtis, one could argue his absence was self-imposed, albeit indirectly, by his 'choices', first, to use heroin and, second, to fund his later addiction through a chaotic criminal career that was likely to result in repeated periods of imprisonment. In chapter 9, though, we question the extent of 'free will' and 'choice' in respect of the sustained use of 'poverty drugs' such as heroin. Our focus on his case – and that of Curtis – is to show how in the most unlikely of circumstances (i.e. of homelessness, joblessness, problematic drug use, crime, imprisonment), young fathers like these can express sentiments and aspire to lead lives quite at odds with the mean portraits of 'absent fathers' offered in the underclass literature (Murray, 1990; 1994; Dennis and Erdos, 1993).

Family planning? Choice, fate and circumstance

If neither financial calculation nor life-style choice were significant elements in explaining young parenthood in East Kelby, perhaps a better explanation can be found in young people's descriptions of the steps they took to plan for parenthood?

In seeking to understand why the UK has the highest rates of teenage pregnancy in Western Europe, the Social Exclusion Unit (1999b) suggests that ignorance about contraception and its relatively limited use by young people is important. We did not ask interviewees directly about this, but the evidence we have fits with the findings of Tabberer et al. (2000) that stress young people's *lack* of planning in respect of contraception and potential pregnancy. According to the Social Exclusion Unit (1999b: 28), 'the first conscious decision that many teenagers make about pregnancy is whether to have an abortion or continue with pregnancy'. Further, and in support of Burghes and Brown (1995), some interviewees explained how they became parents as a result of contraceptive failure. Once pregnant, few reported seriously considering adoption or abortion: 'young people in more deprived areas appeared to disapprove strongly of abortion' and Teesside has the fourth lowest national percentage of conceptions to under 20 year olds that lead to abortion (SEU, 1999b: 59). Turner's study (2004: 237) found that there was no evidence that:

> young women from disadvantaged areas view teenage motherhood as beneficial and as a means to economic independence and adult status. Rather ... once pregnant, women from disadvantaged areas are more likely ... to reject abortion and perceive fewer negative implications of being a mother.

'Falling' pregnant

Despite a near consensus about the best age and circumstances in which to have children, a number of women, and young mothers in particular, talked of parenthood in fatalistic terms and expressed little in the way of a planned approached to it (epitomised by the preferred phrase 'falling pregnant'). Elizabeth (19 and on NDYP) did not have children, unlike many of her friends. Free of the responsibilities of parenthood, she said, 'I've got my life ahead of me'. She added, though, 'if I fell pregnant now I would love it. It wouldn't bother me at all.' Similarly, Carol-Ann (24, employed) said she would be happy to have children 'whenever they come along'. Ellie (26, student) agreed that 'they'll come when they sort of come'. Many interviewees expressed the same outlook, that if they found they were expectant parents they would accept this as part of life. Kayleigh (17, Youth Trainee, no children) was the most explicit:

> *Kayleigh*: But if it happens now, it happens, doesn't it? It's just life. If it happens, it happens, if it doesn't, it doesn't —— I'd just take it as it comes and cross like that bridge when it comes to it.
> *RM*: Yeah, but if you were planning to? Let's say you were thinking of —
> *Kayleigh*: No! 'Cos you don't plan anything because it never works anyway, I've learnt that.

In reading the transcripts of interviews with young people in East Kelby and trying to make sense of the apparent contradiction between their subjective viewpoints about parenting and the objective facts (as expressed in national leagues tables and statistics concerning the place), we kept coming back to this interview extract. Kayleigh's short, pithy comment seemed to resonate with what many of those who *were* parents were telling us and to suggest a different way of understanding patterns of parenting in poor neighbourhoods.

Bounded agency, socio-scapes and 'the sense of future possibilities'

Karen Evans and colleagues introduce the concept of 'bounded agency' to describe people's structurally rooted, 'subjectively perceived frames for action and decision' (2001: 24):

> the notion of bounded agency can be ... further elaborated through the metaphor of social actors moving in a social landscape ... [this sees] agency as being both temporally embedded and bounded, *influenced in the chances of the present moment by past experiences and the sense of future possibilities.* (2001: 25, our emphasis)

This is a useful metaphor. We would also stress the *spatial* dimensions of young people's social landscapes by highlighting the way that local cultural knowledge and values bound individual choices and actions. It is at the local level that young people learn informally – particularly from friends and family and through their own lived experience – 'a sense of future possibilities'; the culturally sanctioned ways of being a young person and becoming an adult. And it is at this level that they learn how such knowledge fits (or does not) the formal 'structure of opportunities' offered to young people through education, training and employment.

In their study of south London youth, Ball and colleagues (2000a: 149) also recognise the spatiality of the social and cultural horizons visible to groups of individuals. These 'socio-scapes' are mental maps of the scope of opportunities and limitations as perceived by young people and spring from deeply entrenched divisions of class, ethnicity and gender. They are also mediated by place. This spatial dimension, this 'geography of exclusion' (Sibley, 1995), helps to differentiate social horizons for young people who might otherwise share similar social characteristics. Thus, the socio-scapes visible to the white, working-class interviewees in Ball et al.'s study of London contained a seemingly greater range of possible careers, opportunities and identities, and were less tightly bounded – to use Evans et al.'s phrase – than were those perceived by ours in East Kelby.

How does this help us understand young parenthood in East Kelby? How do these concepts relate to what Kayleigh told us? Let us quote one more useful study before we return to our own. Drawing upon Bourdieu's ideas of cultural capital, Thomson (2000: 424) investigates the 'local moral economies' that were observed in two locales with sharply contrasting social and economic conditions (one, 'Forest Green', being in an affluent, middle-class, commuter-belt town, the other, 'North Park', being a deprived, public housing estate). These different social worlds valued quite different forms of social, cultural and physical capital. Consequently, the young people there operated with quite different 'logics of sexual practice'. In North Park – which appears similar to East Kelby – 'an economy of physical and symbolic capital meant that young men had much to gain from the cultivation of sexual reputations and young women from the experience and authority of motherhood' (2000: 425). These gendered forms of cultural capital and logics of sexual practice made sense and had currency within their places but in North Park – unlike Forest Green – were unlikely to have much exchange value outside of this domain (see chapter 10). It is this difference in class-structured life possibilities that leads Arai (2003: 212–13) to question current policy discourses towards young mothers:

> Policy makers find it hard to believe that young women, often in the least auspicious circumstances, might actually *want* to be mothers.

Young women may not say as much; to do so is to invite censure in an age in which it is considered strange to want to have children so young... policy makers come from class backgrounds that celebrate the idea of 'being in control'... the apparent fatalism of young mothers partly reflects their class background, with its relatively limited life options, but it also reflects a genuine desire for a maternal role.

Plans that never work

Like Thomson and Arai, we suggest that young people's outlooks on parenthood are rooted in broader, but localised, class cultural experiences and values. This is crucial to understanding the complicated, ambiguous accounts we gathered. When Kayleigh remarked, in respect of whether or not to start a family, that she had learned 'not to plan anything because it never works anyway' she was expressing a sentiment that cropped up frequently and across the topics in our interviews. Accounts of recurrent unemployment, of experiences of school and college, of encounters with criminal and drug economies, of housing moves – as well as of parenting – all contained, to greater or lesser degree, aspects of this resigned attitude to the future (we return to this issue in chapter 10). Bourdieu's characterisation of individual habitus as 'a system of lasting and transposable dispositions' (1997: 95), learnt from the class cultural context and personal experience, helps explain this. Theirs was an inherent view of the world in which things happened to them and where the room for personal agency – for strategically mapping out their futures and then taking progressive steps towards cherished goals – was severely circumscribed (Ball et al., 2000a). Their 'sense of future possibilities' was tightly bounded by 'past experiences' (Evans et al., 2001: 25). Plans 'never work anyway'.

Thus, young parents – and those, like Kayleigh, who were not yet parents – described their biographies and imagined their futures in terms that emphasised the same lack of choice and control. Whilst we think there is much to commend in Arai's questioning of current policy perspectives (above), we are less sure that we can interpret 'young' motherhood as being as freely chosen. There are hints of a similar argument in the existing literature. Craine comments, briefly, that young, lone motherhood is 'less the product of irresponsibility than the result of a fatalistic ethos generated within a context of institutionalised economic and social insecurity' (1997: 143). Phoenix also uncovered an attitude – most common among those young mothers who perceived the poorest employment prospects – of 'not minding whether or not they conceived' (1991: 64). Wallace (1986: 101) talks about young women 'drifting' into parenthood because of lack of clear alternatives. Finally, the Social Exclusion Unit concludes that a young woman who 'sees a clear future for herself through education and work' is less likely to become a parent at an early age than one who sees 'no reason not to get pregnant' (1999b: 22).

We think our and others' accounts of the fatalism induced by the lack of choice, poverty and other lived experiences of social exclusion come closer to helping us understand patterns of parenting in places like East Kelby than do theories that stress the supposed irresponsibility, immorality and calculative planning of the young 'underclass'. They also help explain how a place ranking high on all indices for teenage pregnancy, 'illegitimacy' and lone parenthood can have young residents who express determinedly conventional, unremarkable views about the way in which they might *wish* to become parents.

Being a young mother

The fact that the young mothers achieved this status before achieving the sort of financial and employment security that the majority had hoped for meant that their experience of parenthood was, for most, one redolent of social exclusion. We concentrate on mothers, rather than fathers, because – bearing the brunt of domestic and childcare work – they had far more to say about parenthood.

Restricted social lives

> When I just had Lucy I didn't have any money but I'd still go to the town, window-shopping. In the summer I used to take her to the parks, but now I've got both of 'em it's impossible.
>
> (Amy, 20, non-employed mother)

Whilst young mothers typically talked about the joys of being a parent, most, like Amy, also experienced more limited social and leisure lives, compared with their teenage years, because of the constant demands on their time of caring for young children and the financial hardships of parenthood and running their own houses (Roberts et al., 1990; Kay, 1996). Linda (21) was asked to describe her activities across a typical week:

> What I do? —— take me son to school, come back, usually go shopping or something. If it's a Tuesday go to the market and Saturday go over to Donna's [her sister's house] and that's about it. Weekends? I don't

do anything. Town with Steve [her partner] and then sometimes to a car boot sale on Sunday —— we just go and have a look round, don't buy anything, just passes an hour or so away.

For this group of young mothers, early teenage 'street corner society' and later involvement with commercial, town centre leisure were replaced by domestic socialising as people became older, formed stable partnerships, established their own households and became parents: 'I don't go to the town...my town bits out of the way. I've got a kid, I'm married and it's sort of "forget the town". It's for young girls who wanna get fixed up more than anything [laughs]' (Linda). Many of the older interviewees described how their peer networks were now smaller and more tightly defined than in their teenage years. This general narrowing down of social networks was particularly pronounced for economically disengaged young men in their late teens (see chapter 4) and for young mothers. In both cases, friendship networks became comprised predominantly of others in the same position.[9] And for both groups, leisure and socialising became centred – again – on their immediate neighbourhood. Some men continued with 'street corner society' but for the mothers we interviewed home-based leisure became the norm (Roberts et al., 1990; Loader, 1996).

The following is from an interview with Gail (17) and her sister Carrie (21). Gail had one young child, was expecting another and had grown out of her 'going out, teenage years':

Gail: I used to go to *The Capital* [nightclub] and places like that —— [but] I'm too much in my ways now. I don't miss it [going out]. I'm used to lights out, curtains shut, Joe [her son] on the settee. I sit on the chair and watch the telly and I'm in bed for 10 o'clock. It's just my routine now since we've had the house. Staying in with Malcolm [her partner]. What are you laughing at?
Carrie: She's like an old woman! [*laughing*].
Gail: I am like an old woman ——but I'm happy...[before the baby] I'd have been out with me friends messing about or just sat in our Mam's watching telly. You know the lads round here like they're 17, 18, 19 and they – it grinds [really annoys] me! – sit round the shops drinking cider and that. What's the point in doing that? They're adults now. You don't do that, do you? There's this lass, she's nineteen. She's got a baby. She takes the baby round the shops in the pram and drinks bottles with the lads, out all night —— she's had the baby and hasn't realised how much its gonna have to change. Your life does change. You can't just do what you want to.

Gail's criticism of another young women who she implies has failed to 'grow up' hints at both a particular form of conventional, working-class morality about what is expected of 'good' mothers (see earlier) and an ambivalence implied by several young mothers about their new status. Whilst Gail seemed content with living a newly domesticated social life, the comments of others like Amy and Linda ('I don't do anything') suggest some of the limitations of motherhood as experienced in this socio-economic context.

Labour market detachment

The restrictions on young mothers' social lives were framed by the fact that they tended to hold main, if not sole, responsibility for childcare and domestic work in their households (and, of course, several were 'lone parents'). Consequently, young mothers were predominantly not in employment. The relative poverty associated with benefit dependence and the burdens of domestic work combined to restrict the day-to-day social lives of this group. Some had never been employed, having left school and having had children soon afterwards. Others had given up jobs as a consequence of impending motherhood and not returned. Matching our findings, Webster et al. (2004) explain this primarily in terms of these young women's prioritisation of the mothering role, as traditionally understood. Those with infants regarded their primary role as the care and upbringing of their children. Jobs simply were not sought at this point in their life. Lack of easily accessible, affordable, reliable and good quality childcare was another factor that mediated against the return to work. Childcare arrangements, where they existed, tended to be informal, occasional and arranged between similarly placed friends and relatives.

Many of the young mothers acknowledged as well that there was usually a financial disincentive to returning to employment, given the range of benefits to which their households were now entitled. As shown earlier, there was little evidence that motherhood was sought *because* of the availability of these benefits (Roberts et al., 1990). That said, once *in receipt* of them, young mothers were wary of seeking the poorly paid work that might be available to them because of the likely detrimental impact on family budgets.

Young mothers, social networks and school-to-work careers

Young mothers were not completely detached from education and training. We met one group at an estate-based community centre. Like others in East Kelby, it delivered courses geared towards social and economic regeneration. The courses these interviewees took – in word-processing, basic computer skills, confidence-building, 'positive parenting', and so on – normally ran for a few hours each day and lasted for about six weeks.[10] Several women had exhausted all that was on offer here and were waiting for new ones to commence. Their main appeal, however, lay not in their vocational relevance, but in their social value. Attendance brought the chance to meet other young mothers from the estate (and participants were virtually all young mothers) in a relaxed, warm (i.e. centrally heated) environment that offered subsidised lunches and free crèche facilities. Interviewees liked these courses but did not feel that they would increase their chances of returning to employment. Decent jobs that paid more than benefits were too scarce and they were unlikely to get them anyway. As such, participation chiefly provided a valuable adjunct to their otherwise limited leisure lives and temporary relief from the daily humdrum. As Gail put it, 'They gave me a break from Joe [her son].' They became an accepted, regular part of the day-to-day routines of people like them.

Whilst the local supply and quality of employment and childcare are important in understanding their detachment from the labour market, the personal identities and social networks these young women developed over time also impacted on the nature of their school-to-work careers. The social networks of young mothers on the estates of East Kelby provided valuable resources to individuals who were coping with the hard work, limited budgets and potential isolation that came with parenthood (Johnston et al., 2000). They gave a form of leisure – meeting, chatting and socialising in each others' houses, attending community centre courses – that, together with the daily demands of childcare, filled time and at least partially fended off the boredom that can come with being the parent of young children. They looked after each other's children when the need arose. Money was also lent informally between them when budgets were particularly tight. Critically, these social networks also reinforced a positive sense of self-identity and purpose: they felt engaged in a normal, respectable, socially necessary and valued activity – mothering.

Potentially these shared ways of getting by, of offering mutual support and making the best of what was available could limit individuals' ability to break free of their restricted circumstances. These social networks of similarly placed women mediated the options perceived to be open to them. In describing, and occasionally justifying to us, their current situation, these interviewees would identify themselves *as mothers*, rather than as, say, unemployed. Their peer groups reinforced the view that 'the mothering option' was respectable and legitimate, against more populist media (and academic) accounts of them as irresponsible, deviant members of a welfare-draining underclass (Murray, 1994). Their own respectability was defended by condemnation of those other local women regarded as disreputable mothers (e.g. who drank with young men on the street). Immersion in this peer group, and adoption of this shared identity and the limited leisure and social lives that accompanied it, could inhibit personal progress toward new identities and activities.

For instance, Sarah (23, a mother of two) faced hostility when she attempted to re-engage with full-time, further education. When first interviewed, Sarah commented that a network of other single mothers on her estate provided a good deal of emotional and practical support. At second interview and since announcing her intention to return to college, however, these women had been far from friendly, passing critical comments when they met at the school gate to collect their children. In chapter 4, we noted how Annie (24) had also decided to return to college, against the wishes of her then boyfriend, who was keen on them starting a family, and been met with 'bickering and bitching' from young mothers on her estate. They reproached Annie for thinking she 'was summat' (i.e. somehow 'better' than other women in her neighbourhood). Annie described the constraining effects of this 'Orchard Bank attitude':

> You'll never get on, you won't. You'll just stay in the same rut all the time, I think personally. That's my attitude towards it. It's just got a dull —— it's dim and it's just the same faces in and out, same thing, nothing ever changes, you know... The odd few will take a step in their lives but it's easy to get in that rut... I mean, I'm not downing them. You get it everywhere —— I think I felt as if I was gonna go down the plug with everybody else, sort of thing.

Summary and conclusions

Despite what various statistical indices suggest – and underclass theories assert – young people in these poor neighbourhoods had solidly conventional attitudes to parenthood. We have attempted to explain this paradox of subjective viewpoints and objective indicators in terms of lack of planning in respect of parenthood and the generally fatalistic outlooks on the world possessed by our interviewees (a theme returned to in chapter 10). People *'fell* pregnant', morally objected to abortion, did not consider adoption and had learned through life experience that plans, in respect of parenthood as with much else, 'never work anyway'.

Rational, calculative strategies were absent (in all but one case) but welfare payments *became* crucial to surviving as a parent in poor neighbourhoods. Although we have concentrated in this chapter on the experiences of mothers, the (albeit few) stories we gathered from young fathers also raises questions about their usual depiction in media and some academic renditions about 'families without fatherhood'.

The morality that dismissed the possibility of abortion extended to important, deeply held views about what it meant to be a good mother. Unsurprisingly, women bore the brunt of domestic labour and childcare. Although most in the sample (including those who were mothers) might have wished to delay, none regretted having children and all talked of the joys of parenthood. For young mothers, parenthood meant that social and leisure lives became centred on closer circles of relatives, neighbours and friends, most of whom were also young mothers. Because these interviewees were emotionally and morally committed to mothering and because opportunities for decent, rewarding employment (supported by appropriate childcare arrangements) were few, this group was, for the time being, now largely detached from the labour market. Young mothers tended to live socially, economically and geographically circumscribed lives and the concept of social exclusion had some descriptive purchase here.

The social networks and leisure activities that young mothers described were obviously valuable in coping with the material, social and emotional hardships that they faced. They provided practical, informal support and a sense of positive identity and social inclusion. Paradoxically, inclusion in the networks that helped cope with the conditions of social exclusion (e.g. poverty, isolation) could simultaneously inhibit individuals from taking steps that might help them escape these conditions. Once tied into these supportive social networks, their daily routines and accepted norms, it became difficult to break free of the localised, sub-cultural definitions of what it means to be a young mother in East Kelby and the informal rules and sanctions that went with this. Very similar processes operated in respect of the transitions of some of the young men we interviewed (see chapter 4). Both groups – economically disengaged men in their late teens and young mothers – led leisured lives which were now largely restricted to their own estate and which hinged around a smaller range of friends and acquaintances than they knew in their school days.

This focus on the importance of social networks in understanding the transitions of these young adults allows us to consider – briefly here, but in more detail in chapter 10 – the relevance of the fashionable concept of 'social capital'. Social capital usually refers to the potential advantages that can come from long-term commitment to the social networks in which people operate (Bourdieu and Wacquant, 1992; Forrest and Kearns, 2001; Putnam, 2000).

Most contributions to the research literature stress the advantageous ways that social capital, through reciprocal relationships of trust and mutual support, can act as the springboard for efforts to regenerate socially and economically deprived locales (Putnam, 1996; Richardson and Mumford, 2002). Like Webster et al. (2004), this study highlights the potentially negative consequences of strong 'bonding social capital' (i.e. the connections between individuals, their families and closest friends).

It was certainly the case that strong bonds across our informants' social networks helped in coping with life in poor communities: for example, in respect of job search (as described in chapter 6), in respect of living in a high crime locale (chapter 8) and, as discussed in this chapter, in respect of the experience of young motherhood. Yet investment in these highly localised social networks partly explained why few had established 'bridging social capital' – *beyond* their immediate circle of family and friends – to wider, more socially varied networks that might provide access to more promising avenues for individual progress (Strathdee, 2001). We uncovered some evidence that the trust and loyalties engendered through strong, local ties could be inhibiting. Webster et al.'s follow-up study (2004) shows how localised, social networks become even more significant in the later lives of young adults in poor neighbourhoods and can continue to restrict their transitions. One of the aims of the next chapter is to examine further the significance of place – and young adults' curious commitment to living in these poor neighbourhoods – in explaining their transitions.

8
Housing Careers and the Significance of Place

Living here, it's brilliant.
(Martin, 20)

Introduction

The movement from the parental home (or living in care[1]) to independent living is one of the key dimensions of the transition to adulthood (Jones and Wallace, 1992; Coles, 1995; Jones, 2002). 'Independent living' does not imply complete financial and emotional independence. As noted in chapter 7, for instance, many young parents continued to rely on support from their families and friends, and from the state through welfare benefits, after they had left home. As we will see, connections to family networks and to place emerged as particularly important in understanding the housing careers of these informants. Housing decisions and moves articulated with individuals' varied and changing perceptions of their home locales and, before suggesting some conclusions, we review informant's complicated, sometimes contradictory feelings about the poor neighbourhoods in which they had grown up.

Housing careers: leaving home or staying?

The interviewees' housing situations and careers showed many similarities with those reported more generally in respect of young people (Rugg, 1999). For instance, in line with what we know of the general lengthening of the period of dependency on parents (see chapter 2), just over half of the sample still lived with their parents, never having moved out. The majority reported strong, close relationships with their parent(s) and siblings and felt no need to leave home just yet, especially when the financial costs of independent living were recognised to be significantly higher than the small sums they typically paid to their parents. Asked whether he was happy living at home, seventeen-year-old Richy said, 'Yeah, cushty [very good], £10 a week!' This weighing up of financial costs was clear in eighteen-year-old Alison's careful approach to moving out:

> I wouldn't move out at the minute, I want a better job... with a good wage that I can, like, live off and be able to afford a car on it... I want about £150, £200 a week. I don't wanna get myself in a place where I've got a car, can't afford petrol, got a house, can't afford to buy shopping and can't afford to go out anywhere.

The remainder had left home and made varying numbers of steps in their housing career with different reasons underlying these. Four women had left as teenagers when they became pregnant; parenthood and/ or new partnerships were here, as elsewhere, a common reason for establishing independent households. Several others specified various 'family problems' as the cause of their departure. At sixteen, Claire moved into a council flat by herself 'because I couldn't stand me Dad, he was a drunk'. 'Yo-yo' housing careers, involving sometimes quick and/or repeated returns to the family home were not uncommon (Du Bois-Reymond, 1998; EGRIS, 2001), often due the financial strain of managing a tenancy:

> That's why I gave it up because, like, barmaiding, sometimes I was only getting, like, £40, £48 a week. And they were taking, like, £9 council tax and then rent and then my water and my electric... it wasn't worth me working. At the end of the week I had nowt to buy food and I had to go and get it off our Mam and I thought 'I might as well be back at home'. (Sophie, 19)

These sorts of patterns and processes are common to the housing careers of young people in general, for instance as reported in Ford et al.'s recent study of the housing pathways of young people in five contrasting locations in England (2002).

Local nomadism: 'unplanned' and 'chaotic' housing careers

There are several aspects of this sample's housing experiences, however, that do seem to differ from those reported in other studies (e.g. Rugg et al., 2004). The first is the frequency of the moves made. Over half of those who had left the parental home had made over five moves in their housing career (compared with less than a third of Ford et al.'s sample) and ten of these had made more than ten moves. More frequent movers often had housing careers marked by their early onset (e.g. in their early to mid-teens). Sarah, for instance, left home at the age of fifteen after violent arguments with her mother and moved with friends into a private rented flat in Kelby town centre (the first of over a dozen housing moves before the age of 23). She said: 'we had no money for food. We had nothing. All we were doing was going out on a weekend and then just going and doing our YTS and that was it. It was horrible.'

As with Sarah, frequent movers tended to be those who experienced the most instability and insecurity in other aspects of their lives. Here, violent and/or emotionally traumatic relationships with family members and partners sometimes triggered escape attempts that resulted, for instance, in rough sleeping, accommodation in women's refuges or various forms of 'hidden homelessness'. For example, following rows with, and between, her parents Tanya left home at sixteen and began a housing career that, by the age of 21, had involved more than ten changes of address. She now had little contact with her mother and siblings and none with her father. Her baby was currently being 'looked after' in public care until Tanya was able get free of her heroin addiction. At the time of interview, her accommodation involved shuttling between friends' houses and homeless hostels. Tanya and Sarah aside, severely chaotic housing careers tended to be followed by young men with histories of family conflict, problematic drug use and crime. Part of the explanation for the frequency of their moves was their repeated experience of committal to and release from Young Offenders Institutes and prison, which occasioned their relatively rapid movement around different housing positions (e.g. parental homes, with grandparents, care homes, bail hostels, friends' flats and houses, penal institutions, rough sleeping).[2]

From their larger, more statistically representative survey, Ford et al. (2002) suggest a typology of different sorts of youth housing career. All of those in our sample who had left the parental home had what Ford et al. categorise as 'chaotic' and 'unplanned' housing pathways. None seemed to match the other categories they describe, all of which involve greater degrees of planning, family support and moves in response to employment or educational opportunities. This is not to imply that *no* family support was lent to the moves our interviewees made, nor that some of those still living with parents might one day make more planned housing moves. The reasons why some remained with parents was exactly because they wanted to bide their time until they were in a better position to establish independent living (see Alison's comment, earlier).

One of the striking facts of these people's housing careers was their localisation. By the second round of interviews, only one of the 88 had chosen to live away from East Kelby (Carol-Anne, who had moved to West Yorkshire to live with her boyfriend). One or two young men had moved away, temporarily. These had been very short-lived, ill-fated attempts to seek employment. Nearly all had lived in East Kelby all their lives, and many had remained on the same estate.

Yet, Ford et al.'s characterisation of these sorts of pathway as reflecting 'limited choice' does not fit with our interviewees' experiences. One notable difference between the findings of their more general survey and our study is that they found that the private rented sector – 'housing of the last (or only) resort' (*ibid.*) – often underpinned 'unplanned' and 'chaotic' pathways. Hall (2002) describes how privately rented accommodation is central to the youth housing market. The relative abundance of social housing in East Kelby means, however, that its young adults have easy access to it compared to young people in other urban areas (Social Exclusion Unit, 1999b). Even single young men, like Curtis, had been offered a council bedsit (which he had refused because he needed somewhere for his young son to sleep, when he had access rights: see chapter 7).[3] Private tenancies were relatively rare. Ford and colleagues note that the constraints of local housing markets is a key factor in shaping housing careers, and the availability of social housing in East Kelby helps explain, we think, the frequency of moving our study uncovered. In part, this also helps us understand why apparently nomadic housing careers were constrained to moves *within* East Kelby.

Living in poor neighbourhoods

To understand the housing experiences of our interviewees properly we need to appreciate their feelings about the neighbourhoods in which they lived. As with school-to-work careers, we cannot theorise housing careers only by reference to the local structure of opportunities (e.g. the relative availability of social housing). Many informants, probably the majority, *chose* to remain in wards that have been described as some of the 'most miserable places in England' in which to live (Burrows and Rhodes, 1998). Why do young people stay in poor neighbourhoods?

Knowing and being known: the importance of family and social networks

The most important explanation relates to the embeddedness of these individuals in close, locally concentrated family and social networks. Consider Carol-Anne's answer (at first interview, before she moved away) to our question about living in Primrose Vale – and Catherine's about Orchard Bank – both wards rated in the top five most deprived in England:

> *Carol-Anne* (24): I like it. It's good. It depends which part you live in. Where we live, it's quite quiet and it's good. All our family live dead close together anyway...I've got a cousin lives at number 2. One lives at number 9, one 16. We live at 26 and my auntie lives at 30. All in the same road, and then, like, I've got two cousins that live round the corner on another road and then a cousin that lives in Orchard Bank.
> *RM*: So what are the good things and the bad things?
> *Carol-Anne*: The good thing is, like, they're always there if you need 'em. You're just dead close and good, but the bad things is, like, they all know what's going on. If anything happens, they're, like, 'Oh yeah, we know about that already' and you haven't even walked out the door [*laughing*].

> I'm quite happy here 'cause I know a lot of people and I know the area so I just stay around here. Been round here since I was a kid so I know a lot of people and everything, so I'd rather just stay round here...I mean I've got me Mam, me Nana, me uncles and aunties. They all live in Orchard Bank, so I wouldn't move away.
>
> (Catherine, 19)

These family ties were strong enough to pull young adults back, even when they had made the move to 'independent living'. Sophie (19) had recently secured a new tenancy on another council estate after becoming pregnant, but spent most of the time at her mother's house, only returning 'home' to sleep. She, like her sister Amy, told us she could not imagine living anywhere but Orchard Bank. Carol-Anne was the only interviewee to move away from Kelby during the course of this fieldwork and, when interviewed as part of a later, follow-up study (Webster et al., 2004), she remarked that 'leaving home was the best thing and the worst thing I've ever done', explaining the negative aspects of this in terms of her separation from family. Whilst young women (lone mothers in particular) explained their desire to stay near to their families for emotional and practical reasons (e.g. support offered in terms of childcare), many young men had similar views. Leo (18) explained that he wanted to 'stay round here' so that he could be 'close to me Mam and Dad. Like, if anything did happen, I'd be, like, sort of there for 'em, you know what I mean?' He, like other interviewees, expressed the *interdependent* mutual support offered in families.

Being rooted in local social networks that extended beyond family also emerged as an important factor in positive evaluations of this place. In chapter 6 we documented the significance of informal social networks in seeking jobs. The same has been found in older studies of the unemployed (e.g. Marsden and Duff, 1975). Kelvin and Jarrett (1985: 30) comment that 'in the search for work, the value of informal networks militates against mobility. Networks, whether based on the family or friends, depend on people's roots in a locality: they take time to establish.' Moving to other towns would isolate individuals from networks and practices they knew to be effective in getting work: 'You're, like, friendly with everybody round the area and when you go away it'll take time, won't it?' (Broderick, 18). Numerous instances of this and other sorts of support were given. Martin gave one of the most upbeat assessments of the communality of neighbourhood life:

> *Martin*: Living here, it's brilliant. We have no problems with anyone. We know all the thugs and the thieves and whatever but everyone's okay — It's a lot better if you know someone and something goes wrong. You can always call on people. They're always quite loyal in that sense. If you have problems, you can call on them.
> *JM*: Do you think there's a great community spirit?
> *Martin*: It depends on what you call community spirit. It's really an underground kind of thing. It's the backing —
> *JM*: Kind of, you know, support?
> *Martin*: Yeah, everyone supports you. Neighbours come over and they wanna borrow money until they get paid, things like that. You know you'll get it back, so — You can always rely on everyone else. If you're stuck, someone'll help you.

We would not wish to romanticise everyday life in these poor neighbourhoods. Martin, too, was notably cautious about accepting our suggested term 'community spirit'. He interlaced his positive commentary on East Kelby with, albeit passing, acknowledgement of the problems of living here (e.g. of thieving, thuggery, poverty). Virtually all interviewees recognised the same difficulties. They were particularly vociferous in their condemnation of the effects of heroin dealing and use, and associated criminal victimisation, on them, their families and neighbourhoods (see chapter 9). Allan (21), whose family had been burgled ten times, said:

> These council estates, phwoah! It's a hard graft growing up in these, you know? It's full of TWOCs ['taking cars without the owner's consent'] and it's just the heroin that does my head in. Seeing people rotting away on it. It's a disgusting drug, that.

Yet some interviewees wondered whether less troubled places would experience the same sort of social inclusion and support; whether the hardships they collectively endured gave rise to, or at least encouraged, informal ways of coping which, in turn, generated a strong sense of attachment to the place. Kearns and Parkinson (2001: 2105) say that 'as a response to discrimination and exclusion, residents of deprived communities often engage in a high degree of mutually supportive behaviour'. Broderick's comments hint at this:

> Like you've gotta watch your back everywhere you go and everything... just when you, when they leave the house, they'll walk past and say, 'Here, Broderick, you're round the area, just watch our house while I'm out'. I'll say, 'All right' and then I'll just keep and eye on their house while they're out.

Zack (23), Martin's friend, was unusual in that he often visited other parts of the country. He captured the ambivalence implied in many accounts of this place and underlined Martin's statement that knowing and being respected by important, criminal networks on these estates was influential in experiencing life here as liveable:[4]

> Every time I come back to Primrose Vale, it's home. As soon as I see the A66, I know I'm home and I feel dead relaxed, as if it's a weight off your shoulders...I don't like the place!...You're secure, that's what it is. It's a security blanket; the place where you were raised... Every area is different. Areas with money – if you've got loads of money you're respected 'cos who your family are and what money you've got. Round here, it's if you're hard as fuck [tough/violent]. Or if you're a drug dealer, you're respected. If you do things within the community, you're respected...A lot of people do [want to move away from Primrose Vale]. People who aren't involved in the circles of knowing *people*; knowing *the* people. There is hard people

in every estate —— You have to know the big, well, not just the big people but they have to know people, do you know what I mean? And they have to know the kids that are knocking about on the street.

Some interviewees were obviously better connected to criminal networks than others. Broderick had been a small-time player himself and Zack referred vaguely, with a nod and a wink, to his contacts in drug supply chains. Others, like Martin, had had virtually no criminal involvement but, with Zack, was well known in Primrose Vale for his informal youth work on the estate (MacDonald and Marsh, 2001). As in Johnston et al.'s study (2000), several interviewees insisted that there was practical value in possessing a personal or family reputation that was respected in the circles that maintained sometimes violent, informal social control on these estates (circles that seemed to overlap somewhat with those engaged in particular forms of crime). Informal surveillance of each others' houses (as a deterrent against burglary), the return of stolen possessions following burglaries and the settling of personal feuds by 'hard' intermediaries were all given as examples. One of our stakeholder interviewees said he knew of streets in East Kelby where 'one lad would do your leccy [fix your electricity meter so that bills were reduced] and another would bring round [stolen] kids' clothes for you. It's just a way of getting by.'

The normality of social exclusion

Regardless of whether the majority who made appreciative remarks about their home locales were as accepted by/accepting of local criminals, drug dealers and street gangs as Zack suggests, *familiarity* with the place *was* key to understanding why most wished to stay. Gillian (16) said of her estate, 'Oh, I love it. It's just, like —— the shops are close by, friends are close by, everything really'. Even people like Ellie (26), who were less happy about living in Primrose Vale, described becoming accustomed to the signs of social decline:

> You can see, like, you know, glue bags and needles and that kind of thing, but that's just something else which has become sort of everyday —— going for a walk with the dog past a burnt out car and it's the most normal thing in the world to see. I dunno —— something that sounds like a car backfiring but it could just as easily be somebody shot.

Most had very limited lived experience of places outside Kelby. They had little to compare it with. They did not really know how their contemporaries in more prosperous locales fared and without a more global vantage point (like that provided by national league tables of deprived areas) it was difficult for them to perceive in full the inequalities of social polarisation. When they were provided with this sort of insight, as when the local newspaper picked up on the report that named Primrose Vale as one of the most miserable places in England in which to live (Burrows and Rhodes, 1998), its accuracy was denied: 'It was on the news and in the Chronicle. I don't think it's true. I don't think it's as bad as that. I think there's worse places' (Elizabeth, 19).

Designation of the 'excluded' necessitates reference to the 'included' (Sibley, 1995). This extends to self-designation. None recognised the term 'social exclusion' and only a handful felt that it described their lives, once it was explained. All by the fact of their residence confronted the *objective* problems of social exclusion (i.e. of growing up in a poor, high-crime, high-unemployment locality). Few felt, however, that the problems they *did* experience were particularly unusual or noteworthy; a finding also uncovered in a survey of residents perceptions of crime in these parts of the town (Kelby Borough Council, 1999). Why we, as researchers, should be interested in them, was a common question. Perhaps because Kelby has so many deprived wards (17 out of 24 are classed as such), interviewees were able to reel off lists of other parts of town that they imagined being 'worse' than their own. 'Crime was everywhere,' according to Peter and, speaking of Orchard Bank, Fox said:

> It's really fine, actually, in that you don't get people breaking into your house often. You don't get people smashing your windows, unlike places like Willowdene [another deprived part of Kelby]. We've been broken into a couple of times but we couldn't help that.

Whilst a few interviewees volunteered the names of more affluent wards – 'quieter' places with 'nicer houses' where people were 'posher' (Mally) – that so many people and parts of this town experienced similar problems was a further reason why interviewees expressed bemusement at the idea that they might somehow be different (i.e. 'socially excluded'). Together this (largely) unquestioned acceptance of the normality of their experiences of growing up in poor neighbourhoods, their familiarity with the place and their inclusion in strong, supportive family and social networks meant that most saw no reason to leave East Kelby. Alex (23, a New Deal participant) answered our question about why she wanted to stay: 'I dunno. I've been brought up there. I know it. I know most people round there, so I'd rather just stay round there'.

The problems of poor neighbourhoods

To be clear, interviews contained recurrent, extensive discussion of the problems associated with living in these neighbourhoods; the facts of which make the expressions of attachment given by the majority of interviewees' even more remarkable. Accounts of the social decay caused by crime and locally embedded drug markets dominated; Lupton et al. (2002: 2) also describe how in the deprived areas they studied 'neighbourhood problems were mainly associated with markets for heroin and crack' and Wilson says similar things about the US ghetto experience (1996: 9). Experiences of direct criminal victimisation were widespread.

Criminal victimisation

Fear of burglary was common and reflective of high rates of burglary in poor neighbourhoods in Teesside. The house in which Catherine lived with her parents had been burgled six times, for example. When they lived in Townville – another deprived area in Teesside – Martin's family home had been burgled thirteen times in twelve weeks (but, perhaps because of his family's connections here, not once since they had moved to Primrose Vale). Others reported how their cars, or those of other family members, had been broken into (e.g. to allow the theft of car radios), stolen and sometimes found burnt out after TWOCs. Experiences of victimisation also included: the mundane (thefts from sheds, garages and washing-lines); the bizarre (Rebecca talked about how a stranger had entered her house and 'started shooting up [heroin]'); the depressingly repetitive (being kept awake at night by 'joy-riders'); and the near-comical (Kate, who was bulimic, said: 'I had a drawer full of sweets and I used to just scoff them and these kids come in and pinched it!').

Interviews also referred to more serious, violent crimes they or others they knew had experienced. When she was working in a betting shop, Ellie had been the victim of an armed robbery: 'Basically, I had a shotgun put in me face.' Malcolm's father had been hospitalised by some 'druggies and alcoholics' whom he had chased, after they had been throwing stones at the family house. Carrie had been attacked and robbed (for drug money, she thinks) by a gang of young men, one of who was an ex-boyfriend. Her current depression resulted from this incident and, she said, the fact that her participation in the ensuing court case, via video-link, had not led to a prosecution. Others described, variously, being raped, the disappearance of a friend who had been working as a prostitute, the murder and suicide of associates connected to the local drug economy, and the deaths of friends in stolen cars that had crashed.

Although this was not true for all instances and types of crime, there appeared to be some connection between the degree of embeddedness of informants and their families in these neighbourhoods (and the particular social networks attached to them), and the chances of them being the victims of crime. For instance, as in Johnston et al.'s study (2000), newer arrivals to East Kelby – or those with less in the way of local, extended family networks – seemed more likely to be burgled. Malcolm said that his 'family was getting tormented' because they were new to the area: 'the house was an easy target'. Susan believed the reason why she had been burgled by (she thought) the father of her baby daughter and subjected to a violent street robbery (in which her baby daughter's jewellery was stolen) was because she had dissociated from a local peer group that included her previous boyfriend. As we described earlier, those who were better connected were not immune to criminal victimisation but could sometimes draw on these connections to help reduce the risks of, for instance, being burgled and to deal with the consequences if it did happen. Thus, fear and experience of crime (some of it serious) was not uncommon, leading some to give much more depressing accounts of the place:

> *Mally* (19): I just don't like Orchard Bank...I've been living here for 19 years. I hate the place —— There's TWOCs, there's burglars and all that and also that pub over there. I don't like that place either. It's bad news...It's mainly a rough place...It's mainly the people who think they're hard and all that, just the ones who think they're macho, 'cause they've got a name for theirselves, everyone's scared of them ——
> *JM*: Do you think it's quite a scary place to live for a young lad?
> *Mally*: It is indeed, yeah...Like, I'm outside on the nights and I'm looking around and there's, like —— I'm not sure of meself.

Theorising crime in poor neighbourhoods

We asked informants how they explained the crime that blighted their neighbourhoods. Chapter 9 examines the accounts and explanations of those with more extensive involvement in crime. Here we give space to the ideas of those with little or no history of offending, chiefly because their answers are useful in understanding the central question of this chapter: how individuals experience and make sense of living in poor neighbourhoods.

Across the interviews, informants reached for the whole gamut of criminological theories of crime, including: *genetic predisposition* ('they've

got thieving blood in 'em', Whitey); *immorality* ('the young just don't
know right from wrong', Sam); *peer pressure* ('it's 'cos of who they hang
around with', Lindsay); *negative peer group role models* ('when you're
young you look up at the people who're bad and you wanna be just like
them, in with the gang', Kayleigh); *socio-economic marginality* ('it's nothing
to do, lack of work, lack of money', Chrissie); *poor parenting* ('it's definitely
the way that they've been brought up', Catherine); *negative paternal role
models* ('his Dad's a criminal, been banged up in jail, so it's his Dad's
influenced him, that's another reason', Sam); *dependency culture* ('its too
much hassle to get up and go to work when they can just pinch stuff
from a shop or off a washing-line', Sarah); *risk behaviour* ('they enjoy the
thrill of it', Fox); and *drugs* ('all they pinch for, burgling for, is the drugs,
innit?', Linda).

Some offered several of these 'theories of crime' in the same interview.
When pushed about why they, as individuals, were *not* criminally inclined,
the usual answer – if one was attempted – referred to the positive influence of their parents. Once again, interviewees reached for shorthand
versions of underclass theory in which 'bad' parents produced 'bad',
criminally inclined children. This was sometimes despite the facts of
their own family history (e.g. of siblings who, unlike them, had become
embroiled in criminal careers) and of their own occasional offending.
Leo (18) opted for a classic, 'parents to blame' thesis before acknowledging
its limitations:

Leo: It's the environment they live in, innit? The families they come
from, what their Mams and Dads are like. So if you grow up —— say
like your Mam's a heroin addict, she goes out thieving or your Dad's
always in jail, he does burglaries. Nine times out of ten you're gonna
grow up and be doing exactly the same thing as your Mam and Dad.
JM: So what about you? You got involved in it a little bit?
Leo: A little bit. Well, I come from... just like a normal like family
sort of thing but when I was sixteen I just said to me Mam and Dad,
'I can do what I wanna do. I can leave home if I wanna. I can leave
school if I wanna.' They were trying to talk to me, but I didn't take it
in. I do think back and I think, 'Well, I'm an idiot'. I could've got
into college and done things like that but I didn't really take much
interest at the time 'cos of the people I was knocking about with, the
wrong crowd.

Thus, the way that interviewees often sought to differentiate themselves
and their families socially and morally from 'criminal others' – and

offered authoritarian, illiberal perspectives on the causes of crime and the 'rough justice' that should befall criminals – had much in common with the way that many also talked about 'dole wallahs' (see chapter 6) and 'bad mothers' (chapter 7). This is not to suggest that interviewees' fear and descriptions of criminal victimisation are simply phantoms of media-fuelled, local mythology. If anything, we were struck by the way people seemed to *understate* the clear, everyday, personal problems of crime in their communities. Rather, the way they interpreted their *cause* chimed with the way they also theorised other social problems. This was another example of the untutored attempts of people living in such communities to make sense of social decline and, simultaneously, to distance themselves and their families from the negative, moral labels that are applied to people in poor neighbourhoods. Perhaps the strongest evidence against the 'bad parenting/bad parents' thesis is the fact those interviewees who *had* been involved in serious offending and dependent drug use *also* described, usually remorsefully, their own parents' conventional morality and (failed) attempts to keep them on 'the straight and narrow'.

Local social divisions

Problems of crime were a key reason why a significant minority expressed more critical views about living in East Kelby. In addition – and related to this – some people reported little of the supportive neighbourliness and attachment to extensive social networks described by others. For a few, familiarity bred contempt, not a sense of connectedness. Because he was now unemployed Leo (18) spent more time around his family home in Orchard Bank. This intensified his boredom and his dislike for the area and its residents:

> It's stressing me out. You see the same ugly faces every day...I've lived round here for like 14, 15 year, you see? Every day you go out the front with a fag and you see 'em stood there; the same faces every day.

For these and other reasons, some harboured dreams of leaving East Kelby. Here Lisa, Emma and Claire – all young mothers – directly contended with one of the key ideas of underclass theory, the cultural inheritance of an underclass way of life, and in so doing demonstrated the distance between such theories and their lives:

> *Claire*: Luke [Claire's son] is gonna grow up on a council estate. It's a vicious circle. He'll probably live in a council estate with no money.

I'd like to have been able to get out, live somewhere nice, show him that you don't need to be on the dole and then have kids.

Lisa: It's not just that though. When you're living on a council estate, there's a lot of drugs — there's a lot of crime — and I don't want mine getting involved with any of that.

Emma: No, I don't.

RM: And do you think he will? It's an interesting idea, that 'vicious circle' —

Emma: So we've gotta stop it now. We've gotta get out of it now and set an example —

Claire: Before they're old enough to —

RM: When you say, 'Get out of it', do you mean physically leave?

Emma: Yeah, leave the council estate, yeah.

Lisa: Well, just leave, get out of the council estate.

RM: So you couldn't stay here and make your life better whilst being here?

Emma: No, because there's that much around you. You can't stop what's going on around you.

Lisa: If you start walking around and you get a top job and you're walking round in suits, they'll say, 'Who does she think she is?'

Emma: Your house would be getting burgled every five minutes and your car getting nicked and —

Lisa: It's all to do with jealousy.

Emma: I agree with that.

Lisa, Emma and Claire focus on the potential social consequences of living on these council estates. Others were also critical of social housing. Local authority housing stock, housing bureaucracy and allocations policy were the subject of much complaint. Amy said, 'if you want somewhere nice you've gotta buy it, don't you?' (home ownership, perhaps by buying a council house, was regarded as a long-term goal by most in the sample).

The reason why some were more positive than others about (staying in) East Kelby also partly reflects the different parts of it in which they lived. Our interviews and visits to these neighbourhoods confirmed how internally differentiated socially excluded places can be: 'Where my Mum lived, her road's very quiet and it is a nice place, but you go round the corner and it's like Beirut!' (Marje, 23). Parts of East Kelby have gained reputations as 'sink' estates; others remain buoyant examples of 'respectable' working class housing. Murie talks of 'polarization *between* different estates' (1998: 29, our emphasis), but our sample operated with mental maps by which separate, small pockets of the same estate (and their residents) were deemed 'good' or 'bad', which led some to view the latter as 'no-go' areas. These were associated primarily with what Stuart (26) called 'the bad element – smack-heads, the thieves, the youngsters who they're moving in'. Martin (20) clarified this for us: 'I mean it's a zonal thing in Primrose Vale. You've got a good bit, a not so good bit and a bad bit.'

Byrne (1995) has described how local housing markets and local authority housing placement policies have consolidated processes of economic marginality and helped separate out socially included and excluded locales in Teesside. Murie (1998: 29), too, discusses how local authority housing officers reinforce socio-spatial exclusion by channelling:

> the respectable households towards stable, non-problematic estates so as not to put those estates at risk. The rough and non-respectable applicants and, disproportionately, those from minority ethnic groups are channelled towards estates with problems, partly because they will not make them any worse and partly because they are the only people likely to accept offers on these estates.

Our interviewees – young people and 'stakeholders' – observed this same process of 'residential sorting' (Lupton and Power, 2002). Drugs workers complained to us about 'fascist housing officers' reserving the 'crappiest housing' for their clients. They also reported that private landlords – acting as, or in liaison with, pimps – took a role in housing young, female care leavers in the same street, sometimes at the same address, thus spatially concentrating the problems of prostitution in Kelby. Overall, several interviewees criticised the decisions of housing officers to locate together socially excluded households and individuals (such as the unemployed, single young men or young, single mothers) in particular corners of East Kelby, resulting in those neighbourhoods taking on a particular, negatively labelled character (Foster, 2000). The main response of older, more affluent, more 'respectable' working-class householders can be one of abandonment and flight (Wilson, 1987; Byrne, 1989). Over time, spatial processes operating at this level can serve to harden and widen local social divisions between the included and the excluded, corralling the latter in precarious 'estates on the edge' (Power, 1999).

The idea that once respectable neighbourhoods were declining because the local council deliberately housed, to use Lupton and Power's terms, 'families with problems'/'problem families' in close proximity, was rehearsed by interviewees who were both 'beneficiaries' and 'victims' of this policy. Adrian (15) talked about the 'trouble families' that 'the whole green next door to ours completely consisted of'. He went on: 'I think that was the place they put them. You know, they have places where they gang them all together and shut them out of society'. Speaking of the same area, Lisa (20) said:

> there's loads of single mothers on this green, right. I think they've put us all up there with all the trouble-makers, just because we're single mothers, that's what I think. [It's] like, an undesirable place, just because, like, we're single mothers, we have, like, no — like, they don't wanna put us somewhere nice 'cos we're single mothers.

Elizabeth (19) was biding her time, living at home with her parents until she could afford to leave the area. Her views of the social housing that might be available to her locally (and of living in East Kelby *per se*) were coloured by what she perceived as a council 'dumping policy':

> I would like to live with me boyfriend, but not until we've both got jobs and we can both afford it. I don't wanna live in a little council house in somewhere I don't wanna be — like Regency Road! That's probably where they'd put me... because there's so many empty houses. They try and put everybody there — because I haven't got a kid or nothing, they'd try and put me in flats and I don't wanna live in flats. That's why I wanna wait until I've got money 'cos then I can get a private rented house or something. But I'd never live in the flats... They're horrible, they're full of smack-heads and just nasty people who I don't wanna be near.

Regency Road was where Richy (17) lived. He gave an even more precise, spatial mapping of local, social divisions (a depiction exactly the same as that given by others):

> Regency Road – it's, like, it's a long street, it's a long road. Like, there's the top part, that's just full of boarded up [i.e. derelict] houses. There's the bottom part, that's full of, like, people who muck about, do you know? Pinch cars and stuff like that and, like, there's the middle bit, just, you know like where we get on with your neighbours, you know? Yeah!

Summary and conclusions

This chapter has been about the housing careers of young adults in poor neighbourhoods, the significance of place in these and the way interviewees described growing up in some of the most deprived parts of the country. Around half the sample remained living with parents and tended to describe strong family bonds, to appreciate the emotional and financial support that they received and were often biding their time in the hope of better establishing themselves in employment. Those that had left the parental home tended to recount unplanned and sometimes chaotic housing careers (Ford et al., 2002). Multiple moves were common and spurred by events in other spheres of their lives such as the onset of parenthood, the formation/cessation of partnerships or turbulent relationships with family, friends and partners (but not the sighting of employment or educational opportunities, as typical of the more planned and student pathways described by Ford and colleagues). Unsurprisingly, then, our study showed a preponderance of those housing pathways associated with 'instability, poor conditions, limited choice and exclusion' (Ford et al., 2002: 4). Those with the most moves and most chaotic housing careers were likely to be those with the most difficult and troubled lives in general. In virtually all cases, moves were confined to their home neighbourhoods.

We explain the localisation of these informants' housing careers, and the fact they were able to make moves to independent living regardless of much progress in the labour market, partly in terms of the relative availability of social housing in East Kelby (supported as well by other welfare benefits). Given the multiple problems of social deprivation that cohere in the estates of East Kelby, young people's physical and affective attachment to the place is surprising. For the majority, supportive networks of family and friends induced deep loyalty and helped make life liveable. Whilst all recognised the problems that affected their estates, their familiarity with the place – and their unfamiliarity with places where social conditions and life chances might be different – meant that they rejected definitions of themselves as 'socially excluded'. In fact, their accounts of mutual support in the face of adversity were more redolent of a feeling of social inclusion.

A substantial minority expressed much more critical views about living in East Kelby. Perhaps because they were less embedded in extensive, local, social and family networks, they felt less of the supportive neighbourliness that others described. Local social divisions also emerged as important in understanding interviewees' differential assessment of place.

These young adults operated with finely drawn, mental maps of their estates in which some neighbourhoods were more or less associated with social problems. The housing allocations policy of the local authority was implicated in a process of 'residential sorting', and in some interviewees' eyes the decline of particular parts of East Kelby, whereby single-parent households, young unemployed people and those with records of crime and dependent drug use were allegedly rehoused in specific streets.

Experiences of criminal victimisation, of different degrees of seriousness, were common in the interviews. Together, crime and the sometimes related problems of a local drug market provided by far the most common complaints about living in East Kelby. Other problems were referred to – for example, of 'post code' discrimination, whereby people felt they had missed out on jobs simply because of the negative reputation of their estate – but these were relatively infrequent. Subjective 'theories of crime' were numerous but tended towards positions which resonated with the authoritarian moralising of cultural underclass theory. Few offered more structural, sociological explanations for crime or the other problems of their neighbourhoods. It is perhaps strange that discussion of, say, the hardships of unemployment or insecure employment was so scarce. We think this can be explained by the immediacy of the problem of crime – ever-present fear of burglary, for example, demanded that they be alert to this problem - and the relative newness of the local drug economy (see chapter 9). Economic marginality, experienced as recurrent unemployment and unstable employment, appear to have become background 'facts of life' in these neighbourhoods. For these young adults, this was their whole experience of the labour market (see chapter 6). As such, economic marginality was not worthy of much mention (until we enquired more directly about it). In the next chapter we discuss more directly the development of criminal and drug-using careers, based on interviews with those engaged in them; a discussion which is quite at odds with the underclass theories popular amongst many of the interviewees.

9
Journeys to the Margins: Drug and Criminal Careers

> It's the heroin. It's wrecking everybody's life. I mean there's people dying off it. There's girls going selling their bodies for it. There's lads burgling or getting a hold on a lass and making them be a prostitute for the heroin, robbing people and that. I hate it, me.
>
> (Gail, 17)

Introduction

The alleged anti-social behaviour and crime of young people is a common feature of arguments about the socially excluded underclass. Reflecting their general theoretical take on these debates, some commentators see youthful deviance as emblematic of the rise of a 'demoralised', dangerous class (Murray, 1990; 1994; Dennis, 1994) whilst others prefer to understand it as cultural adaptation to restricted socio-economic circumstances; a 'delinquent solution' to blocked opportunities (Wilson, 1996; Craine, 1997).

Surprisingly, few commentaries on social exclusion, however, have prioritised discussions of youth drug use. It often appears among the social pathologies said to typify socially excluded places but there has been little close analysis within this literature – or that related to youth transitions – of exactly how, and the extent to which, illicit drug use can become a central element in the social exclusion of young people. This is despite the fact that rates of illicit drug use in Britain tend to be much higher in poor neighbourhoods (Advisory Council on the Misuse of Drugs, 1998), that 'serious' drug use has tended historically to be concentrated in Britain's most deprived areas (Pearson et al., 1987; Parker et al., 2001) and that 'most of the new young users

170

taking up heroin can be described as socially excluded' (Parker et al., 1998a: vi).

In our study, illicit drug use – combined with persistent criminality – emerged as a crucial factor in shaping some of the most intractable experiences of social exclusion. For the majority of interviewees, drug-driven crime was *the* central fact that explained most of the problems of East Kelby; a view shared by some of the professional workers to whom we talked (Wood and Vamplew, 1999; Page, 2000).

In this chapter we consider the nature and significance of criminal and drug-using careers for processes of social exclusion and youth transition. Of course, many of the people we talked to had little, if any, notable engagement with either crime or drug use.[1] Some displayed criminal careers but had only a fleeting acquaintance with illicit substance use. A few had more concerted experience of the latter but minimal offending. Nevertheless, the prolonged combination of the two had dramatic, personal consequences for the individuals concerned and affected the quality of life of all those young people to whom we talked.

Understanding criminal careers

Conceptually, our interest throughout this book has been to understand young people's transitions as being comprised of analytically separate but empirically interdependent, multiple careers. A biographical focus allows exploration of how individual factors (e.g. family circumstances, engagement with peer networks) interact, at different stages, with the structured opportunities facing youth (e.g. access to decent employment or training, the possibilities presented by local drug and criminal markets) in shaping the form and direction of criminal and drug careers.

The best-known British research on criminal careers is that by Farrington and colleagues (1994; 1995; see Webster et al., 2003 for a fuller discussion). Interested in the 'longitudinal sequence of offences committed by an individual offender' (1994: 511–12), Farrington regards criminal careers as part of a wider set of anti-social behaviours that develops in childhood and amplifies in later life: 'hyperactivity at age 2 may lead to cruelty to animals at 6, shoplifting at 10, burglary at 15, robbery at 20, and eventually spouse assault, child abuse and neglect, alcohol abuse, and employment and accommodation problems later in life'. Studies in this positivistic vein typically draw on larger-scale, longitudinal cohort data to measure risk factors that predispose individuals towards criminality (e.g. high impulsivity, low intelligence, poor parenting). Farrington reports that

13–15 is the peak age for the onset of a criminal career and the peak age for desistance is between 21 and 25 years; a large proportion of those with chronic offending 'might have been identified with reasonable accuracy at age 10' (1994: 566).

We would not deny the influence of this sort of approach to criminal career, nor the descriptive match between some of the findings that come from it and those of our own study. Our general, theoretical stance is different, however. For us, too little room is given in orthodox criminological studies to understanding both the active role of young people and the particular historical, cultural and socio-economic conditions of neighbourhoods in the making of criminal careers. An ethnographic approach can help us understand criminal careers close-up; as they unfold in time and place, from the point of view of participants who simultaneously face, and make, limited choices in respect of this and the other careers that make up youth transitions. Given the evidence in this chapter, we argue that it would be difficult to comprehend an individual criminal career without also considering concurrent, wider experiences of transition not normally surveyed in criminology.

We also take issue with the determinism inherent in much criminal career research (for exceptions see Little, 1990; Sampson and Laub, 1993; Craine, 1997; Laub and Sampson, 2003). Fieldwork uncovered many instances of individuals who did not pursue full-blown criminal and/or drug-using careers, but who might have been predicted to do so (given the risk factors that could have been ticked off against them). For instance, contrary to some theorisations of crime in poor neighbourhoods (e.g. Dennis, 1994; *The Guardian*, 5 April 2001), our study found little correlation between family type and later criminality. Only four (of 20) of those who reported frequent, longer-term offending were brought up in lone-parent families.[2] Even when they had begun, criminal careers, as with other types, did not always follow a steady course. Unpredictable 'critical moments' sometimes turned people away from criminal careers, sometimes towards them.[3]

An ethnographic approach that encompasses a focus on criminal careers within a broader appreciation of youth transitions can provide a useful corrective to more deterministic, positivistic theories of criminal career (see also Smith and McVie, 2003; Little, 1990).[4] This perspective can also provide a useful counterweight to sociological writing on youth crime that plays down the individual decision-making that underlies criminal careers; that, in turning its gaze to the social structural factors that create criminogenic conditions, overlooks the criminal choices and actions of young people (Craine, 1997).

Gender, women and crime

This chapter is mainly about young men. Proportionately far fewer females in East Kelby (as elsewhere) offend or pursue the sort of extended criminal and drug-using careers that are the main focus of this chapter (Campbell, 1993; Farrington, 1995; Graham and Bowling, 1995; Kelby Borough Council, 1999). As a consequence, nearly all the case study material that we gathered on this subject came from men and particular forms of mas-culine identity (see chapter 4; Campbell, 1993; Collison, 1996; Simpson, 2003) were important in understanding the onset of criminal/drug careers, the types of crime committed, underlying motivations for drug use and the process of desistance.[5]

Nevertheless, interviewees like Gail (quoted in the introduction) described how young women can also became embroiled in sometimes dangerous, destructive life-styles. The form that these processes took tended to be gender-divided. Of greatest significance in understanding the most hazardous forms of drug-crime involvement for young women in Kelby is the combination of abusive family and partner relation-ships, a burgeoning, exploitative, local 'sex industry' and the widespread availability of cheap, addictive drugs.

Kelby is notorious for street prostitution, attracting male 'punters' from across the north of England. We interviewed staff from a project that helped young women 'exit the street' (their account is very similar to that provided in recent studies: Bean, 2002; Pearce, 2003). These 'stake-holders' interpreted local prostitution as a form of child/sexual abuse (a point forcibly made by Pearce's study); many had first become prosti-tutes in their early teens (or before). The workers' case-loads were comprised of women who virtually always had been the victims of earlier (sometimes continuing) abusive, violent relationships with men (generally partners, but sometimes relatives), who forced and then controlled their prostitution. Many had spent periods 'looked after' in care and virtually all had run away from parental or care homes at some point. These interviewees pointed to heroin, often supplied by partners/pimps, as a key factor in entering people into, and keeping them locked into, prostitu-tion (i.e. they 'worked' for their own and their partners' drug money). Heroin also helped women cope psychologically with the repeated degradations and dangers of their work. They, like some of the young people we interviewed, noted the recent murder and disappearances of local women who had worked as prostitutes.

Phoenix would criticise this interpretation of prostitution. She says that 'the rhetoric of victim-hood operates to render redundant discussions of young people's agency and poverty' (2002: 363). For her, it is more appropriate to understand prostitution as 'part of the survival strategies of young people in their attempts to negotiate actively the socio-economic conditions they inhabit' (*ibid.*: 372). The limits of our own research material make it impossible to take sides here. We did, however, meet one young woman whose narrative was short on volition and which matched very closely the descriptive contours of accounts given by staff from the 'exiting the street' project (and we rely on their account to fill in some of the gaps left by Leila, when we interviewed her).

Leila's story

Leila (18) had been brought up by her mother, her father having left before she was born. At thirteen, life seemed 'normal'. She had been 'in the top classes at school' and 'liked it'. Things started to go wrong shortly afterwards.

She told a hair-raising, complicated story in which it was difficult to ascertain the detail and causal sequence of events. She referred to the difficulties associated with a change of school, 'lots of family problems', her running away from home and then being 'kicked out' by her mother, moving in with her father, her friend (aged fourteen) having a child by Leila's father[6] (who was a drug dealer and owner of an 'escort agency'), him offering Leila work as an 'escort' ('£100 an hour and anything on top is your own'), culminating, still aged thirteen, in Leila attempting suicide. Her housing career thereafter consisted of, first, a spell in a mental hospital, then moves between five different care placements (before the age of fifteen), followed by a 'mother and baby home' (Leila had a child when she was fifteen but 'as soon as I was sixteen they kicked me out'), time in two homeless hostels (one of which she had to leave after receiving death threats from her 'boyfriend' of the time and his turning up at the hostel with a gun) and a succession of rented houses. In five years she had had over a dozen addresses; a clear example of the sort of destabilising 'accommodation pinball' (Brown, 1998) that often accompanies 'careers in care' (Biehal et al., 1995; Coles, 2000a).

At fourteen, she had been 'let down by schools' who would not accept her when she was pregnant. At fourteen she had a job, three nights a week, as a dancer in a nightclub. She also started using heroin, 'cold turkeying' herself a year later, then relapsing into crack cocaine use (coming off that with the help of the local drugs service). At fourteen too she began working as a prostitute on the streets of Kelby (and did so for a year and a half): 'I just can't remember anything about it – I was too high.'

Although Bean (2002: 169) says that, for young women like Leila, the 'hopes of achieving conventional roles [are] remote', Leila at eighteen was trying to do just this. She had been living in a housing association property for six months, had a new boyfriend (aged 40) who owned his own business, was taking a part-time college course in counselling and doing some associated voluntary work, whilst 'living on the social'. She was now seeing her mother again (but still felt this was a 'bad relationship') and said that she wanted to study more in the future. She regretted having her daughter so young. She said that in a few years 'I wanna start getting a mortgage together, have a business or a good job, well-paid job and, like, hope my daughter's doing well'. We were unable to contact her for a second interview.

We present this brief cameo in order to highlight one particularly malign set of socially exclusionary experiences that threaten vulnerable young women in this place. We also give it, as the first example in this chapter, of an individual biography of crime, victimisation and drug use that is impossible to understand without simultaneous attention to the other careers that make up, and the circumstances that constrain, youth transitions in this place.

The consolidation of young men's criminal careers

In chapter 4, we describe how *early* criminal careers often emerged in the context of persistent truancy and the purposelessness of disengaged peer groups (Stephen and Squires, 2003). This was mainly petty, leisure-time crime. In our study the transition to more serious acquisitive crimes such as burglary and robbery was usually, but not always, related to the emergence of careers of dependent drug use.

The drugs–crime nexus

Limitations of space allow us to note only some overall findings about illicit drug use (see MacDonald and Marsh, 2002, for a full discussion). Although united by common residence in poor neighbourhoods, interviewees had markedly different experiences of and orientations to drugs. The largest single group were, or had been, archetypal recreational drug users and viewed the use of cannabis, amphetamines and ecstasy, for instance, as a normal part of their 'leisure-pleasure' landscape (Parker et al., 1995; 1998b; 2001).[7] Coexisting in the same place, however, was another substantial group, who displayed wholly anti-drug sentiments and distanced themselves from their use and from users. Some of these claimed to know no one who used drugs and little or nothing about drug issues. These were not the 'drug-wise' individuals spoken of in the popular theory of drug 'normalisation' (*ibid.*). We think this theory is overstated and concur with those who prefer a more differentiated understanding of the appeal of *some* drugs for *some* young people in *some* contexts (Shiner and Newburn, 1997; 1999; South, 1999; Shildrick, 2002).

Drug behaviour was a central axis by which interviewees differentiated themselves. Abstainers and recreational users both abhorred 'smack-heads' and blamed heroin for the decline of their neighbourhoods. Both these groups also shared transitions in which illicit drug use was largely *unimportant* in processes of social inclusion and exclusion.

As numerous, authoritative studies have concluded (Parker and Newcombe, 1987; Hough, 1996; Bean, 2002; Simpson, 2003), the relationship between drug use and criminality – the 'drugs–crime nexus' – is complex, multifaceted, rarely uni-directional and sometimes not present (i.e. one can exist without the other). Our conclusions are similar. Some, like Ellie, had no criminal record apart from her near-dependent, persistent use of amphetamines (solely funded through legitimate work). Several others told us life stories in which crime and drug use both featured but often not in ways which appeared directly, immediately related. One or two people had lengthy records of offending but had wholly avoided 'problematic drug use' (but did describe instances of drink-fuelled attempted burglary or assault).[8] Nevertheless, the hardest cases of social exclusion revealed to us were those in which criminal careers became embroiled in careers of dependent drug use (or vice versa).

The combination of criminal and drug-using careers

> That's the way it goes. Start off smoking a bit of ganga, breaking into cars and pinching car radios and then you end up on heroin and that and it fucks you up.
>
> (Jason, 21)

Eleven informants had careers of sustained (and what they regarded as problematic) dependent use of opiates. They had used heroin, in some cases combined with cocaine and/or crack cocaine, usually on a daily basis over months and years. The central elements of their narratives were very similar and provide the opportunity to consider the inter-relationships between drug and criminal careers. We describe one case in order to detail the factors that seem important in making sense of these sorts of transition.

Richard's story

Richard was 20 when first interviewed in a Young Offenders Institution. We talked to him again, ten months later, in a probation hostel in Kelby. His mother worked as a cleaner and his stepfather was a bricklayer. His natural father left the family when Richard was aged four, working abroad as a scaffolder for much of Richard's childhood. More recently some contact had been re-established, with the pair occasionally meeting for a drink on Friday evenings.

Richard spent much of the first years of secondary schooling involved in 'loads of truancy' with friends, sometimes shoplifting to relieve the boredom (receiving two police cautions for these offences). He said of this period: 'I think I went off the rails a bit with my Dad being away.' His mother tried to deter his truancy: 'She used to give me a good hiding.' At fourteen, he began to concentrate on his schoolwork and gained five GCSEs – 'not great, not rubbish grades'. The number of times Richard swapped between uncompleted YT and NDYP schemes, low-level jobs and unemployment may have been higher than the majority, but the nature of his school-to-work career was unexceptional (see chapters 5 and 6).

What set him apart from the majority of the sample, and united him with an important minority, was his engagement with a concerted criminal and drug-using career. Richard described how he and his friends made the shift from cannabis to heroin use:

> We'd all been smoking tack [cannabis] for ages. Ever since we were fourteen or fifteen. We'd smoke it all day and it'd get to the point where it had no effect. It wasn't getting us stoned ... [so] ... me and my friends thought we'd have a daft go at it [heroin] and before we knew it a few of us were [cold] turkeying and then we all were. Hooked. It's dead hard to come off —— they say 'once a smack-head, always a smack-head'. Maybe they're right.

Addiction now drove his shoplifting: 'I had no choice about that really. It was the only way I had of funding the smack.' He estimated that he committed around 150 separate thefts from shops in different towns around the north-east during this period (having been 'barred out' of Kelby town centre by private security guards aware of his criminal record). At one point he was making around £300 a day from selling on stolen goods and 'most of it was going on heroin'.

Richard was ambivalent about heroin, acknowledging that it was a 'bad drug' in terms of the collateral damage it brought to him and his family, but quickly adding that he:

> liked it — I thought it was good and I was having it everyday. I thought it was brilliant. Just made you sleepy and dead relaxed. A good feeling. It made all your worries go away...but when I look back now I just wish I'd never done it...it's affected me mentally as well as physically. It just puts me to shame. I feel a lot of guilt. I just feel sick for what I've done to her [his mother], like what I must have put her through — You just don't think about what you're doing when you're on smack. All you think is heroin – where do you want to go for a mooch [to thieve], where to score a bag [purchase heroin], where to do it [to administer the drug]. If you pinch off you're sister, you don't think about it. It's a vicious circle. When you stop, you start to think about it. I don't want to get into it no more.

At eighteen, a stab at drug desistance (aided by a methadone programme) was concluded by a rapid sequence of events that led him back to heroin. His mother accused Richard of stealing some of her jewellery (which he denied) and ejected him from the family home. He became homeless, staying with his sister and then sleeping rough in a derelict house. At this point he was hospitalised following a violent assault by a group of young men. His doctor arranged for Richard to move into hostel accommodation shortly before Christmas. This step in his housing career precipitated a further stage in his drug/criminal career, as he explained in a tearful interview:

> *RM*: So what went wrong?
> *Richard*: Well, I was just like down, you know? It was the first time me Mam's kicked me out — I felt low and sick cause I wasn't with me Mam over Christmas — I was in the hostel for Christmas and New Year and I got mixed in with a few lads who were on drugs and, like, I was having a go now and again and I ended up an addict [again] so I had to go out and burgle for it and that.
> *RM*: So straight back into heroin?
> *Richard*: Yeah, and I ended up getting caught 'cos I was no good at it, as I now know!

Richard was charged with commercial burglary (smashing a window and stealing a pair of shoes from a shop). The first interview with him was when he was on remand awaiting a court appearance on this charge. He saw imprisonment as a 'definite choice, to do me rattle [the physical withdrawal from heroin dependency]. The solicitor said that I could get bailed to me Mam's, but I wanted to go inside to help me get off it.' He received a three-month sentence. Shortly afterwards he was prosecuted for a further heroin-related shoplifting offence and spent another period on remand. Perhaps because of a particularly sympathetic report from a Probation Officer, he then received a non-custodial sentence, part of the conditions for which involved residence in a bail hostel and participation in another methadone treatment programme.

We interviewed him for a second time in this hostel, where he spoke of his determination to 'go straight' and resist the lure of heroin, which was made more difficult by the constant temptation provided by co-residents continuing to use (without the knowledge of Probation staff). Asked why he recurrently relapsed into heroin use, he said:

> It's 'cos I don't occupy myself. No job to keep me busy. It does me head in just wandering around. Nothing to do. So I end up knocking around with me old mates. I just get back into it. I don't have enough to do. I just hang around here. Play pool. Go to me sister's. I need more purpose. I want to go to college. I wish it would come around quicker.

His aim to re-enter education was a vague one. He did not have a particular college or course in mind. He spent his days completing some basic literacy worksheets (provided by his Probation Officer), administering his methadone, undergoing tests (to detect illicit heroin use), visiting his sister and looking forward to occasional drinking sessions with his father. His main ambition remained to be reunited with his mother, who still resisted contact with her son, and to 'have grand kids for her one day'.

Crossing the Rubicon: the transition from recreational to dependent drug use

The received wisdom in the UK drugs research literature is that recreational and dependent users are distinct, separate groups. The former are 'sociable, sensible, and morally aware as non-users' (Perri 6 et al., 1997: 45); like most young people, they view 'taking hard drugs and actually injecting as anathema: a Rubicon they will never cross' (Parker et al., 1998b: 132). Dependent users of heroin are, on the other hand, 'from the edges' (Parker et al., 1998a). The 'basic identi-kit of the most likely heroin user' would list 'poor school performance and attendance, light parental supervision' and having grown up 'at the wrong end of town' on 'the poorest estates'. Parker et al. conclude that:

> the least worst scenario is that heroin *trying* does not become accommodated within the far larger 'recreational' drugs scene but remains predominantly associated with *degrees* of social exclusion. (1998a: 45–6, our emphases)

The issue, though, for poor neighbourhoods in East Kelby is that this risk profile would perfectly match a large proportion of their young residents. They all experience 'degrees of social exclusion'. Some, as we have noted, resist drug use of any sort and – for many – drug careers presently extend only to recreational drugs. This and other studies suggest, however, that the Rubicon dividing recreational and dependent heroin use is being bridged by an apparently growing number of young people, like Richard, in poor areas of the north-east (Johnston et al., 2000; Simpson, 2003). Rebecca, a local drugs worker, said:

> I see a lot of heroin users who went through that thing in the late 80s/early 90s when E [ecstasy] was out, who did the dance thing, who did that rave scene, and did all that and then fell into heroin use later on. They say, 'I can't believe I'm here, I'm so ashamed of being here because, you know, I used to call them [verbally abuse heroin users] and now I am one'. If I had a pound for every time they say that! They really honestly think that they can [just] try it; it's the *trying*, the *trying*.

Changing drug markets and the appeal of 'poverty drugs'

In chapter 10 we argue that we can only properly understand the microprocesses of youth transition that are represented in stories like Richard's by placing them in the spatial and temporal context in which they took place. Here we stress the significance of changing local drug markets (see Pearson et al., 1987; Parker et al., 1998a; Taylor, 1999; Lupton et al., 2002).

Until the mid-1990s, Kelby was not regarded as having a major heroin problem (Pearson et al., 1987). Police, drugs workers and young people told us, however, that heroin entered the Teesside 'scene' in a substantial way in the mid-1990s: at exactly the moment identified as the start of 'the second wave of heroin outbreaks' in Britain (Parker et al., 1998a). Since then it 'not only hosts [heroin] outbreaks but is the dealing/ distribution base for surrounding towns' (*ibid.*: 37–8). By the late 1990s, Teesside dealers were claimed to offer the cheapest heroin in the UK

(*Evening Gazette*, 21 October 1997; Munro, 1999) with consumers apparently travelling from across the northern region to make purchases (*Evening Gazette*, 1 June 2000). One drugs worker told us that she had even heard of occasions where £1 'bags' have been sold, compared with a typical price of £5–10 nationally (Lupton et al., 2002). Despite its relative cheapness, Kelby has been identified as one of the worst areas affected by drug crime (Home Office, 2003; see also Bennett, 1998; Foster, 2000; Johnston et al., 2000), and high-profile, 'a dealer a day' policing has become geared to disrupting low- and mid-level drugs markets.[9] The upsurge in local heroin use – and, since 1998, crack cocaine (Lupton et al., 2002) – has re-profiled the work of drugs agencies. A shift towards serving recreational users in the early 1990s was later reversed and one agency has increased its staffing from three to nineteen to cope with up to twenty new clients a week seeking consultations about heroin. These agencies see increasingly younger clients, some of whose first experience of illicit drugs was of heroin. Teesside is said to have proportionately more under twenties starting drug treatment than anywhere else in the UK; with children as young as twelve seeking rehab. programmes (*Evening Gazette*, 9 November 2000) and becoming enmeshed in the dealing of heroin (*ibid.*: 16 July 2003).

Thus, stories like Richard's are – for this place – novel ones. Interviewees who were in their mid-twenties and who had long-term, recreational drug-using careers reported no contact with heroin when they were passing through their teens (in the late 1980s). Other drugs (or solvents) had become their 'drug(s) of choice'. Now heroin was 'everywhere'.[10] Younger interviewees like Richard had encountered it at critical points in their drug careers and in their transitions to adulthood more generally. By 1996, when Richard was sixteen, heroin had become widely available in East Kelby and he and his peer group made a speedy transition from recreational to problematic drug use. He said:

> Heroin came into Kelby in about '95, didn't it? I had a go at it in '96. I didn't even *know* it was heroin. It was just brown powder on a bit of foil. Like tack. No one was bang on to it [knew much about it] then. Didn't know it was heroin or what the risks were.[11]

Some writers have suggested that this apparent lack of knowledge, the dearth of health education campaigns about it since the late 1980s and the availability of cheap, smokeable heroin may all have been factors behind young people's susceptibility to this new heroin outbreak (Pearson et al., 1987; Parker et al., 1998a; 2001). Rebecca had worked for drugs services for several years. She remembered how police had successfully targeted local cannabis dealers (following tip-offs rumoured to have come from a major, new heroin supplier) and produced 'an absolute drought in 1996', how at the same moment 'someone had targeted this fucking town for heroin' and how street dealers switched from trading cannabis to trading 'dirt cheap' heroin to their ill-prepared clients (under the name of 'brown' and bearing a physical resemblance to cannabis resin).

This rapid transformation in the local drugs markets – and young people's apparent lack of preparedness when faced with the choice of heroin – highlights the need for a re-evaluation of drugs policies and services. Perri 6 and colleagues argue that effective drugs strategies must work at 'empowering local networks to work with young people in ways that engage with local youth cultures' (1997: 45) and that we cannot design such strategies unless 'we understand that the motivations of young people are rooted in opportunities and constraints that can only be understood at local level' (*ibid.*: 8). Our findings shows these observations to be astute ones. Coexisting in the same neighbourhoods at the same time are substantial numbers of young people who seem to have made clear anti-drug choices and, living alongside them (sometimes literally, in the case of siblings), young people whose lives have become fully absorbed into problematic drug use. To understand how and why some overcome the local cultural barriers to problematic use where others do not, we also need to appreciate the particular appeal and 'conditions of existence' of different forms of drug use to different groups of young people (1999: 86, Taylor cited in MacGregor, 2000).

An important distinction emerged in informants' descriptions of drug use. Recreational users often talked about drugs in terms of the joys of 'leisure and pleasure' lifestyles. Heroin users reached for quite different words to explain its attraction. Like Richard, they talked variously about 'not having a care in the world' after using heroin, about it 'taking all [their] worries away' and it 'wiping away all the bad things that have happened'. Drugs workers talked of the 'cotton wool' effect of heroin. Given the profile of the new, young heroin users of the 1990s as the 'socially excluded', and the meanings given to its use by these informants, it is not too difficult to understand heroin *in this context* as a poverty drug; a form of self-medication for the socially excluded, a drug that is compelling because its pharmacological effects 'blank out' the day to day realities of their social exclusion. Goldberg puts it well:

> much of what I have observed in the field can be best explained by the attempts of problematic consumers to escape – escape from the

past, from the present, from society, from their feelings, from everything that passes through their heads, and from not having any future. (1999: 133)

Going straight: desistance in criminal and drug-using careers

In reviewing the development of the criminal and drug-using careers of young men in Kelby (some of whom were originally part of our study), Webster et al. (2003: 15) stress the importance of social networks:

> At teenage local social networks were important in accompanying, supporting and encouraging criminal and/or drug-using identities, offered protection and criminal opportunity, kept the momentum and excitement of lawlessness and drug use going, provided skills and contacts and crucially offered a means of entering illicit local markets in drugs and stolen goods.

Such networks eased the transition to offending. Many of our interviewees described how they also acted as the main obstacle to desistance. Even when people had come to a point where they felt a desire or a need to 'go straight' they perceived no easy way forward. This was true of all those with extended criminal careers, but particularly exemplified by those interviewees for whom these had become entangled with drug careers. Dependent heroin users were virtually unanimous on this point; their lives since mid-teenage had been lived within social networks that reinforced drug behaviour. Escaping these networks was crucial to going straight. For many of them imprisonment often provided a welcome opportunity to do their 'rattle' (albeit under a harsh, non-therapeutic regime).[12] A few had even purposefully sought a prison sentence (rather than probation supervision) as a way of escaping the recurrent drug temptations they encountered 'on the street'. Release from prison was normally viewed with trepidation because it signalled a return to the environment that had generated their initial drug dependency: 'you're just going back to the same place, the same group of people and it's easy to get back into it' (Stu, 20). Richard's plan 'to go straight' hinged around reintegrating with non-drug-using friends that he knew from earlier days:

> I'm planning to go out drinking with some of the lads from Primrose Vale. That's what I used to do before I got kicked out [of his mother's house] . . . I've already written to a few of 'em. I used to talk to them

when I was on it [heroin], like when I used to pass them. I didn't used to like stand and knock about with 'em. I'd always be on my way somewhere, going for a score [to purchase heroin] or summat.

Distancing oneself from localised, peer networks that shared the same delinquent predisposition was – among other factors – crucial in strategic attempts to desist from crime. Moving to a different neighbourhood or starting a job or training scheme opened up the possibility of forming new friendships. This process was often described as part of the business of getting older. Others talked about how the same, earlier friendship group had collectively abandoned wrongdoing. Repeated questioning to try to uncover the mysterious secret whereby criminal careers stop, led Richy (17, YT trainee) to say: 'We've just grown out of it. We've all changed. I think it's about growing up, actually. Simple as that.' The fact that their crimes 'weren't that bad anyway' (and had not incurred custodial sentences) also meant that the distance back to more conventional paths of transition was not too great. Paul (16) envisaged a similar process of growing out of crime: 'When you get to about 20 you wanna, like, do something with yourself and like stop being a rogue and causing violence and stuff . . . you don't wanna be doing what sixteen-year-olds are doing, TWOCing cars and everything.'

Leo's interview highlighted many of the processes, events and decisions that underwrote the move to desistance expressed by many. Now eighteen and unemployed, he reflected on his days as a truant: '[I would] get up and used to go round [the corner] and they all used to be sat there, thirty of them, sat on one little corner, smoking and drinking at 9 o'clock in the morning'. How did he feel now about his earlier life?'

Leo: I class meself as a lowlife, doing that. Should have been doing summat else better for meself. I should have been back at school doing me exams. I just thought it was good at the time. Buying bottles of cider from the shop. Getting into fights. Go by people's cars, smash the windows, pop the tyres, stuff like that. Get drunk.
JM: Why do you think you changed?
Leo: When I first left school I went straight into a job you see, so I had to buck my ideas up. If I done something wrong and I got a fine, half my wages would be going —— the lads I know, they're always saying, 'Why don't you come round?' It makes you feel sad 'cos you've like knocked around with them that many years, but at the end of the day I had a job. I need[ed] to keep my job. I've got a car, I need to keep my car . . . like, I'm on the dole now but I don't think I'll go and

do this now and pinch his radio. I don't think that no more, know what I mean? I don't bother with heroin addicts no more [his previous group of friends]. If I got mixed in with 'em again I'd be worser, I'd be getting arrested every week...one of the lads, I seen him a few weeks ago and he has a job and I say, 'Is it a change?' He's got a kid to support. That's what's changed him and he didn't want heroin addicts going to their house and saying, 'Oh, he owes us 50 quid' and taking all the kid's clothes and toys. He's changed and I've changed. Don't think about going down and doing a burglary or mugging someone.

Changes in school-to-work and family careers were identified by many as particularly significant in motivating changes to criminal (and drug-using) careers. Leo, for instance, managed to step from school to a job, working in a factory. He loved driving, passed his test and eventually bought his own car (a traffic accident resulted in his losing this job and being off work for six months). Leo's luck in getting a job immediately post-school (he was one of the few to do this) was crucial in separating him, at a crucial juncture, from passing days with his peers. Many of 'the old crowd', he said, made a transition soon after to heroin use, more serious criminality and imprisonment. For Leo, the risks associated with continued delinquency – loss of wages that helped pay for his car – was an obvious, immediate, material disincentive. He now had something to lose. Even though he was now unemployed, the experience of the material benefits and discipline of work had facilitated his resolve to turn away from delinquency. Stephen and Squires (2003: 159) also found in their study of longer-term criminal careers that 'legitimate paid employment' was 'one key factor' in helping individuals stop offending.

For others, the process of 'growing out of crime' (Rutherford, 1992) was underwritten by another aspect of transition: parenthood (Laub and Sampson, 2003). Leo alludes empathetically to an acquaintance who has changed his previous heroin-using, criminal ways because of fatherhood. Several people, young men and young women, who had, to that point, been pursuing criminal and drug-using careers also stated that becoming a parent had been the main, if not sole, factor that stopped them. This was a 'critical moment', usually unplanned, that demanded personal reflection. The direction-less, drift of youthful delinquency (Matza, 1964; 1969; Simpson, 2004) was superseded by the purposefulness of parenting. Parenthood consumed time, energy and money and many, but not all, of those young men previously engaged in morally questionable activities professed very conventional, normative views about fathering. Providing suitable role models, family income and protecting households from the risks of continued criminality became common commitments. Curtis (21) stated matter-of-factly: 'I've done every single drug you can name...I've done heroin as well. I've done it all. I stopped because Angela fell pregnant with the baby. So I stopped it because of the baby.'

Liam (27) looked back on lengthy, complicated and interlinked criminal and drug careers. He had had two custodial sentences (for attempting to smuggle drugs into prison for a friend and for pulling out a replica firearm in a drunken altercation with the police). Since his most recent time away he had worked as a volunteer for a local youth charity (see below) and was attempting to turn away from crime. A key moment in this process, which had caused him 'to really open my eyes', had been when he had heard, during a phone call from prison, his young children opening their presents on Christmas morning. Liam stressed the different ways that work, for him, was important in deterring crime:

> I get respect for working, 'cos I'm doing something. I can't sit around doing nowt. I get bored too easy. I start going down the wrong path and get into trouble. The two times I got into trouble – the one with the gun and the one with the drugs – was because I'd stopped working and I was doing nowt and I was bored...Yeah, it's pride. It's all it is. I like to go to work...I don't want my kids growing up seeing me just sat on my arse all the time 'cos they'll just do the same. They'll think 'he never worked, why should we?' You need to be a good role model and the only way to do that is to have respect for yourself, have pride and have a job.

Just as the perceived purposelessness of school had provided the context for the drift into delinquency – and later unemployment meant informants like Liam sometimes went down 'the wrong path' into more serious crime – the availability of purposeful activity in which individuals could invest their time, energy and identity helped in the shift away from drug and criminal careers. Employment and parenting were important in this respect and so were some local agencies. One of these was Primrose Vale Youth Action (PVYA), set up by Martin and Zack, two of our interviewees, following the death of Martin's father and the suicide of one of their close friends. Its motto – 'for the youth, by the youth' – captures the motivation behind this grass-roots, estate-based attempt to win small-scale funding for positive leisure. Several interviewees described how involvement with the sports, leisure and personal development activities laid on by PVYA had helped them in reorienting their lives away from the more anti-social aspects of street corner society. Many of the same interviewees went on later to attend another, better established local voluntary organisation in East Kelby that had the same purpose. Participation in their organised leisure activities and vocationally-oriented, basic short courses helped to fill their time and divert their energies into more positive activities. Roy and his friends used to go to one such centre nearly every day: 'In there you can learn activities – it's not just playing pool like in a normal youth club – learn how to handle yourself and stuff like that.' Several of these young men reported the same experience and talked very positively of going along together, supporting each other informally. What was particularly interesting in the descriptions of these two agencies was how they stood out from the generally negative depiction given by most of the sample of most of the training and employment organisations that they had encountered (see chapters 5 and 6). The wholly voluntary nature of young people's participation, the fact that they encouraged attendance by pre-existing friendship groups, that they were not explicitly geared towards employment outcomes (that might be perceived as pointless) and that they were run by people whom participants perceived as understanding the pressures they faced (in some cases through direct experience), are all factors that help explain this.

The factors that seemed to help desistance were not easily achieved and nor was the surrender of long-run crime and drug use as simple for others as put by Curtis, earlier. Notably, he was one of two interviewees whose (limited) experience of heroin use had not resulted in addiction. Webster et al. (2004) also report that the establishment of stable partnerships, parenthood and employment in the lives of those with long-term criminal and dependent drug-using careers are critical factors in both motivating and sustaining desistance. They also note, however, that for those with long-term heroin dependence, 'going straight' in the long term is best understood as an aspiration that is highly contingent on other factors (such as the availability of suitable drug treatment regimes and disengagement from previous peer networks).

For this sub-group in particular, 'growing out of crime' via involvement in the purposeful activity associated with standard aspects of transition was very hard to initiate and sustain. A normative reorientation away from the prevailing values of 'the street' had difficulty taking hold in the absence of alternative, mainstream routes forward. Matthew (19) was a recurrent heroin user and had served several custodial sentences.

Reflecting on his frustrating attempts to get away from his past, he describes the pressures against going straight:[13]

> First day I was out [of YOI] this time I was thieving, do you know what I mean, miss? I'm just sick of it, doing the same thing over and over again, getting locked up and that...if I had the money, miss, I wouldn't even do it — even a 100 quid a week would do me. Yeah, I could get £200 a week at the turkey factory but I could get that in one day off one [stolen] car...but I'm sick of all these places. I've seen too much of it. When I was fifteen, to tell you the truth miss, when I first came in [to a secure unit] I thought it was just a bit of fun. I've just grew out of it each time, do you know what I mean? I grow out if then I get back into it...I'm sick of pinching, I'm sick of doing all the crime and that. I wanna chill out for a good bit, do you know what I mean?... [but] the lads my age and a bit older, they're all into crime. I'm close to them. I dunno, but I think it's hard making new friends and that again. It's hard, but I would like to do it miss, 'cos it's doing me 'ead in. I'm sick of being in here all the time.

Economic marginality was an experience for all the sample, but effective (re)engagement with employment was doubly difficult for those with often extensive records of offending and imprisonment, even when they were prepared (as most seemed to be) to surrender the more lucrative proceeds of crime for the wages of local poor work.[14] Many did make attempts to access training and educational courses, in and out of prison, to improve their qualifications and labour market chances. Successful completion of these (against numerous counter pressures[15]) at best placed them at the back of long queues for jobs and in competition with similarly qualified individuals who benefited from the absence of a criminal history. For some, continued failure to (re)enter employment and continued 'hanging around' provided the context for relapse and the end, for the time being, of fragile efforts to 'go straight'. Richard is a case in point. Serving a second sentence in a bail hostel and apparently determined to stay off heroin, he worried that he had 'no job to keep [him] busy'; he needed 'more purpose' and was fed up just 'wandering around'. He bemoaned the fact that his (hazy) aspiration 'to go to college' had not 'come around quicker'. We now know he relapsed into heroin-driven crime shortly after this (Webster et al., 2004). Spending many years in and out of prison, on heroin and out of work also limited the opportunities for this group to establish stable, loving partnerships. 'Settling down' was inhibited by their commitment to male friends, to drugs and to crime.

Whilst others in the sample were making efforts to progress, the school-to-work, family and housing careers of this group were held on pause as they struggled to disentangle themselves from crime and drugs.

Summary and conclusions

Confirming popular and academic representations of socially excluded locales, our interviewees felt that dependent drug use – and related crime – was significant in explaining the decline of their neighbourhoods. Nevertheless, informants had markedly different orientations towards drug use, and drug behaviour was a central axis by which youth here differentiated themselves. Both abstainers and recreational users abhorred 'smack-heads' and shared transitions in which illicit drug use was largely *irrelevant* to understanding their social and economic marginalisation.

A main aim of this chapter has been to understand ethnographically the processes whereby a minority of young people in such places evolve careers of dependent drug use and crime and the consequences of these for their broader transitions. Our findings eschew the inherent determinism of much criminal career research; interviews were full of unpredictable instances of individuals turning away from, or towards, deviant behaviour. Examining how criminal and drug involvement is embedded within the broader, complicated facts of young people's unfolding lives, rather than focusing on how individual criminality might be predicted by early risk factors, allows us, we think, to understand better young people's different and changing transitions and the significance of offending, and drugs, in them. Leila's case provides an extreme example of this argument. Her immersion in street prostitution and heroin dependency might not have been predicted by her life prior to the age of thirteen and nor would the emotional depths she plumbed during her teenage years predict her later promising efforts to reach a more conventional adulthood.

Leila's biography allowed us to glimpse one severe set of exclusionary processes that affect some vulnerable young women in Kelby. Whilst by no means uncommon here, the majority of men and women in our study recounted forms of criminal career that were different and that are likely to be common in other poor neighbourhoods. Very many of the sample reported offending in their early teenage (predominantly infrequent, petty shoplifting). For the majority, their transgressions ceased there. Two key movements can be identified in the consolidation of the most serious, longer-term criminal careers.

The first of these was the hardening up of school disaffection into full-blown disengagement, exhibited in frequent, persistent truancy. Long-term engagement with street corner society further established oppositional identities and was the cornerstone for the evolution of most, but not all, careers of crime that extended beyond early to mid-teenage. Dull truant time was enlivened by the camaraderie of shoplifting jaunts, other petty thieving and speeding around the estates in stolen vehicles: crime as leisure for bored, out-of-school teenagers. For some, this marked the early phases of criminal apprenticeships (Little, 1990). They began to learn the routines of more acquisitively-oriented offending (e.g. how and what to thieve from cars) and were drawn into local criminal markets (e.g. the best shops and pubs for fencing stolen property, the market rate for 'knock-off gear', etc.). For many, though, these sort of infringements – coupled with underage drinking and recreational drug use – marked the extent, and end-point, of criminal careers.

In general terms, we describe a process whereby the large numbers involved in (petty) offending in early teenage gradually lessened as the years passed. The second, most significant 'moment' – which helped to drag out a smaller number of individual's criminal careers into later periods and to transmute them into something more destructive – is when heroin enters the scene. It would be foolish to argue that all persistent youth offending is and has always been rooted in drug dependency. Craine (1997) shows how economically marginal transitions can readily generate minority 'alternative careers' of crime, regardless of any contact with poverty drugs. Our purpose, however, has been to document the situation as we found it among the people we talked to, not as might have been the case in Kelby prior to the influx of heroin. We are confident that the form of drug-crime careers we have concentrated on here now explains much of, and the most pernicious examples of, the youth offending in this locale.

Thus, dependent use of heroin and cocaine was clearly implicated in the exclusionary transitions of a smaller sub-set of interviewees. As Little (1990: 139–40) puts it:

> by choosing to continue with his criminal lifestyle, the young offender closes a number of doors which might otherwise have led to conformity and extended liberty, particularly such important options as those which hold out the promise of education, employment and security.

In our study, this closing down of options for more 'mainstream' life-styles and identities was confirmed by the 'choice' to use heroin. For individuals like Richard, the close combination of drug and crime careers became central to an understanding of unfolding biographies. Drug dependency fuelled increasingly desperate acquisitive criminality (Bennett, 1998; Edmunds et al., 1999). He had failed to complete several government training programmes, had been employed only once (and briefly), had been unemployed recurrently, had become estranged from his family, had been homeless and slept rough, had a lengthy and worsening record of offending, had been imprisoned twice and, at the age of twenty, was living in a bail hostel, struggling to maintain his commitment to a methadone programme and scratching around trying to find ways, beyond heroin, to fill tedious, direction-less days.

In chapter 10 we raise questions about the descriptive purchase provided by the concept, but we would argue that if anyone is 'socially excluded', Richard is. Cases like his represent perhaps the most intractable forms of social exclusion that we uncovered. In line with criminological research, others described processes of 'growing out of crime'. Desistance was motivated and facilitated by normal aspects of youth transition such as the getting of jobs, the forming of partnerships and parenthood. Separation from previous peer groups and immersion in purposeful activity seemed crucial in 'going straight'. The problem, though, is that the cumulative effects of sustained, heroin-driven crime – often largely 'empty' school-to-work careers punctuated by repeated spells of imprisonment – make this resolution much harder to achieve. People like Richard are unlikely to appear attractive as potential employees, partners and fathers. With purposeful activity to engage energies and through which to redefine personal identity, liberating oneself from addiction was hard enough. Without it, relapse was common. Heroin helped 'fill the void [and] make life bearable' (Foster, 2000: 322).

It is important to stress the novelty of stories like Richard's, at least in the context of this place. Even fifteen years ago we would have struggled to find a similar one in East Kelby. This reminds us again that the sort of biographies of exclusion that they relate cannot be read off as some defect of an immoral, inter-generationally transmitted underclass culture. Leila's case aside, to the best of our knowledge, their parents were not heroin addicts, criminals or anything but despairing of their children's wrong turns. Something happened here to make these experiences possible. Throughout we have stressed the theoretical value in attempting to understand how young people's multiple and interdependent careers take shape in relation to the legitimate (and illegal) opportunity structures that prevail in a locality. Critical here has been the changing local drug market and the influx of heroin at a particular historical moment;

a moment in which many of these interviewees were leaving school and facing the depressing limitations of the formal labour market. Educating young people about the hazards of problematic drug use is, of course, a laudable exercise, as are attempts to control their supply. But given that the social and economic experiences that gave root to these individuals' drug careers are shared by all young people in East Kelby – and that more 'excluded youth' now seem to be crossing the Rubicon to heroin use – for us the most fundamental, long-term political challenge is to combat the social and economic conditions that create the demand for poverty drugs. We take up this theme again in the final chapter.

10
Disconnected Youth? Conclusions

What have we learned about youth transitions in some of Britain's poorest neighbourhoods? How closely do the experiences described here connect with popular and influential theories of the excluded, underclass? The first half of this chapter considers these questions in the light of our findings. The second locates the answers we give in a more panoramic discussion of the socio-economic, historical and geographical contexts that help us comprehend more fully the biographical narratives that have formed the basis of this book. We conclude with a brief, critical foray into contemporary policy debates about the social exclusion of youth in poor neighbourhoods.

Youth transitions in poor neighbourhoods

Different transitions and multiple careers

The first, obvious conclusion is that there is not one single, uniform way of growing up in poor neighbourhoods. A context of social exclusion does not generate just one way of getting by (Johnston et al., 2000). The transitions to adulthood that these people were making were unique: a banal point, but one worth making given the partial way in which 'underclass youth' are often portrayed. Three interviewees – Sarah, Jason and Martin – are selected here to demonstrate this argument (they appear at various points in earlier chapters, and are discussed in more detail in MacDonald and Marsh, 2001).

Sarah (23) was a single mother and university student after teenage years marked by turbulent relationships with family, friends and partners and a chaotic housing career (see chapters 5 and 8). Jason (21) was serving his tenth term 'inside' – an outcome of extended and dangerous criminal and drug-using careers (see chapter 9). In contrast, Martin (20) was married, in relatively steady employment and working hard for the local youth organisation he had co-founded (chapter 8). In comparison to the detailed, contrasting narratives recounted by these three – and the other 85 people we interviewed – depictions of a unitary, 'new rabble' underclass culture appear simplistic caricatures, concentrating as they do on one sort of negative response to socio-economic dislocation (Murray, 1994). This is our first point of objection to conservative underclass theory; it does not allow for the diversity in transitions and outcomes uncovered by this study.

This differentiation in the *lived experience* of young people in poor neighbourhoods is in part explained by the wider view of transition taken here. Unlike many youth studies, school-to-work careers were not our only focus. Although these *are* critically important in understanding the general, longer-term outcomes of transitions (Webster et al., 2004), from the perspective of young people – their unfolding biographies paused in the moment of the research interview – other things sometimes *felt* more important *at that point* and took prominence in the way that they, and we, interpreted their lives. Because transitions to adulthood are multifaceted, the influences on individual's experience of them – and outcomes from them – are diverse. For instance, for the two sub-groups who recounted narratives most redolent of social exclusion, issues beyond the labour market seemed most significant in understanding their current situation. For some, damaging careers of heroin use had become the primary fact that explained most of the rest that went on in their lives. For others, motherhood had become central, superseding previous employment ambitions; an experience in this context typified by socially and materially restricted lifestyles. The two dimensions of transition that are alluded to in these examples – family and drug-crime careers – were the ones that most differentiated the current situations of the sample.

Flux, complexity and unpredictable 'critical moments'

Thus, although class, ethnicity and place united our interviewees, their subjective *experiences* of transition were different. The combined influence of school-to-work, family, housing, leisure, criminal and drug careers also meant that individual transitions were complex, fluid and unpredictable. Encounters in one sphere could have dramatic repercussions in another. Unpredictable 'critical moments' had unpredictable consequences. Physical and mental ill health was very widespread among interviewees and their families, unsurprisingly so given what we know about the socio-spatial concentration of health inequalities (Mitchell et al., 2000; Tees Valley Joint Strategy Unit, 2002; Macintyre, et al., 2002). The extent of reported ill health (particularly of personal and parental psychological problems, such as depression) suggests that, in hindsight, a closer analysis of young people's 'health careers' might have proved valuable in understanding these transitions. Experiences of loss – particularly of bereavement and parental separation – proved to be especially important in shaping the course of individuals' lives thereafter. Again, though, *how* such events impact on transitions would be unknowable without the benefit of interviewees' *retrospective* biographical accounts.

Seemingly treading uneventful, conventional paths until that point, a few interviewees (like Sarah and Jason) highlighted family traumas as the moment when they started 'going off the rails'. Learning at the age of eleven that her 'father' was not her biological father was identified by Sarah as the 'critical moment' (Johnston et al., 2000; Thomson et al., 2002b) or 'turning point' (Hodkinson and Sparkes, 1997) that set in train a series of turbulent relationships with family members and boyfriends, which in turn motivated a chaotic, nomadic housing career. According to Jason, the onset of his long criminal career could be traced back to the separation of his parents, also when he was eleven, and his father's ensuing alcoholism. Conversely, in Martin's case the death of his father caused him to redouble his commitment to local community work and to his job. Webster et al. (2004) show how these sorts of family trauma can – sometimes within the same biography – become the psychological triggers for the onset of *and* desistance from criminal careers.

These interviewees collided with the numerous hardships that typify socially excluded places. Direct, cumulative experience of *inter alia* poverty, personal and family ill health, criminal victimisation, unemployment, poor schooling, problematic drug use, homelessness, and so on undeniably affected the sort of lives they led. Exactly what sort of effects such experiences might have, at the level of the individual case, is much less certain.

Two examples: interviews revealed several instances of individuals re-engaging with, or disengaging from, education despite earlier encounters that might have suggested that this would not be the case (see chapter 3). Several people who could have had all the requisite risk factors ticked off against them did *not* pursue full-blown criminal or drug-using careers (see chapter 9). Indeed, as with Webster et al.'s follow-up study (2004), this research struggled to identify any *background* factors that seemed to play a causal role in separating out more 'delinquent' transitions from more 'conventional' ones. Interviewing siblings who followed quite different paths confirmed our wariness about the 'actuarial positivism' present in some contemporary criminology (Young, 1999). Transitions were contingent; buffeted by unanticipated critical moments, they were a complex set of twists and turns. A key conclusion is, then, that transitions of whatever sort do not roll on deterministically to foregone conclusions.

Individuated transitions, shared marginality

Furlong and Cartmel (1997) argue that the increased complexity and room for personal decision-making ushered in by the restructuring of youth transitions engenders in young people an increased sense of personal autonomy (and culpability, should their 'choices' not work out). In accounting for their life histories, our informants usually prioritised their own actions and shied away from social structural explanations. This has been found in studies of the 'excluded' elsewhere. Murad (2002a: 43 and 44) describes the 'strong feeling of guilt' at 'not having succeeded in life' encountered in interviews in other parts of Europe. In our study, feelings of personal failure and regret imbued, for instance, nostalgic memories of school and remorseful accounts of attempts at desistence from drug-crime careers that quickly turned to depressing relapse.

Biographical interviews are perhaps more likely than other research methods to uncover atomised, subjective theories of 'personal troubles' (Mills, 1970) such as these. In asking questions about the *multiple* careers that make up transitions, we may necessarily be led into emphasising the diversity and differentiation of experience (Ball et al., 2000b: 48) when, in fact, the economic substructure of young people's lives (Roberts, 2000) is shared and constant.

Transitions – at the level of the *individual case* – were marked by uncertainty, fluidity and flux. School-to-work careers demonstrated this most clearly (Craine, 1997). Moving *into* and *out of* casualised, low-paid, insecure jobs was a typical feature of the interviewees' post-school careers (Furlong and Cartmel, 2004). The same applied to college courses and training schemes; far fewer were completed than were started. The revolving doors of YT schemes metamorphosed into the revolving doors of NDYP programmes. By their early twenties, some had transited through all these different statuses. Rapid, 'multiple re-locations' (Fergusson et al., 2000) between government schemes, college courses, 'poor work' and unemployment became the norm (the same applied to locally nomadic, chaotic housing careers).

The *frequency* of changes differed, but the *nature* of interviewees' school-to-work careers was much the same (i.e. leaving school with poor educational qualifications and then circulating round the various 'options' available at the bottom of the local labour market). Our efforts to identify more (or less) 'successful' examples of school-to-work career foundered on the fact that they were all broadly the same in nature. All were included in these unstable, marginal careers. The entire sample could be categorised as economically marginal, despite differential levels of school achievement, truancy, disaffection, and so on. Although most held on to the official rhetoric that educational qualifications equalled greater likelihood of rewarding employment, the experience of their post-sixteen labour market careers in East Kelby did not provide much supporting evidence. Consequently, a minority forcefully argued that this meritocratic claim was bogus, arguing that individual economic fortunes were more dependent on connection to informal, neighbourhood social networks (i.e. 'who you know') and chance.

So, whilst the details of individuals' transitions differed – with most contrast being provided by differential participation in family and drug-crime careers – overall the interviewees were united by a common, enduring experience of economic marginality.

Youth (sub)culture and transitions

The separation of 'two traditions' of youth research has become a common focus of complaint among those interested in this field (see chapter 2). Although this argument is sometimes overstated[1] (see MacDonald et al., 2001), it is still true that the study of youth culture remains marginal to mainstream British research on transitions. The project reported here was a study primarily of transitions. Yet we think our book shows that there is value – for both traditions of youth research – in attempting to conceptualise and research the way that issues of youth culture impact on youth transition, and vice versa.

Whilst there is not the room here to develop a fuller argument, there still appears to be some mileage in drawing on older subcultural approaches in attempting to theorise – in relation to class and place – the transitions of young people in poor neighbourhoods (MacDonald and Shildrick, 2004). If we take 'youth culture' broadly to refer to the values, identities and practices that are shared by socially stratified groups of young people, then an adequate analysis of transitions would *necessarily* involve exploration of youth culture. The study of the structural aspects of transitions and the policy questions that flow from this (e.g. the way that the changing, pre- and post-sixteen institutions structure opportunities for youth and influence processes of inclusion and exclusion) *requires* the study of youth cultural experiences and identities. We could not have understood, for instance, the transitions of 'socially excluded' groups such as young mothers and the young men of 'street corner society' without attention to the impact of leisure careers and localised, peer networks on gendered self-identities. Conversely, it would have been impossible to comprehend how leisure careers changed and how individuals became engaged in different local, cultural networks without tracking the influence over time of their respective school-to-work, housing and family careers.

Disconnected youth? Explaining transitions in poor neighbourhoods

In chapter 1 we reviewed theories of the underclass and concepts of social exclusion. How closely do they connect with the sorts of transition we have described?

Against the (cultural) underclass thesis

Despite the generally hostile reception to Murray's writing in Britain, our starting position was that underclass theories are not necessarily mistaken. Having conducted research that we think overcomes some of the methodological shortfalls of previous studies, we are now convinced that they are. To us, conservative theories of a dangerous, welfare-dependent underclass are plainly, simply wrong. The evidence for this conclusion is present throughout the preceding chapters and we select here only some key findings.

We followed the approach *most* likely to reveal localised, 'minority underclass cultures' (Payne and Payne, 1994), i.e. 'not clipboards and multiple choice questionnaires' but 'long conversations conducted over weeks and months' (Murray, 1990: 70) with residents of a place apparently most conducive to underclass formation. Yet we could not find 'the underclass' (Morris, 1993).

Clearly, in East Kelby there was no shortage of the 'classic early warning signals' claimed to signify its existence. High rates of crime and unemployment bedevil these neighbourhoods. Single parenthood and 'illegitimacy' run at rates significantly higher than the national average. Interviewees lived these things. Yet narrative accounts of their experience resisted explanation in terms of a theory that understands all or any of these social phenomena as the outcome of a distinct, separate underclass *culture* constituted around 'the deplorable', immoral responses of a 'different kind of poor people' (Murray, 1990: 3). Although individual and collective experience of 'welfare dependency', unemployment, single motherhood and crime was plentiful, these were not the cultural choices of a generation disconnected from the moral mainstream. On the contrary, the values, morality and goals of interviewees, in virtually all cases and respects, were stubbornly normal.

Interviewees imagined becoming parents in 'the right way' at the 'right time', expressing careful judgements about the importance of establishing stable partnerships and employment *prior* to parenthood. 'Hyper-conventional' attitudes to getting jobs predominated, despite the fact that casualised, 'poor work' was what people usually got. Scouring thousands of pages of interview transcripts produced only four short extracts which described in any way positively the experience of unemployment (and these all referred to very brief spells). A handful resisted claiming their welfare entitlements and all regarded 'benefit dependency' as a way of surviving, not a way of life. Fraudulent 'fiddly work' *was* condoned in general, but only if it provided a necessary, incremental, short-term boost to meagre welfare benefits. Several interviews spontaneously turned a key tenet of underclass theory on its head: being raised by poor, unemployed parents did not mean offspring inherited a taste for idleness, but rather a sharper determination to avoid the same for themselves. Very many interviewees *were* quick to condemn others around them as work-shy 'dole wallahs', as irresponsible 'bad' mothers or as mired in criminality. Murray heard exactly the same in his brief visits to poor communities in Britain, taking them as direct evidence of a widening division between the 'deserving' and 'undeserving poor'. We interpret them differently; as the rhetorical attempts of people to distance themselves from negative reference groups and to defend personal and family reputations against the continuing stigma that attaches to poor people and neighbourhoods.

We could go on but, in dismissing underclass theory, we are *not* suggesting that our sample led untroubled lives or was innocent of the troubles that other local people faced. The traditional, 'respectable' working-class goals described to us rarely translated into practice, but again we dispute underclass theories' overemphasis on the agency of individuals in creating the situations they find themselves in. Conservative underclass theory fails to appreciate that individuals can react quite differently to apparently similar events *and* that this reaction is not fixed, clear or predictable (across cases or within individual biographies). A static view of 'underclass culture' ignores the complex and changing life experiences of young people who find themselves in difficult circumstances. As such, this approach fails to grasp that experiences beyond individual control or the orbit of personal morality can impact severely on young lives. In other words, writers like Murray overstate the choices and underplay the constraints facing so-called underclass youth.

One might argue, though, that those young men with long-term criminal and drug-using careers provide ample evidence with which to substantiate cultural underclass theories. There is no doubting the damage that they had caused their families, their local community and themselves. Theirs were stories of wasted potential and fruitless intervention by the criminal justice system. Most had largely 'empty' school-to-work careers and a few showed no inclination 'to go straight'. Surely here we have the living embodiment of 'the dangerous class'?

Again, we raise reservations. This sort of 'life-style' was only one among many. It was by no means dominant, even among economically marginal young men in this prime underclass locale. The 'delinquent solution' was followed by some but not most and, as such, Murray's diagnosis of one, deviant, dangerous culture 'contaminating the life of entire neighbourhoods' overstates the case (1990: 195). More importantly, the choices that underpin criminal careers cannot be understood as a pure reflection of personal immorality or cultural estrangement. One reason why Murray's perspective receives much less scholarly acclaim than Wilson's (1996: 55) is because of the latter's more careful analysis of the sociological context that shapes the behaviour of the 'ghetto poor':

> This is not to argue that individuals and groups lack freedom to make their own choices, engage in certain conduct and develop certain styles and orientations, but it is to say that these decisions and actions occur within a context of constraints and opportunities that are drastically different from those present in middle-class society.

'Hard lads' like Jason and Stu insisted that they were the authors of their own life-stories, would blame no one else for their wrongdoing and would oppose any analysis that positioned them as the unreflecting victims of social circumstance. Nevertheless, in explaining transitions we need to appreciate the context in which such choices are made; how the agency of these young men – and all the other interviewees – was bounded (Evans, 2002) by the balance of opportunities afforded by the formal and informal economies. In particular, the dramatic reshaping of the local drug market in Teesside in the mid-1990s had enormous repercussions for young people vulnerable to the lure of 'poverty drugs', most of whom, to that point, had relatively petty, sporadic criminal careers. Subsequent, entwined careers of dependent drug use and crime progressively closed down the possibility of legitimate 'choices'. Focusing on the way that changing drug markets, local youth culture and the limitations of the formal labour market interact in a context of social exclusion seems a more promising way of understanding these sorts of transition than theories that interpret them simply as the outcome of an inter-generationally transmitted culture of deviancy (Perri 6 et al., 1997).

Social exclusion: 'poor work is the big story'

Few youth researchers would sign up to the wilder claims of conservative underclass theory. The concept of social exclusion has come to be a more popular way of describing the multiple, socio-economic difficulties encountered by disadvantaged young people. Dominant paradigms put exclusion from the labour market, for young and older people alike, at the top of the policy agenda. Similarly, the versions of underclass theory that have been more warmly received in youth studies are those that think of young people as possible underclass members because of their *structural* exclusion from employment (Roberts, 1997a).

We certainly would not want to underestimate the problem of joblessness for East Kelby young people. Unemployment was common; the default status to which many returned repeatedly. Of those who had been out of school for a few months, only one had never been unemployed. Likewise, only a minority of those who had left school displayed careers in which employment was completely absent. Some of this latter group were individuals that had pursued extended criminal and drug careers that led them progressively away from employment. Others prioritised 'the mothering option' and – *for the time being* – had become detached from the labour market. The point, however, is that even for some of these most inexperienced, unqualified young workers, in a place beset by high levels of joblessness, employment remained possible, albeit usually in the form of severely casualised 'poor work'. Even some of those with the most uninspiring work histories and lengthy records of imprisonment also occasionally managed to get jobs during spells 'on the out'. The most likely contenders did not display the 'obdurate refusal of poor work' (Byrne, 1999: 21) said to typify the excluded underclass (Mead, 1997).

Accordingly, accounts of social exclusion that posit the complete, permanent excision of young people in poor neighbourhoods from the world of work seem mistaken. For the same reason, policy initiatives to count and respond to distinct, static categories such as 'NEET young people', 'the unemployed' or indeed 'the employed' at any one time - or to estimate the success of New Deal programmes by counting those with 'positive outcomes' a few months after completion - rather miss the point (SEU, 1999a; Britton, et al., 2002). The flux of transitions meant that virtually all interviewees had occupied these different statuses at one time or another, usually on several occasions. An individual's labour market status at one moment did not predict where he/she would be at the next. As Bhalla and Lapeyre (1997: 428) put it 'the concept of precarious employment may be of greater value in explaining social exclusion than the more usual concept of unemployment'. In short, social exclusion is best understood as a process or longer-term experience, not a fixed, stable category reducible to, and measured by, current joblessness.

This confirms findings of other research in the same locality (MacDonald, 1994; 1997c; Johnston et al., 2000) and elsewhere (e.g. Furlong and Cartmel, 2004). It supports theories that explain economic marginality not in terms of the exceptionality of young people as part of a permanently excluded, wholly redundant underclass, but in terms of the restructuring of employment in post-industrial, 'flexible' labour markets (Morris, 1994).

Drawing on research from the 1980s, Ashton and Maguire make the same point. They traced the growth of careers of 'sub-employment' for young adults who moved between government schemes, low-skilled jobs and unemployment. Labour market restructuring and the spread of poor work meant that sub-employment became 'much more widespread... no longer confined to the unskilled... [and] very much part of the experience of a large section of the working class' (1991: 48). The research here supports this view. Many of our young interviewees reported that, even if their parents had previously enjoyed more Fordist forms of employment, they were now similarly economically marginal (working on short-term contracts, in under-skilled jobs, unemployed, 'retired', 'on the sick' or otherwise economically inactive).

David Byrne's incisive interrogation of 'social exclusion' reaches similar conclusions: 'the degree of dynamic change in circumstances over time makes the notion of a permanently excluded underclass absurd' (1999: 70). He complains that 'what is absolutely missing' from many accounts of the socially excluded is 'the significance of the combination of low wages, insecure employment and dependence on means tested benefits supplements to low incomes... poor work is the big story' (1999: 69). The need of post-industrial capitalism for a 'flexible', reserve army of labour means that low-paid work punctuated by unemployment becomes the 'normal experience' for many of the working-class and 'represents the most significant kind of excluded life in our sort of society' (*ibid.*: 74).

Byrne's theoretical discussion resonates with the details of our empirical study: unemployment, job insecurity and poor work have become common *working-class* experiences, rather than the preserve of an underclass stranded beneath them.

Social inclusion and social capital: the paradox of networks

The second issue that we draw attention to in critiquing the concept of social exclusion is that it does not connect in a straightforward way with the *subjective* experiences of young people from localities which, by all objective definitions, were socially excluded.

As well as economic non-participation, social scientific commentaries on social exclusion are often interested in disadvantaged individuals' participation in community life, their social networks and their social support. On these scores, it would be difficult to class our interviewees as excluded. Many *felt* included. In different ways and degrees, informants were *connected* to the life of their estates in ways untypical of residents of those apparent paradigms of social order: middle-class, suburban neighbourhoods (Baumgartner, 1988). There is a strange contradiction in policies to reverse decline in socially excluded areas by trying to beef up neighbourly activity: 'normal Britain (or "socially included" Britain) doesn't have community centres' (Kleinman, 1998: 10).[2] Although it is fashionable to explain the decline of poor neighbourhoods in terms of their apparent lack of social cohesion, community spirit and social capital (e.g. Etzioni, 1993; Putnam, 1995), the majority here did not seem short of strong, close, supportive relationships. According to Forrest and Kearns (2001: 2141), 'close family ties, mutual aid and voluntarism are often strong features of poor areas' and help people 'cope with poverty, unemployment and wider processes of social exclusion'.

The influence of informal, social networks of family, kin and friends was evident across the different careers that make up youth transitions. Informal peer groups in school were crucial in understanding shifting processes of educational engagement and disengagement. 'It's not what you know, it's who you know' was a common refrain in interviewees' critical debunking of the supposed instrumental value of educational qualifications (chapter 3). In searching for jobs, informants relied on exactly this practice, finding it accurately reflected the realities of their local labour market (chapter 6). The way they 'chose' and assessed post-sixteen training and employment programmes was also mediated through the experiences of others close to them (chapter 5). Leisure lives became centred on neighbourhood-based circles of others like them, especially for young mothers and those young men who were most marginal to the labour market (chapter 4). Young mothers drew on such networks for informal childcare, emotional and financial support and in positively valuing their role and identity (chapter 7). We could not understand the localisation of housing careers without appreciating the powerful hold family networks, in particular, had on young people's surprisingly strong attachment to place. Whilst most acknowledged the problems of living in East Kelby, such as criminal victimisation, knowing and being known by particular types of locally embedded social networks helped ameliorate some of their consequences (chapter 8).

As Perri 6 has pointed out, however, 'we must not celebrate...any kind of network or any kind of social capital. The consequences of a person participating in some networks may be very damaging for everyone else and perhaps, in the longer-term, for themselves' (1997: 21). Involvement in criminal networks was the example of 'destructive social capital' he was referring to here (Webster et al., 2003). In our study, prolonged immersion in street-based, youth cultural activities and identities was crucial in entrapping some participants in criminality and dependent drug use. Desistence depended upon separation from such networks (chapter 9). Being connected to networks can also have other disadvantages. They helped hurry young people's departure from schooling, bolstered resistant 'learner identities' and, for some, played a crucial role in promoting educational underachievement (chapter 3). The collective identities and loyalties engendered by shared commitment to the 'mothering option' sometimes hindered the taking of steps in other directions (chapter 7). Spano sums up similar processes of social exclusion in southern Italy: 'networks based on kinship as well as on friendship can easily become a constraint...by enclosing the subject in a limited social space, they can preclude [the] possibility of having new opportunities, of working out new projects, of maturing new aspirations' (2002: 73). To use Putnam's phrase (2000: 23, cited in Kearns and Parkinson, 2001): 'bonding social capital bolsters our narrower selves'. Perhaps the clearest example of the potentially malign influence of social networks is that usually presented by informants as one of their main benefits.[3]

Perri 6 (1997: 10–11), reviewing Granovetter's (1973) seminal work on networks together with recent studies, concludes that 'the most valuable contacts [for getting jobs] are not the ones with whom they have strong ties, such as kin and neighbours, but those with whom they have weak ties, such as former colleagues, acquaintances and friends of friends'. Compared to the middle class, the social networks of working-class people are more likely to contain strong bonds with a smaller circle of family and friends and a paucity of weak ties 'that are more useful in advancing oneself in the labour market' (*ibid.*). 'Network poverty', as Perri 6 calls it, means that interviewees like ours lacked 'bridging social capital' to more extensive, diverse social networks that would help in transcending the limiting socio-economic conditions in which they lived. In relying upon localised, informal networks for job search, interviewees were constrained to the same sort of 'poor work' done by their social contacts (Morris, 1995). Wilson reports the same in respect of the American 'ghetto poor' (1996: 65) and Morrow (2001) reports very similar findings to our own in respect of disadvantaged young people in a Southern English town. Kearns and Parkinson sum it up neatly: 'the neighbourhood for poorer people has more often served as an arena for "bonding" social capital that enables people to "get by", rather than as a platform for "bridging" social capital that enables people to "get on"' (2001: 2105).

So, paradoxically, whilst connections to local networks could help in coping with the problems of growing up in poor neighbourhoods and generate a sense of 'inclusion', the sort of social capital embedded in these relationships served simultaneously to close down opportunities (Strathdee, 2001) and to limit the possibilities of escaping the conditions of social exclusion (Johnston et al., 2000).

Panoramas of marginalisation

Sociologists, particularly ethnographers, have long been criticised for holding their palms upwards, for research grants, to the rich and powerful whilst casting their eyes downwards to study the lives of the poor and powerless 'as part of the surveillance necessary for their control' (Nicolaus, 1968; Byrne, 1999: 5; Murad, 2002a). One of the most scathing attacks on *youth* sociology has come from Jeffs and Smith (1998: 59; see chapter 2). Among other things, they complain that the field of study has become obsessed with 'picking over the minutiae of young people's lives'. Whilst denying some of them, we would accept many of the criticisms writers like Jeffs and Smith make. In this section we break away from close-up discussion of the 'minutiae' of youth transitions in East Kelby to consider how they connect with some wider sociological debates about place and class.

We think that a truly 'holistic' (Coles, 2000a) theory of youth transitions needs to appreciate the historical, spatial and socio-economic contexts in which they are made.

In the biographical accounts we gathered we can glimpse not only the twists and turns of individual lives as the years unfolded but how these were mediated by the changing set of possibilities and risks afforded to young adults in East Kelby. History, even very recent history, shapes the sorts of youth transitions that are possible. They have a temporal specificity. The most dramatic example of this from our study relates to the transformation of the local drug market in the middle of the 1990s, when many of interviewees were passing through their teenage years. Growing up in this period predisposed individuals to certain experiences (and made others less probable). Had they been borne even ten years earlier the likelihood is that none of their biographies would have become so entwined with heroin (and all that meant for them and their families).

Although some stress the declining sociological importance of place under late modern processes of globalisation (see Brewer, 2000; Waters, 2001), our study highlights the opposite (Jones, 2002). To grasp properly how the sort of transitions we have described have come about requires a discussion of how this *locality* has been subject to *global* processes of change (Cooke, 1989; Harvey, 1989; Brewer, 2000; Chamberlayne et al., 2002); the way that place, under globalisation, recasts youth opportunities. Social exclusion has a geography as well as a history (Sibley, 1995) and, for us, the primary fact that explains youth transitions in East Kelby is the rapid, widespread deindustrialisation of Teesside.[4]

Deindustrialisation, globalisation and place: excluding youth

Raising the level of our analysis draws attention to the changing flow of global capital over the past thirty years, the increased competition between the old economic regions of the Western hemisphere and the newly industrialising ones of the South and East, the subsequent deindustrialisation of the UK's manufacturing heart-lands and the changing economic character of this place (Lash and Urry, 1987; Jordan, 1998; Turok and Edge, 1999).

As we described in chapter 2, the history of Teesside over the past thirty years has been one of remarkably swift economic decline; where the mainstays of economic and community cohesion have been rapidly dismantled by global shifts in capital which, together with failed regional policy, have created 'one of the most de-industrialised locales in the UK' (Byrne, 1999: 93). Once world-famous for its iron, steel and chemical production Teesside has become economically peripheral; a dispensable, global outpost (Robinson, 1990) seemingly cut off from the benefits of a new, knowledge-based global economy (Wilson, 1996; Castells, 2000a; 2000b).[5] As writers like Beynon et al. (1989), Robinson (1990) and Hudson (1989a; 1989b) explain, the character and culture of

Teesside *as a place* has been marked by deference to the whims of national/regional economic policy and the decisions of big businesses, like ICI and British Steel/Corus, owned and controlled at a distance. Later we consider how a history of economic dependency might be reflected in the fatalistic character of youth transitions here, but note for now how in 2004 at a cost of 400 redundancies, the Korean firm Samsung became the latest in the list of sizeable firms to disinvest in the local economy.

The marginality of this sub-region to the main centres of national and international capitalist trade, in the last three decades of the twentieth century, is mirrored in, and *creates*, the economic marginality of East Kelby youth. Teesside's economy, like the transitions of working-class young people here, has become characterised by insecure employment and the stubborn recurrence of unemployment. In chapter 2 we noted the successive waves of government area regeneration programmes that have sought to tackle the consequences of deindustrialisation. Like the successive government programmes encountered by young Teessiders since the late 1970s (with the now replaced YT and the NDYP being the principal ones accessed by our interviewees) these have tended to be experienced as short-lived and only partially successful in reducing the risk of unemployment.

Despite this massive state policy intervention, Kelby is the English town with the most concentrated poverty. East Kelby's wards rank amongst the poorest in the country. In some of them around half the working-age population are jobless. This is not to say that area-based policies do not have a part to play in improving local conditions (Hills et al., 2002; Simpson and Cieslik, 2000), but that they have been unable to *solve* the persistent, long-term and various problems of deindustrialisation, structural unemployment and entrenched poverty. In Kleinman's words (1998: 3), 'local initiatives cannot alone provide solutions to problems whose causes are national or even international'.

Byrne's explanation is that social exclusion is '*inherent* in a market-oriented flexible post-industrial capitalism' (1999: 130, our emphasis). For him, 'exclusion is something done by some people to other people' (*ibid.*: 1). Murad (2002a: 51) says that 'exclusion is the name given to the process of splitting up and reconstructing the working classes... [a section of which] is condemned to continued precariousness'. This macro-level perspective throws into question attempts to understand youth exclusion as the outcome of the micro-level, personal decision-making and agency of individual young people. It alerts us to the role of the state and the economy in creating the conditions in which exclusionary youth transitions become possible; how the distant decisions of trans-national corporations and governments have resulted in the 'wrecking of a region' (Hudson, 1989b), the transformation of part of the local, skilled working-class into an industrial reserve army (Byrne, 1999) and the collapse of the 'economic scaffolding' that previously enabled transitions to stable and secure working-class adult life (Salo, 2003).

In 1974, when 'the lads' in Paul Willis's classic study (1977) were stepping from school into manual, working-class jobs their counterparts in Teesside (i.e. white, working-class young men) were also following what then seemed to be an equally certain cultural apprenticeship, finding employment or apprenticeships at British Steel, ICI or the docks. Then 55 per cent of sixteen-year-olds went into employment. Within the space of two decades the movement of the young working-class into jobs at minimum school leaving age had virtually ceased. In 1994, four per cent of Teesside school-leavers got jobs, the lowest figure ever recorded (MacDonald, 1998).[6]

Murad (2002a: 51) would interpret these statistics as the 'outcome of a failure in the process of inclusion'. The economy has changed to the point that it can no longer accommodate all young people: social exclusion 'selects the most deprived young people, the group that remains after the others have been selected by the labour market' (*ibid.*: 53). Yet, as implied by our study, the spatially concentrated spread of high-skill jobs in the new, global information economy 'does not render obsolete the bulk of poor work' in places like this (Brown and Scase, 1991: 13). The increasingly flexible market of the global economy has led to a growing proportion of jobs at the bottom end of the labour market being of a more temporary and low-paid nature. Indeed, Byrne (1999: 56) argues that social exclusion and the poor work that goes with it is not 'an accidental by-product of capitalist development but absolutely intrinsic' to post-Fordist forms of capitalist accumulation.

Hutton (1995) estimates that the bottom 30 per cent of the population are those trapped in insecure work. For young people in marginal economies, deindustrialisation does not spell 'the end of work' (Rifkin, 1995). The perpetuation of work opportunities in the casualised, secondary labour market helped explain the nature of transitions for a group who might be expected, because of their lack of educational and cultural capital, to have become wholly excised from employment. Their durable emotional, social, moral attachment to work, in a context where such an attitude might be called obsolete, is one of our most startling and perhaps bathetic findings.[7]

Reflexive modernisation and communities of fate

This recent local history of deindustrialisation means that, for working-class young people, transitions represent a 'struggle against exclusionary probabilities' (Murad, 2002a: 46). Our interviews revealed the various, resourceful, resilient ways informants lived with the consequences of economic change; changes which meant that the post-school 'world of work' had become a dispiriting sequence of knock-backs, let-downs, false promises and dead-ends. They had learnt to get by and make do.

From time to time we have noted how transitions here are different from (or similar to) those followed elsewhere, partly reflecting the particular set of limits and opportunities visible in young people's locally-rooted 'socio-scapes' (Ball et al., 2000a). A regular finding across recent youth studies, regardless of their geographical location, is that young people subscribe to longer-term goals common to their class and to society at large (e.g. McDowell, 2001; Stephen and Squires, 2003; Gunter, 2004). The same was true here. And, as elsewhere (e.g. Furlong and Cartmel, 1997), a good number also felt that they might one day achieve them, even if the evidence of the here and now gave little grounds for optimism.

One of the advantages of Ball et al.'s London-based study (2000a; 2000b) over ours is that it sampled young people with a wider range of socio-economic (and ethnic) statuses, allowing some comparison of our informants with young people who possessed more advantageous economic, cultural and social capital. None in *our* study imagined the 'relatively clear, relatively stable and relatively possible' futures – through A-levels and university to professional careers – envisaged by *their* middle-class interviewees (2000b: 51). Predominantly, the 'imagined futures' of our interviews matched ones Ball et al. characterise as 'beset with uncertainties' or riven with 'a sense of aimlessness … of "getting by" and coping on a day-to-day basis … [sometimes] overtaken or dominated by events beyond their control, for example illness, pregnancy, family breakdown, personal crises' (*ibid.*). As a consequence, few East Kelby young people were able or prepared to map out a plan that might lead them to the symbolic markers of adulthood (e.g. a secure job, their own home). Ball and colleagues explain this sort of 'very foreshortened time perspective', this 'refusal of the future, of planning' (2000a: 149), in terms of the heavy constraints of economic circumstances and the damage done to materially disadvantaged young people's 'learner identities' by alienating school experiences. In a study of young people in a Scottish town, Anderson et al. found that 'failing to achieve ambitions in the past *does not affect ambitions* but does limit willingness *to plan* for the future. Poverty and job insecurity, and also the presence of children, inhibit planning, in some cases to extreme degrees' (2002: 1, our emphasis).

Such findings sit uncomfortably with some of the more gung-ho theorisations (and celebrations) of reflexive modernisation (see chapter 2; Giddens, 1991; Beck, 1992; Beck et al., 1994; Cieslik and Pollock, 2002). The diverse, individualised identities and transitional pathways that we mapped out are definitely more risky, fluid and unpredictable than in previous periods. Interviewees certainly engaged in reflexive consideration of their lives. The conclusions reached, though, did not result in individuals 'conceiv[ing] of himself or herself as the centre of action, as the planning office with respect to his/her own biography' (Beck, 1992: 135). *Lack* of planning – what Evans and Heinz (1994) call 'passive individualisation' – was the definitive feature of the majority of the school-to-work, family and housing careers described in this book.

As Spano explains, 'in this new scenario', where the traditional route maps for youth transitions are obsolescent, 'exclusion can be seen as the result of a "deficit of reflexivity"' (2002: 72). It can be, but it should not be. Modish, theoretical attention to the apparent, alleged deficits of working-class culture – in respect of reflexive modernisation or social capital – runs the risk of mirroring the victim-blaming, 'cultures of poverty' arguments of underclass theory. In our case, exclusion is ultimately the result of an historical process of deindustrialisation which has left a broad swathe of Teesside's young working-class vulnerable to economic marginality.

Putting aside the dubious, unpleasant implication that young people in poor neighbourhoods could all somehow 'plan' themselves out of poverty, interesting questions do remain about the unequal distribution of the socio-economic and other resources upon which the ability to (re)construct and plan personal biographies are predicated (Roberts, 1997b). Or, as Spano goes on to say (2002: 72), 'reflexivity...is not an individual resource', freely and equally available to all. Rather, as Bourdieu suggests, 'agents are endowed with habits, internalised from past experiences' which generate 'adapted and continuously renewed strategies, but *within the limits of the structural constraints* by which they are produced and which define them' (Bourdieu, 1997: 166, cited in Murad, 2002b: 111, our emphasis).

We see the truth of this in the *different* ways in which our informants attempted to get by under *shared*, persistent conditions of poverty and economic marginality. The weight of previous experience and current circumstance meant that they had learned not to 'plan anything because it never works anyway' (see chapter 7). This is reminiscent of what young homeless people in Blackman's (1997) study described as 'the fear of the fall'. Cumulative, personal disappointments combined with the pressure of the moment to make the consideration of forward steps too risky. As Lash puts it, there are losers as well as winners in the reflexivity game: 'just how "reflexive" is it possible for a single mother in an urban ghetto to be? . . . just how much freedom from . . . structural poverty does this ghetto mother have to self-construct her own "life narratives"?' (1994: 120). We agree with Lash's implication, and conclude that some contemporary accounts of reflexive modernisation underplay the social structuring of the psychic and emotional resources on which reflexivity depends and overplay the ability of personal life-planning to overcome the class-based, material bases of social exclusion.

We are also a little suspicious about the extent of 'de-traditionalisation' that is expounded in theories of individualisation and the risk society. Our theoretical conclusions match exactly those of Rustin and Chamberlayne (2002: 7):

> just as some versions of the globalisation theory fail to recognise the new structural constraints the have emerged in this new environment, so the theory of 'individualisation' and 'reflexivity' advanced by Giddens and Beck overstates and idealises the 'disembedding' of individuals from social and cultural settings . . . individuals usually remain deeply embedded within social networks and relationships, and they depend on these for their wellbeing.

In a context of '*structured* individualisation' (Roberts, 1997b: 59), young people continue to derive from their class and family backgrounds particular sorts of social and cultural capital rooted in local economic history and conditions (Forrest and Kearns, 2001). Whilst Teesside young people may now make more individualised transitions than did their parents and grandparents, we would speculate that their generally resilient but fatalistic outlook on life corresponds with longstanding elements of local working-class culture. Cultures of class and place still matter. Whilst global capital might only perceive Teesside as 'a (temporary) space for profitable production', this is also a place where people have:

> networks of friends, relatives and acquaintances, where they have learned about life and acquired a cultural frame of reference through which to interpret the social world around them . . . As a result, people have often become profoundly attached to particular places,

which come to have socially endowed and shared meanings which touch on all aspects of their lives, helping shape *who* they are by virtue of *where* they are. (Beynon et al., 1994: 5)

Although some social theorists declare 'the death of social class' (Pakulski and Waters, 1996) in postmodern times and 'the disappearance of the local under global processes' (Brewer, 2000: 173) we, like Brewer, argue that ethnography can reveal the continuing sociological relevance of class and place in understanding lived experience (Forrest and Kearns, 2001). The history and current conditions of East Kelby – a place *made* for working-class people – saturate the biographical narratives we have presented. For instance, in discounting academic schooling, in prioritising reliance on family and friends to get by, in accentuating the positives of community life, in talking up 'the mothering option', in rejecting life as a 'dole wallah' and in describing the central importance of work, these narratives articulated deep-seated, locally embedded, class 'cultural frames of reference'.

A particular feature of working-class history in Teesside has been an historical dependency on a few large firms and nationalised industries for employment. Some business leaders claim that this bred a 'dependency culture' (which has inhibited, for instance, self-employment and small business development: see MacDonald and Coffield, 1991). Deindustrialisation has progressively stripped away the economic structures in which the working-class cultural tastes and outlooks described by our interviews once 'worked' and made sense. Talking of another northern town hit hard by steel industry redundancies, Charlesworth describes 'a once-present state, now lost, in which individuals could *plan* a future, buy a house, marry, have children, live a life that, though constrained by the routines of work, offered some security...' (2000: 10, our emphasis). The vicissitudes of global capitalism and local deindustrialisation means the living of working-class life – here and elsewhere – has now come to depend on rafts of government area regeneration programmes, action zones, schemes, welfare payments and poor work. Insecurity and economic marginality prevail.

Depleted of the industry that brought it into being, East Kelby has become a 'community of fate' (Hirst, 1994, cited in Jordan, 1998). Its young residents have been dispossessed even of the opportunity to make the sort of secure, 'respectable', working-class life known by their grandparents, let alone the opportunity for limited social progress up and away from the working-class condition that was previously possible (Toynbee, 2003). Now marginal to the centres and circuits of the new

global economy, downward inter-generational social mobility characterises their comparative position (Byrne, 1999). In this historical
context of class and place it is perhaps not surprising that young
adults who have experienced the most tangible conditions of poverty
described their biographies and imagined their futures in terms which
emphasised – not the confident, exciting choice-making hypothesised
in some contemporary social theory – but fatalism, lack of choice and
powerlessness.

What is to be done? Inclusion, exclusion and the policy agenda

At this point of a book like this it is usual to make some policy recommendations. These are limited, not just for reasons of space, but also
because what we have to say is brief and relatively simple. Sketching out
a 'wish list' of the numerous policy developments implied by our study
in respect of education, housing, childcare, training, leisure provision,
employment, benefits, drugs, criminal justice, and so on would be
straightforward. On the basis of a mass of recent social research, Darton
et al. (2003) delineate key principles in respect of tackling disadvantage
with which we would wholly concur. Furlong and Cartmel's (2004) call for
an attack on the casualisation of employment and better connections
between training and progressive employment (see Kleinman, 1998), is
an example of a *particular* policy prescription supported by our findings.
Others are now in place (since the time of our fieldwork) or are at least
claimed ambitions of government.

Although 'educational policy alone is unlikely to be sufficient to
eradicate serious inequality' (Feinstein, 1998: 103), education represents
by far the single largest 'social policy' investment in poor neighbourhoods.
For it to work in the interest of social inclusion, rather than against it,
class-based patterns of provision and choice in respect of education and
training need overhauling (Ball, 1993). A necessary condition for this
will be the establishment of rewarding, viable vocational and academic
educational pathways (or mixtures of each), from the mid-teenage years
onwards, that are equally resourced, enjoy equal esteem (amongst young
people, parents and employers), provide the necessary financial support
to young people and which lead to rewarding employment. The revision
of the 14–18 curriculum, the provision of EMAs, efforts to upgrade the
quality of youth training and initiatives to widen participation in
Higher Education are all welcome aspects of this (Social Exclusion
Unit, 2004).

But in this arena, as in others, we are a long way from what is hoped for in government pronouncements (as chapters 5 and 6 show). Announcing policy goals is easier than enacting them. Part of our hesitancy about going into greater policy detail stems from a realistic appraisal of the extent of the interconnected, multiple problems facing 'socially excluded' young people (and a little pessimism about the ability of government to seriously tackle them) (Beynon et al., 1994). Mizen (2003) is the latest of many to describe the repeated failures of government 'vocational policy' over the past twenty years to address class-based underachievement in education. Another example, that we remarked on earlier, would be the apparent inability of area-based policies to resolve the concentrated, multiple problems of poor neighbourhoods. In our view, these must be part of the solution yet Kelby, a town that has perhaps 'benefited' the most from such initiatives, is also now the town with the most concentrated poverty in England.

More importantly, we feel that much of the current policy agenda is, at best, only able to ameliorate the *effects* of poverty, economic marginality and social exclusion rather than tackle the underlying *causes* and conditions that create them (Webster et al., 2004). In a similar vein Osmond and Mugaseth (2004: 124) argue that, rather than developing particularised policies for separate disadvantaged groups, we should 'consider first the wider context of communities within which disadvantaged people live and to see how the collective condition can be improved'. We give one example of our argument, from chapter 9. Devising ways in which to improve drugs education, to control drug supply and markets better and to revise the treatment of addicts are all laudable exercises, but none tackles the social and economic conditions which give 'poverty drugs' their appeal. Despite various initiatives of these sorts over the past ten years, Teesside continues to have some of the deepest problems of drug-related crime and drug dependence amongst young people in the country (Home Office, 2003).

Including youth?

This policy perspective throws into question the sort of thinking behind government programmes towards excluded youth. The policy *prescriptions* that emanate from the Social Exclusion Unit and other branches of government tend to be much more specific than their *descriptions* of the problem and proclaim a fundamental belief in the role that paid work has in forging social inclusion. Whilst the plural hardships of social exclusion may be 'the problem', 'the solution' – the route to social inclusion – is singular: entry into paid work (Holden, 1999; Benn, 2000). This is most obviously the case with the New Deal for Young People programme, promising as it does to move the young and poor 'from welfare to work', but it also applies to the Connexions youth support programme. Connexions aims to provide a co-ordinated, extensive support service for 13–19-year-olds, particularly those 'at risk' of social exclusion (SEU, 2000). Primarily, though, it seeks to engage teenagers in learning and training so that they can more easily enter employment as they move into adulthood. For New Labour, engagement with schools, colleges and training schemes delivers the skills, personal aptitudes and qualifications necessary to secure paid work and, as a consequence, social inclusion. Connexions and the NDYP programme mop up, re-engage and re-orient those who fall by the wayside.

Two related premises are at work here. The first is that jobs (in suitable number and quality) are available to accommodate young people as they emerge from education and training programmes at the end of their teens and in their early twenties. The second is that youth unemployment is, therefore, a symptom of an ill-prepared workforce; the 'fault' of the young unemployed. Our study shows the flaws in this policy approach and how Labour's 'new deal' for youth is failing to secure 'social inclusion' for many young Teessiders, even if we interpret the term in the *narrow* sense of the movement of young adults into relatively rewarding, relatively lasting employment.

We are not saying that employment is unimportant in alleviating social exclusion. On the contrary, paid employment is crucial to overcoming disadvantage and to lifting people out of poverty (Darton et al., 2003). This has not happened, however, for our interviewees. McKnight (2002) describes several statistical trends that help us understand why this might by so, including: the substantial increase, over the past thirty years, in the proportion *of the poor* who are in low-paid jobs; the significant increase, since 1997, in the proportion *of employees* who are in low-paid work; and the greater prevalence of low pay in the north-east (and Northern Ireland) than in any other region of the UK.

Thus, for our informants, entry to employment did not provide a first step on an upward path away from poverty and benefit dependence. The wages they received for the jobs they did were not high enough to lift them out of the category of the 'working poor' (Toynbee, 2003). Even if they had been, these jobs remained insecure and of poor quality. Becoming employed was typically a temporary experience terminated in the main not by choice but by redundancy, by the end of a contract or by 'unfair' dismissal. As Atkinson (1998: 9) argues, 'marginal jobs' which do not 'offer training and prospects for internal promotion' can often trap people in 'low paid and insecure jobs with recurrent unemployment' (Howieson, 2003; Furlong and Cartmel, 2004). In local labour markets typified by pervasive under-employment and unemployment 'a job may only represent a turn in the cycle of poverty' (McKnight, 2002: 98). The policy imperative to move the unemployed into any employment – regardless of its suitability and quality – means that government welfare to work programmes can be accused of adding to the problems of social exclusion, not solving them (Byrne, 1999).

What is missing from the current policy agenda – according to several contributors to a recent, high-level, national policy seminar[8] – 'is a strong regional policy which focuses on raising employment in lagging regions and doing this not just through supply-side measures but also with policies aiming at increasing the number of jobs' (Regan and Robinson, 2004: 24). Another speaker commented, however, that this seems to be 'off the New Labour radar' (Wicks, 2004: 51), despite promising evidence that Intermediate Labour Markets of social enterprises, for instance, can assist the movement into decent employment even in Britain's poorest areas (Marshall and Macfarlane, 2000; Osmond and Mugaseth, 2004). Welfare-to-work programmes appear most successful in the places they are least required, in more buoyant labour markets where the demand for labour outstrips supply. In these places, the majority of young adults will make relatively smooth transitions to employment, regardless of the help offered by New Deal. But 'large areas of the country have employment shortages which make redundant the welfare to work dynamic' (Wicks, 2004: 50).

It is this context which makes our interviewees economically marginal and subject to the casualised 'hire-and-fire' strategies of employers who are safe in the knowledge that the number of young workers available exceeds the number of low-level positions on offer. This is even truer of better quality opportunities. In May 2001, one of the Teesside local authorities advertised three apprenticeships for young people. There were over 400 applications. Even Lawrence Mead (1997: 127–8), a champion of 'workfare' programmes in the United States, has acknowledged that cajoling the workless into the British versions of 'workfare' (such as NDYP) may not be sufficient to secure social inclusion for all:

> Workfare does assume that jobs are available to recipients required to work... I do not presume that the British labour market generates as many jobs as the American. Some regions are historically depressed, particularly in the North, and it might be necessary to create some jobs there if all the dependant are to work.

In summary, then, the problem for government policies that seek youth inclusion via paid work is the same as that faced by the host of schemes and programmes from the 1980s and 1990s that concentrated on the supposed deficiencies of the *supply* side of the youth labour market (see Mizen, 2003). Initiatives like the New Deal for Young People and Connexions will continue to represent only a partial response unless government develops a truly 'joined-up' policy to youth exclusion that addresses more fully the persistent problems of *demand* in places like Teesside: the lack of decent, enduring jobs for young adults (Webster et al., 2004).

Improving the economic context of youth transitions will not in itself resolve all the difficulties facing young people as they grow up in Britain's poorest areas. As Levitas (1998) says, incorporating 'the excluded' back into (better quality) employment will not overcome the social inequalities inherent there, but it would help meet the more limited ambition of reversing the downward trend in social mobility experienced by the 'disconnected youth' of deindustrialised locales. Furthermore – and in agreement with William Julius Wilson's overriding policy conclusion in respect of American ghetto neighbourhoods – we believe that 'increasing the employment base would have an enormous positive impact' (1996: 238) on all the interrelated, entrenched problems of poor neighbourhoods.[9] According to our evidence, it would greatly increase the opportunity for all our interviewees to become more firmly connected to the sort of productive, ordinary lives to which they aspire.

Notes

Chapter 1

1. In the main, we have chosen not to place inverted commas around words that we find problematic (such as 'underclass' and 'illegitimacy'). This is partly a stylistic decision but we also cite the arguments of others who use these terms freely and often uncritically. The book's final chapter will make clear our own perspective on these contentious terms.
2. MacDonald (1997a: 4) offers a working model that conflates structural and cultural theories. The underclass can be understood as: 'a social group or class of people located at the bottom of the class structure who, over time, have become structurally separate and culturally distinct from the regularly employed working-class and society in general though processes of social and economic change (particularly de-industrialisation) and/ or through patterns of cultural behaviour, who are now persistently reliant on state benefits and almost permanently confined to living in poorer conditions and neighbourhoods.'
3. Buckingham's study (1999) is a rare example of serious empirical research that offers support for conservative underclass theory. Although there is not the space here to provide a full critique, we would point out that his quantitative analysis of data from the National Child Development Study operates with very minimalist definitions of underclass membership (e.g. those who have one episode of 'benefit dependence' in a ten-year period and those who do not own their own home). Even then, his findings sit uncomfortably with many of Murray's claims. For instance, Buckingham's sizeable sample contained only one never married man who had fathered a child out of wedlock.
4. The Economic and Social Research Council, the largest funder of social scientific research in the UK, has 'social exclusion' as one of its nine central themes for investigation.
5. The 'cultural' dimension of social exclusion is sometimes referred to as 'the social'. This concerns the degree to which individuals are able to participate in their communities, their attachment to social networks, the degree of social support available to them, their engagement in leisure, etc.
6. In essence, their first two dimensions are different aspects of the 'economic sphere' and boil down to the level of household income (as a measure of consumption) and household members' work status (as a measure of production) (see Burchardt et al., 2002: 34).

Chapter 2

1. The Economic and Social Research Council (ESRC) and Joseph Rowntree Foundation (JRF) each initiated large-scale research programmes during this

period (see www.tsa.uk.com/ycsc/index.html and www.jrf.org.uk/knowledge/findings).

2. The Careers Service categorised those in education, training and employment as statuses 1, 2 and 3.

3. These ideas are developed in more detail in MacDonald et al. (2001).

4. This has been demonstrated in a more recent study of the extended transitions of 'socially excluded' young people (Webster et al., 2004). This study followed the fortunes of some of the young people discussed in *Disconnected Youth?* and Johnston et al.'s (2000) *Snakes and Ladders* as they reached their mid- to late twenties. A key finding is that it was virtually impossible for individuals at this age to escape the cumulative consequences of earlier, economically marginal youth transitions. Where relevant, further reference is made in our book to Webster et al.'s findings.

5. Unlike other de-industrialised northern towns and cities, Teesside's slide could not be explained by capital under-investment but by the concentration of (at times massive) investment in too narrow a range of industries.

6. In a foreword to the plan for the postwar development of Kelby (Lock, 1945: i), its mayor foresaw a bright future for the new residents of East Kelby: 'wherever in will be found health, comfort, convenience, beauty and happiness, in many cases for the first time in the lives of the poor'.

7. 'Joblessness' refers to the proportion of the working-age population who are not in employment. Measuring 'joblessness' rather than 'unemployment' (e.g. benefit recipients) allows for a broader understanding of economic inactivity. Unless otherwise stated the statistics in this section are taken from the Tees Valley Joint Strategy Unit.

8. What East Kelby does have is a relatively stable (predominantly white, working-class) population. Other 'socially excluded', poor areas have more transient and/or ethnically mixed populations. Whilst we maintain that East Kelby provides prime territory for understanding processes of social exclusion characteristic of many of Britain's post-industrial areas – and for pursuing the central questions of underclass theory – it is possible that the forms of community it still possesses serve to limit some of the direst social consequences of poverty (as we argue in chapter 8).

9. Jane Marsh undertook all this aspect of the research and most of the rest. Robert MacDonald interviewed several 'stakeholders' and about one-third of the young people in the sample.

10. MacDonald undertook various youth research projects on Teesside in the late 1980s and early 1990s: this topic rarely featured as significant in young people's accounts then.

11. Those interviewees with heavy experience of the criminal justice system will have had several opportunities to reflect on and present life stories. Others seemed to be considering in depth for the first time the sort of questions we asked.

12. The study by Webster and colleagues (see note 2) also provided the opportunity for a largely new research team to re-examine some of these interview transcripts and our analytical account of them and to re-interview some of the same interviewees: their later study came to very similar conclusions to this one and found no reason to question the veracity of our analysis.

Chapter 3

1. The local statistics quoted in this section are derived from Tees Valley Joint Strategy Unit unless otherwise stated (www.teesvalley-jsu.gov.uk).
2. Our study was not intended to evaluate these initiatives. The majority of the sample had concluded secondary education and had had little direct contact with them. That said, their qualitative accounts of the experience of schooling in this context have some important implications for policies of this sort and we discuss them when appropriate.
3. For instance, 'They'll put you down . . . they don't, like, build your confidence up and that, they always say, "Oh, you're never gonna get a job, you're thick" and stuff like that . . .' (Paul, 16, YT trainee).
4. When we quote, material in square brackets is for explanation. A long dash — indicate a natural pause. That extraneous material has been edited out is indicated as follows: . . . Unless we state otherwise, emphasis (shown by italicised words) is as in the original.
5. We suspect a degree of post-hoc rationalisation in some accounts of educational underachievement. We did not access young people's accounts of school experiences as they were happening and are unsure whether, at the time, these people were actually keen to work harder. Later, we interrogate a theme that was very prevalent across our interviews: a strongly expressed regret for not having worked harder at school.
6. Informants were given the opportunity to select their own pseudonym. 'Fox' was one of the few that did. He was a fan of the TV programme 'The X-files' and its lead character, 'Fox Mulder'.
7. We noted earlier how being placed in a low-ability class exacerbated Broderick's negative attitude to school. In Fox's case, we see how school systems for differentiating pupils can have a *positive* effect, turning disengagement to engagement.
8. We say 'appeared' because some gave fuzzy responses to our questions about qualifications. This partly reflects their embarrassment they felt about the official status of their qualifications: 'Oh God! the highest was a C and then they were all D's and not worth mentioning!' (Claire). Others did not know their results. Roy, for instance, was working by the time they were published. For him, the immediate costs of collecting his results (threatened suspension and loss of pay) outweighed the potential longer-term benefits of knowing them.
9. In Webster et al.'s follow-up study (2004; see chapter 2 n. 4) three individuals had relatively 'successful' school-to-work careers in the longer term. These people had even *lower* levels of qualifications than the under-qualified majority.

Chapter 4

1. One youth service response to the apparent hostility of young people to meeting in youth clubs, to their preference for unsupervised association and to the antagonisms that this can generate with older, local residents has been the development of a 'youth shelter' on one estate near to East Kelby. This modest initiative – similar to a large bus shelter with lighting and seating, situated

several hundred yards from the nearest houses – met with an enormous response, with over 100 young people congregating there on some evenings.

2. Few truants reported that their parents condoned their school absence.
3. The many strategies and policies they had experienced as attempts to control their truancy and to re-engage them with school were seen unanimously as failures: 'you always find a way to get out' (Kate). They deployed energetic schemes to get themselves registered as present at different points of the school day yet missed all lessons, ignored punishments such as after-school detention, were indifferent to the encouragement and threats of Education Welfare Officers and Social Workers, and some even saw temporary school exclusions as a victory. A few of the most recalcitrant truants had been taken on camping trips designed to address their poor behaviour. These were enjoyed but criticised as wrong-headed because they 'rewarded' school disengagement. Others had been sent to various 'vocational training' centres and courses. They tended to abscond from these too, chiefly because they knew no one there and felt the tasks they were given were too menial ('just stacking shelves up, keeping the floors tidy, stuff like that').
4. Although Leanne played down the significance of alcohol in the attraction of 'going out', most interviewees described how drinking was central to young adults' leisure. Their first serious encounters were usually at the start of their teenage years and sharing bottles of cheap cider was reported as a common, unremarkable precursor to their later drinking in the commercialised leisure outlets of the town centre.
5. The crucial exception to this being those people who sustained dependent drug use through acquisitive crime: see chapter 9.
6. A very similar set of processes operated in respect of the young mothers in the study.
7. The ethnographic chapters that followed focused on the more tightly defined, well-known, leisure-based and stylistically spectacular sub-cultures. In some subsequent academic critiques these have (wrongly) been taken to stand for what the CCCS was all about (see Bennett and Kahn-Harris, 2004).
8. Therefore, our evidence stands against more 'postmodern' theories (e.g. Featherstone, 1991; Miles, 2000) which propose that 'older' social divisions by class or place no longer play a significant role in determining youth culture, life-styles and leisure (Roberts, 1997b; Stenson and Watt, 1998).

Chapter 5

1. *JM*: Right, so was it the Careers Adviser who got you into Futures Training then? *Leanne*: No, it was Abigail's Mam said that there was, like, a job going – a two-year course, training. I was interested, so I applied for it.
2. This might partly be explained by fuller counting of those in the 'destination unknown' survey category.
3. Legard et al. (2001) note, however, some 'new' participants may conclude their part-subsidised, FE courses and then find themselves unable to continue into higher education because of the financial costs.
4. This is the aim of an on-going research project with which one of the authors is currently involved.

5. Employment Training (ET) was a year-long government programme for those over the age of eighteen. Previously unemployed participants worked for their unemployment benefits plus £10 per week (and thus, colloquially, ET was understood to stand for 'Extra Tenner'). Only a handful of our sample had participated in it.

6. Others found that they had chosen the wrong course in the sense that it had not met their initial expectations in terms of content or quality.

7. For instance, Alex (23) said of her YT scheme: 'they had no computers . . . well, one or two in the whole building and it was a Business Admin. course'.

8. In addition – and signalling New Labour's focus on area-based initiatives to combat social exclusion – there is also a New Deal for Communities programme (see chapter 1).

Chapter 6

1. Other less frequent elements of job–search strategies included responding to job vacancy notices in the local newspaper, the use of employment agencies and speculative visits to employers' premises.

2. The lack of a driving licence and/or car was often mentioned as a key impediment to getting a job.

3. A broader definition of informal economic activity might also include, however, work in caring for one's own children (see chapter 7) and work in criminal enterprises (see chapter 9).

4. The only difference here is that we came across one or two people whose 'fiddly work' verged on – or was a first step to – fuller criminal activity (Craine, 1997). One example was Claire, who for a short period whilst claiming had, with her boyfriend, 'done fag runs from Dover to Calais' (the illegal importation of cigarettes, to be sold on for cash): 'It was awful. I never got no sleep. Smelly hotels. Absolutely shitting myself going through Customs.'

5. It is difficult to understand the disparities in pay quoted by Broderick, Curtis and others. We suspect that some claimed much higher rates than were actually paid and some reported much lower ones. Alternatively, Curtis's 'job' may have been a YT placement (some confused the two) or the pay for his first week's employment at the factory may have contained deductions for employer-arranged travel to and from work and/or for special clothing. His was the lowest weekly wage quoted across the sample, but many others cited rates of pay which were not much higher (another turkey factory employee reported getting £50 per week). Perhaps Curtis did get £30 for his week's work.

6. Anecdotal evidence from some of mature, working-class, male students at the University of Teesside confirmed that they too regularly accessed work at the turkey factory.

7. Media coverage of asylum-seekers in Britain sometimes points out how they too get drawn into these types of casualised employment (particularly in basic agricultural, horticultural and food-processing industries) for these same reasons. Interestingly, many of the young adults in our study undertook exactly those types of 'poor work' – and in some cases, for exactly those employers (Pai and Leigh, 2004) – said now to be heavily reliant on the employment of asylum-seekers.

8. Boredom was not the only reason that Ellie gave for quitting jobs. She departed one bookmaker's firm following an armed robbery and being threatened with a shotgun.

9. In only one interview did we hear a suggestion of this. This was with Jason and Stu, both of whom had long records of offending, were currently imprisoned and were plotting more lucrative crime (as drug dealers) on release (see chapter 9).

10. By the time of our second interview, Alison had left this job for one in a fast-food outlet. She had still 'loved' it but came to feel exploited because although she had been given supervisory responsibilities, she was still taking home only £85 for a 40-hour week – and had to work Sundays, in order to 'make my money up'.

11. Two informants – Martin and Zack – described the suicide of a close friend who 'hung himself because he couldn't, he wasn't employable, he was getting knock-backs from various people, he was having troubles at home as well.'

12. Some gave answers such as 'there's no work in Kelby, anyway', 'there's no factories anymore', 'businesses are closing down, stuff like'. Explanations like these were few in number, brief and undeveloped.

Chapter 7

1. To reiterate, ours was not a statistically representative sample and, as the fieldwork unfolded, we selected purposefully interviewees who could provide insight into young parenthood.

2. As we will argue, interviewees' plans did not always play out as they imagined. By the time of Darren's second interview (less than a year later) his girlfriend was expecting his child.

3. There were some exceptions. As might be expected, those who were lone mothers tended to accentuate the positive aspects of this situation and some of those who had been raised by a single parent defended their upbringing. Richy said: 'My Mam's a single parent. She's brought me up excellent, I think.'

4. Unless otherwise specified, the statistics in this section are drawn from the web-site of the Joint Strategy Unit (JSU) of the Teesside district authorities (www.teesvalley-jsu.gov.uk).

5. In a similar vein, many in Teesside report undeclared, 'fiddly work' to be widespread yet are unable to cite actual cases with any authority (MacDonald, 1994).

6. The exception was Tanya, whose child was in care whilst she made efforts to come off heroin.

7. Matthew insisted on referring to his interviewer, Jane Marsh, as 'miss', despite being encouraged not to.

8. This is not to suggest that a father who does not reside with his children cannot act as a father at all. For instance, Susan (aged 22) had a child when she was fifteen to a man who was, at the time of interview, serving a prison sentence. Despite his absence Susan felt that he still occupied an important role in her child's life and had an important disciplinary role: 'Tracy [her child] got her school report the other week and it was a bit, not on the good side — she's too talkative and she doesn't listen enough — so I took it up [to the prison]

and I showed 'im the report and he talked to her. I mean, she'll listen to him more than she'll listen to me.'

9. Wilson (1996: 65) reports a similar finding, but says that motherhood, in the American ghetto, brings the greatest social isolation (and we note our discomfort with some of the terminology he uses): 'jobless black females (mostly mothers on welfare) were significantly more isolated from mainstream individuals and families than jobless black males. Welfare mothers interacted with other welfare mothers.'

10. The fieldwork pre-dated the introduction of Sure Start programmes.

Chapter 8

1. A handful of interviewees had, at some time in their lives, been 'looked after' in the public care system. These individuals tended to have the sort of later, chaotic housing careers experienced by others in the study.

2. One of these young men had spent three months 'kipping in a shed of a derelict house'.

3. Curtis said, 'I'm not bothered about sleeping on the streets at night, do you know what I mean? I don't mind. All I want is me nights with my son and I can't have them if I haven't got anywhere to stay'.

4. There were other benefits of local crime. Whilst some resented these offers, others took pragmatic advantage of the availability of cheap, shoplifted goods or contraband cigarettes and alcohol imported from France duty free. Another poignant example of an otherwise law-abiding individual benefiting from crime was when Annie had been given a new, three-piece suite by a friend who was terminally ill. This person had ordered the furniture in her own name, knowing that neither she nor Annie would ever have to pay for it.

Chapter 9

1. Seventy-five of the 88 interviewees gave what we felt were useable accounts of offending behaviour. Of these, over half (n = 41) reported no crime whatsoever, fourteen reported petty, one-off or short-lived offending, and twenty reported more recurrent offending (all of whom had received convictions and ten of whom had been imprisoned).

2. Similarly, the majority of 'frequent truants' came from intact families.

3. The spur to desistance sometimes came from particularly traumatic 'critical moments'. Lisa used to be 'in with a crowd getting into trouble and doing drugs' until she was raped by one of them. Zack explained how 'the turning point' in his life was when 'my best mate hung 'imself'. He had 'calmed down now', given up 'all sorts of mad stuff' and committed most of his time to running an informal, voluntary youth group (more of which later).

4. Bob Coles alerted us to the similarities between the argument of this chapter and Michael Little's *Young Men in Prison* (1990). Whilst providing a more detailed, social psychological focus on the episodes that comprise a criminal career than we do, our study confirms many of his findings (e.g. the importance of peer networks in confirming criminal identities, the movement from petty

to more serious crime as careers progress, the absence of familial cultures of delinquency).

5. However, one or two young women in the study reported earlier criminal careers that shared some similarities with those of young men.

6. This is the only direct instance from our study that we know of a parent apprenticing or otherwise encouraging their child toward a criminal life-style. All others reported the opposite.

7. Terms such as 'dependent' and 'recreational' drug use have contested meanings (Goldberg, 1999) and are used in different ways by different authors. Rather than use inverted commas throughout, we note this here.

8. Although drunkenness in our study was rarely the driving force behind repeated criminality, that is not to say that drink-related crime was insignificant. It impacted on individual case histories (Broderick, for instance, was imprisoned for an unprovoked, vicious assault on a stranger during a drink-soaked night out) and on the leisure lives of East Kelby young adults. In chapter 4, we mentioned how some preferred to avoid nights out in the town centre partly because of the potential for getting caught up in violence. For women but particularly men, 'avoiding trouble' – that is, being assaulted or being called on to react aggressively to perceived threats or slights – meant 'staying local' and enjoying evenings in neighbourhood pubs and clubs or at home.

9. The policing response has also incorporated educational programmes in which reformed heroin addicts describe the error of their ways to secondary school pupils and calls for greater medical prescription of heroin to Teesside's long-term users (*Evening Gazette*, 16 July 2003).

10. Many interviewees claimed to be able to identify numerous dealers of heroin and crack cocaine resident in their neighbourhoods.

11. We are unsure about this claim, even though it has been implied in other studies. In an earlier quotation, Richard implies that he and his friends chose heroin because of the deteriorating hit they were getting from cannabis.

12. 'Rattle' refers to the process of heroin detoxification.

13. Mathew insisted on calling Jane Marsh 'Miss' throughout his interview.

14. In only one interview did we hear what might be regarded as unrealistic pay aspirations. This was with Jason and Stu, both of whom had long records of offending, were currently imprisoned and were plotting more lucrative crime (as drug dealers) on release (see MacDonald and Marsh, 2001). They said they knew 'lads who "were on the out" who were earning £450 per week working at ICI. We should earn that! Taxis, night-clubs, trainers, a good haircut – it all adds up. How much does it cost the government to keep us in here [prison] for a week? They should just give us that money and I'd stop doing crime.'

15. In a letter from prison Danny described how on release from his previous sentence he had failed to attend an interview for a place on a welding training course at a local college: 'It was the Careers Service [in the last YOI] that arranged it for me. I got out but the interview was another two months away and I never really thought about it after a few weeks. Daft really 'cos I would've done sound as well. I never cared much then though. I've thought a lot now so I'll give it 100 per cent next time around! I'm still interested in getting on a course. I'm not as keen as before about welding, like, but I'm gonna

try my luck with a place on landscape gardening. If not then I'll go with welding. Either one's still a bonus.'

Chapter 10

1. Some of the most interesting, recent accounts of youth transition have shown how youth (cultural) identities are 'made up' in relation to the changing markets of post-sixteen education, training and employment and the 'new urban economies' (Ball et al., 2000a; Fergusson et al., 2000).

2. Toynbee (2003: 129–30) makes a similar observation: 'It is strange that it is always the people with fewest resources who are expected to galvanise themselves into heroic acts of citizenship... since no-one ever demands the residents of Mayfair get involved with their street lighting and pavements, why should these people whose difficult lives and lack of money make it harder?'

3. For a more detailed, theoretical discussion of the relationships between social networks and social exclusion, see Phillipson et al. (2004).

4. The other key globalising trend that occurs to us as particularly relevant to our discussion concerns the local effects of the global drug economy. Arguably as a partial consequence of Teesside's de-industrialisation (and the related poverty of many of its residents), Kelby has become a global outpost of a developing (inter)national/regional heroin trade. Despite vociferous local policing, the town still hosts what are reported to be cheapest sales of heroin in the country. In 2002, Afghanistan produced its highest ever harvest of opium, topping the world league of heroin production. This has been linked in press coverage to an increase in younger, pre-teens and 'the working young' using heroin (*The Observer*, 6 July 2003). A more panoramic account of the transitions of some of our informants would necessitate discussion of this aspect of the illegal global economy and how it impacts directly upon the lives of young residents of poor neighbourhoods in Britain.

5. 'Those living in poor areas are not excluded *by* globalisation... they are excluded *from* globalisation' (Kleinman, 1998: 6).

6. In prioritising deindustrialisation in our analysis we would not wish to romanticise Teesside's industrial heritage. As Webster et al make clear (2004: 32), working-class life was 'characterised by hardship, the dangers of heavy industries and rigid and oppressive sexual divisions of labour'. Similarly, although women's employment has risen substantially during this period of de-industrialisation much of it remains part-time and low paid and female joblessness rates in East Kelby remain high (see chapter 2).

7. 'What is so striking is that despite the overwhelming joblessness and poverty, black residents in inner-city ghetto neighbourhoods actually verbally endorse, rather than undermine, the basic American values concerning individual initiative' (Wilson, 1996: 179).

8. Senior representatives of the Labour government, the Conservative opposition and leading 'think-tanks' debated the Joseph Rowntree Foundation's principles for tackling disadvantage in Britain (Darton et al., 2003). An interesting consensus emerged which acknowledged the unresolved problems of widespread economic inactivity and continuing, regionally concentrated unemployment

and the potential for employment creation policies, amongst other things, to combat these (Joseph Rowntree Foundation, 2004).

9. For instance, Donnison (1998: 18) argues that: 'strategies for improving economic opportunities will exert the most powerful, immediate influence on crime rates. People who claim to be wanting to reduce crime without doing anything about unemployment or the quality of jobs at the lower end of the labour market are, at best, ignorant.'

References

Abrams, F. (2004) 'Outcast', *The Guardian*, 16 March.

Advisory Council on the Misuse of Drugs (1998) *Drugs Misuse and the Environment*, London: Stationery Office.

Alcock, P. (1994) 'Back to the future', in Murray, C. *Underclass: the Crisis Deepens*, London: Institute for Economic Affairs.

Allen, J., Cars, G. and Madanipour, A. (1998) 'Introduction', in Madanipour, A., Cars, G. and Allen, J. (eds.), *Social Exclusion in European Cities*, London: Jessica Kingsley.

Allport, G. (1979) *The Nature of Prejudice* (third edition), Massachusetts: Addison-Wesley.

Anderson, M., Bechhofer, F., Jamieson, L., McCrone, D., Li, Y. and Stewart, D. (2002) 'Confidence amid uncertainty: ambitions and plans in a sample of young adults', in *Sociological Resarch On-line*, 6, 4, 1–22.

Apple, M. (1986) *Teachers and Texts: a Political Economy of Class and Gender Relations in Education*, New York: Routledge.

Arai, L. (2003) 'Low expectations, sexual attitudes and knowledge: explaining teenage pregnancy and fertility in English communities', *The Sociological Review*, 51, 2, 199–217.

Ashton, D. and Maguire, M. (1986) *Young Adults in the Labour Market*, Research Paper 55, London: Department of Employment.

——(1991) 'Patterns and experiences of unemployment', in Brown, P. and Scase, R. (eds.), *Poor Work: Disadvantage and the Division of Labour*, Milton Keynes: Open University Press.

Ashton, D., Maguire, M. and Garland, V. (1982) *Youth in the Labour Market*, Research Paper 34, London: Department of Employment.

Ashworth, C., Hardman, J., Woon-Cjia Liu, Maguire, S., Middleton, S., Dearden, L., Emmerson, C., Frayne, C., Doodman, A., Ichimura, H. and Meghir, C. (2001) *Education Maintenance Allowance: The First Year, A Quantitative Evaluation*, Research Brief 257, London: DfEE.

Atkinson, A. (1998) 'Social exclusion, poverty and unemployment', in Atkinson, A. and Hills, J. (eds.), *Exclusion, Employment and Opportunity*, CASE Paper 4, London: CASE.

Atkinson, J. (1984) 'Manpower strategies for flexible organisations', *Personnel Management*, August, 28–31.

Atkinson, R. and Kintrea, K. (2001) 'Disentangling area effects: evidence from deprived and non-deprived neighbourhoods', *Urban Studies*, 38, 12, 2277–98.

Auletta, K. (1982) *The Underclass*, New York: Random House.

Bagguley, P. and Mann, K. (1992) 'Idle, thieving bastards: scholarly representations of the "underclass"', *Work, Employment and Society*, 6, 1, 113–26.

Bagnoli, A. (2003) 'Imagining the lost Other: the experience of loss and the process of identity construction in young people', *Journal of Youth Studies*, 6, 2, 203–18.

Baldwin, D., Coles, B. and Mitchell, W. (1997) 'The formation of an underclass or disparate processes of social exclusion?', in MacDonald, R. (ed.), *Youth, the 'Underclass' and Social Exclusion*, London: Routledge.

Ball, S. (1981) *Beachside Comprehensive*, Cambridge: Cambridge University Press.
——(1993) 'Education markets, choice and social class: the market as a class strategy in the UK and USA', *British Journal of Sociology of Education*, 14, 3–19.
——(2003) *Class Strategies and the Education Market*, London: Routledge/Falmer.
Ball, S., Maguire, M. and Macrae, S. (2000a) *Choice, Pathways and Transitions Post-16: New Youth, New Economies in the Global City*, London: Routledge/Falmer.
——(2000b) '"Worlds apart" – education markets in the post-16 sector of one urban locale 1995–8', in Coffield, F., *Differing Visions of a Learning Society: Research Findings Volume 1*, Bristol: Policy Press.
Banks, M., Breakwell, G., Bynner, J., Emler, N., Jamieson, L. and Roberts, K. (1992) *Careers and Identities*, Milton Keynes: Open University Press.
Bates, I. and Wilson, P. (2004) *Independent Learning and Social Inequality*, Leicester: Youth Work Press.
Bates, I. and Riseborough, G. (eds.) (1993) *Youth and Inequality*, Buckingham: Open University Press.
Baudrillard, J. (1988) *Selected Writings*, Oxford: Oxford University Press.
Bauman, Z. (1998) *Work, Consumerism and the New Poor*, Buckingham: Open University Press.
Baumgartner, M. (1988) *The Moral Order of the Suburb*, New York: Oxford University Press.
Bean, P. (2002) *Drugs and Crime*, Devon: Willan.
Bell, J. (2003) 'Beyond the school gates: the influence of school neighbourhood on the relative progress of pupils', in *Oxford Review of Education*, 29, 4, 485–502.
Bell, T. (1985) *At the Works*, London: Virago.
Beck, U. (1992) *Risk Society: Towards a New Modernity*, London: Sage.
Beck, U., Giddens, A. and Lash, S. (eds.) (1994) *Reflexive Modernization*, Cambridge: Polity Press.
Becker, H. (1963) *Outsiders: Studies in the Sociology of Deviance*, Glencoe, IL: Free Press.
Benn, M. (2000) 'New Labour and social exclusion', *The Political Quarterly*, 309–18.
Bennett, A. (1999) 'Sub-cultures or neo-tribes? Rethinking the relationship between youth style and musical taste' in *Sociology*, 33, 3, 599–617.
——(2000) *Popular Music and Youth Culture*, Basingstoke: Macmillan.
Bennett, A. and Kahn-Harris, K. (eds.) (2004) *After Sub-culture*, Basingstoke: Palgrave.
Bennett, T. (1998) *Drugs and Crime: The Results of Research in Drug Testing and Interviewing Arrestees*, Home Office Research Study 183, London: Home Office.
Bentley, T. and Gurumurthy, R. (1999) *Destination Unknown: Engaging with the Problems of Marginalised Youth*, London: Demos.
Berger, P. and Berger, B. (1972) *Sociology: A Biographical Approach*, New York: Basic Books.
Beynon, H. (1997) 'The changing practices of work', in Brown, R. K. (ed.), *The Changing Shape of Work*, Basingstoke: Macmillan.
Beynon, H., Hudson, R., Lewis, J., Sadler, D. and Townsend, A. (1989) '"It's all falling apart here": coming to terms with the future in Teesside', in Cooke, P. (ed.), *Localities: The Changing Face of Urban Britain*, London: Routledge.
Beynon, H., Hudson, R. and Sadler, D. (1994) *A Place Called Teesside*, Edinburgh: Edinburgh University Press.
Blackman, S. (1995) *Youth: Positions and Oppositions*, Aldershot: Ashgate.
——(1997) 'Destructing a giro', in MacDonald, R. (ed.), *Youth, the 'Underclass' and Social Exclusion*, London: Routledge.

Bhalla, A. and Lapeyre, F. (1997) 'Social exclusion: towards an analytical and operational framework', *Development and Change*, 28, 413–33.

Biehal, N., Clayton, J., Stein, M. and Wade, J. (1995) *Moving on: Young People and Leaving Care Schemes*, London: HMSO.

Bourdieu, P. (1990) *The Logic of Practice*, Cambridge: Polity Press.

——(1997) *Outline of a Theory of Practice*, Cambridge: Cambridge University Press.

Bourdieu, P. and Wacquant, L. (1992) *An Invitation to Reflexive Sociology*, Cambridge: Polity Press.

Bourgois, P. (1996) *In Search of Respect*, Cambridge: Cambridge University Press.

Brent, J. (2001) 'Trouble and tribes: young people and community', *Youth and Policy*, 73, 1–19.

Brewer, J. (2000) *Ethnography*, Milton Keynes: Open University Press.

Briggs, A. (1963) *Victorian Cities*, London: Odhams Press.

Britton, L., Chatrick, B., Coles, B., Craig, G., Hylton, C. and Mumtaz, S. (2002) *Missing Connexions*, Bristol: Policy Press.

Brown, G. W. and Harris, T. (1978) *The Social Origins of Depression*, London: Tavistock.

Brown, J. (1998) *Family and Adolescent Support Services: A Social Services Inspectorate Survey*, London: National Institute for Social Work.

Brown, R. K. (1997) 'Introduction', in Brown, R. K. (ed.), *The Changing Shape of Work*, Basingstoke: Macmillan.

Brown, P. (1987) *Schooling Ordinary Kids*, London: Tavistock.

Brown, P. and Scase, R. (1991) 'Social change and economic disadvantage', in Brown, P. and Scase, R. (eds.), *Poor Work: Disadvantage and the Division of Labour*, Milton Keynes: Open University Press.

Brown, P. and Crompton, R. (eds.) (1994) *A New Europe? Economic Restructuring and Social Exclusion*, London: UCL Press.

Brown, S. (1995) 'Crime and safety in whose community?', *Youth and Policy*, 48, 27–49.

Bryman, A. and Burgess, R. (eds.) (1994) *Analyzing Qualitative Data*, London: Routledge.

Buck, N. (1992) 'Labour market inactivity and polarisation', in Smith, D. (ed.), *Understanding the Underclass*, London: Policy Studies Institute.

Buckingham, A. (1999) 'Is there an underclass in Britain?', *British Journal of Sociology*, 50, 1, 49–75.

Burchardt, T., Le Grand, J. and Piachaud, D. (2002) 'Degrees of exclusion', in Hills, J., Le Grand, J. and Piachaud, D. (eds.), *Understanding Social Exclusion*, Oxford: Oxford University Press.

Burghes, L. with Brown, M. (1995) *Single Lone Mothers: Problems, Prospects and Policies*, London: Family Policy Centre/JRF.

Burrows, R. and Rhodes, D. (1998) *Unpopular Places? Area Disadvantage and the Geography of Misery in England*, Bristol: The Policy Press.

Bynner, J. and Parsons, S. (2002) 'Social exclusion and the transition from school to work: the case of young people not in education, employment or training', *Journal of Vocational Behaviour*, 60, 289–309.

Bynner, J., Chisholm, L. and Furlong, A. (1997) 'A new agenda for youth research', in Bynner, J., Chisholm, L. and Furlong, A. (eds.), *Youth, Citizenship and Social Change in a European Context*, Aldershot: Ashgate.

Bynner, J., Elias, P., McKnight, A., Pan, H. and Pierre, G. (2002) *Changing Pathways to Employment and Independence*, York: Joseph Rowntree Foundation.

Byrne, D. (1989) *Beyond the Inner City*, Milton Keynes: Open University Press.

——(1995) 'Deindustrialisation and dispossession', in *Sociology*, 29, 95–116.

——(1999) *Social Exclusion*, Milton Keynes: Open University Press.

Campbell, B. (1993) *Goliath: Britain's Dangerous Places*, London: Methuen.

Carlen, P. (1996) *Jigsaw: A Political Criminology of Youth Homelessness*, Milton Keynes: Open University Press.

Carlen, P., Gleeson, D. and Wardhaugh, J. (1992) *Truancy: The Politics of Compulsory Schooling*, Buckingham: Open University Press.

Cars, G., Madanipour, A. and Allen, J. (1998) 'Social exclusion in European cities', in Madanipour, A., Cars, G. and Allen, J. (eds.), *Social Exclusion in European Cities*, London: Jessica Kingsley.

Carter, M. (1966) *Into Work*, Harmondsworth: Penguin.

Castells, M. (2000a) *The Rise of the Network Society* (second edition), Oxford: Blackwell.

——(2000b) *End of Millennium*, (second edition), Oxford: Blackwell.

Chamberlayne, P., Rustin, M. and Wengraf, T. (eds.) (2002) *Biography and Social Exclusion in Europe*, Bristol: Policy Press.

Charlesworth, S. (2000) *A Phenomenology of Working Class Experience*, Cambridge: Cambridge University Press.

Chatterton, P. and Hollands, R. (2002) 'Theorising Urban Playscapes', in *Urban Studies* 39, 1, 95–116.

Cieslik, M. and Pollock, G. (2002) 'Introduction', in Cieslik, M. and Pollock, G. (eds.), *Young People in Risk Society*, Aldershot: Ashgate.

Clarke, G. (1982) *Defending Ski-jumpers: A Critique of Theories of Youth Sub-cultures*, Paper 72, Centre for Contemporary Cultural Studies, University of Birmingham.

Clarke, J., Hall, S., Jefferson, T. and Roberts, B. (1976) 'Subcultures, cultures and class: a theoretical overview', in Hall, S. and Jefferson, T. (eds.), *Resistance through Rituals*, London: Hutchinson.

Cleveland County Council (1986) *Cleveland Structure Plan: People and Jobs*, Economic Development and Planning Department, Middlesbrough: Cleveland County Council.

Cockburn, C. (1987) *Two-track Training*, Basingstoke: Macmillan.

Coffey, A. (2001) *Education and Social Change*, Buckingham: Open University Press.

Coffield, F. (2000) 'Introduction: a critical analysis of concept of a learning society', in Coffield, F., *Differing Visions of a Learning Society: Research Findings Volume 1*, Bristol: Policy Press.

Cohen, P. (1997) *Rethinking the Youth Question*, Basingstoke: Macmillan.

Cohen, P. and Ainley, P. (2000) 'In the country of the blind? Youth studies and cultural studies in Britain', *Journal of Youth Studies*, 3, 1, 79–95.

Cohen, S. (1980) *Folk Devils and Moral Panics*, (second edition), Oxford: Martin Robertson.

Coles, B. (1986) '"Gonna tear your playhouse down": towards reconstructing a sociology of youth', in *Social Science Teacher*, 15, 3: 78–80.

——(1995) *Youth and Social Policy*, London: UCL Press.

——(2000a) *Joined up Youth Research, Policy and Practice: An Agenda for Change?*, Leicester: Youth Work Press.

——(2000b) 'Slouching towards Bethlehem: youth policy and the work of the Social Exclusion Unit', in Dean, H., Sykes, R. and Woods, R. (eds.), *Social Policy Review 12*, Newcastle: Social Policy Association.

Coles, B., Rugg, J. and England, J. (1998) *Young People on Estates: The Role of Housing Professionals in Multi-agency Working*, Coventry: Chartered Institute of Housing.

Collison, M. (1996) 'In search of the high life', *British Journal of Criminology*, 36, 3, 428–43.

Cooke, P. (ed.) (1989) *Localities: The Changing Face of Urban Britain*, London: Routledge.

Corrigan, P. (1976) 'Doing nothing', in Hall, S. and Jefferson, T. (eds.), *Resistance through Rituals*, London: Hutchinson.

Craine, S. (1997) 'The black magic roundabout: cyclical transitions, social exclusion and alternative careers', in MacDonald, R. (ed.), *Youth, the 'Underclass' and Social Exclusion*, London: Routledge.

Crawshaw, P. (2004) 'The logic of practice in the risky community', in Mitchell, W., Bunton, R. and Green, E. (eds.), *Young People, Risk and Leisure*, Basingstoke: Palgrave.

Crowther, D., Cummings, C., Dyson, A. and Millward, A. (2003) *Schools and Area Regeneration*, Bristol: Policy Press.

Cullingford, C. and Morrison, J. (1996) 'Who excludes whom?', in Blyth, E. and Milner, J. (eds.), *Exclusion from School*, London: Routledge.

Dahrendorf, R. (1987) *The Underclass and the Future of Britain*, 10th Annual Lecture, Windsor.

Darton, D., Hirsch, D. and Stelitz, J. (2003) *Tackling Disadvantage: a 20-year Enterprise*, York: Joseph Rowntree Foundation.

Davies, M. (1990) *City of Quartz*, London: Verso.

Dean, H. (1991) 'In search of the underclass', in Brown, P. and Scase, R. (eds.), *Poor Work*, Buckingham: Open University Press.

Dennis, N. (1993) *Rising Crime and the Dismembered Family*, London: Institute of Economic Affairs.

Dennis, N. and Erdos, G. (1992) *Families without Fatherhood*, London: Institute of Economic Affairs.

Denny, C. (2003) 'Analysis: profits of loss', *The Guardian*, 25 November.

DETR (2000) *Index of Multiple Deprivation*, London: Department of the Environment, Transport and the Regions.

DfEE (2000) *Secondary School Performance Tables*, London: Department for Education.

——(2001) *Secondary School Performance Tables*, London: Department for Education and Employment.

Dolton, P., Makepeace, G., Hutton, S. and Audas, R. (1999) *Making the Grade*, York: JRF/York Publishing Services.

Dolton, P., Dyson, A., Meagher, N. and Robson, E. (2002) 'ROUTES: Youth Transitions in the North East of England', *ESRC Youth, Citizenship and Social Change Research Briefing*, 3.

Donnison, D. (1998) 'Creating a safer society', in Jones Finer, C. and Nellis, M. (eds.), *Crime and Social Exclusion*, Oxford: Blackwell.

Du Bois-Reymond, M. (1998) '"I don't want to commit myself yet': young people's life concepts', *Journal of Youth Studies*, 1, 1: 63–80.

Duncan, R. and Edwards, R. (1999) *Lone Mothers, Paid Work and Gendered Moral Rationalities*, Basingstoke: Macmillan.

Easton, H. and Heggie, J. (2003) 'The missing link? Using life grids as a feminist qualitative research tool', *3rd Annual Irish Postgraduate Conference*, Dublin, University College.

Edmunds, M., Hough, M., Turnbull, P. and May, T. (1999) *Doing Justice to Treatment: Referring Offenders to Drugs Services*, DPAS Paper 2, London: Home Office.

EGRIS (European Group for Integrated Social Research) (2001) 'Misleading trajectories: transition dilemmas of young adults', in *Journal of Youth Studies*, 4, 1: 101–18.

Employment Service (1997) *New Deal for Young People in Teesside: Delivery Plan*, Middlesbrough: Employment Service.

Epstein, J. (ed.) (1998) *Youth Culture: Identity in a Postmodern World*, Oxford: Blackwell.

Etzioni, A. (1993) *The Spirit of American Community*, London: Simon and Schuster.

Evans, K. (2002) 'Taking control of their lives? Agency in young adult transitions in England and the new Germany', in *Journal of Youth Studies*, 5, 3, 245–70.

Evans, K. and Heinz, W. (1994) *Becoming Adult in England and Germany*, London: Anglo-German Foundation.

Evans, K. and Furlong, A. (1997) 'Metaphors of youth transitions: niches, pathways, trajectories and navigations', in Bynner, J., Chisholm, L. and Furlong, A. (eds.), *Youth, Citizenship and Social Change in a European Context*, Aldershot: Ashgate.

Evans, K., Rudd, P., Behrens, M., Kaluza, J. and Woolley, C. (2001) 'Reconstructing fate as choice?', *Young*, 9, 3, 2–28.

Farrington, D. (1995) 'The development of offending and anti-social behaviour from childhood', *Journal of Child Psychology and Psychiatry*, 36, 929–64.

Farrington, D. (1994) 'Human development and criminal careers', in Maguire, M., Morgan, R. and Reiner, R. (eds.) *The Oxford Handbook of Criminology*, Oxford: Clarendon Press.

Featherstone, M. (1991) *Consumer Culture and Postmodernism*, London: Sage.

Feinstein, L. (1998) 'Which children succeed and why', *New Economy* 5, 2, 99–103.

Felstead, A. and Jewson, N. (1999) 'Flexible labour and non-standard employment', in *Global Trends in Flexible Labour*, Basingstoke: Macmillan.

Fergusson, R., Paye, D., Esland, G., McLaughlin, E. and Muncie, J. (2000) 'Normalized dislocation and new subjectivities in post-16 markets for education and work', in *Critical Social Policy*, 20, 3, 283–305.

Fevre, R. (1991) 'Emerging alternatives to full-time and permanent employment', in Brown, P. and Scase, R. (eds.), *Poor Work: Disadvantage and the Division of Labour*, Milton Keynes: Open University Press.

Finn, D. (1987) *Training without Jobs*, Basingstoke: Macmillan.

Foord, J. (1985) *The Quiet Revolution: Social and Economic Change on Teesside 1965 to 1985*, A Special Report for BBC North-East, Newcastle: BBC.

Ford, J., Burrows, R. and Rugg, J. (2002) 'Young people, housing and the transition to adult life', *ESRC Youth, Citizenship and Social Change Research Briefing*, 1.

Fornas, J. (1995) *Cultural Theory and Late Modernity*, London: Sage.

Forrest, R. and Kearns A. (2001) 'Social cohesion, social capital and the neighbourhood', *Urban Studies*, 38, 12, 2125–43.

Forsyth, A. and Furlong, A. (2003) *Losing Out? Socio-economic Disadvantage and Experience in Further and Higher Education*, Bristol: Policy Press.

Foster, J. (2000) 'Social exclusion, crime and drugs', in *Drugs: Education, Prevention and Policy*, 7, 4, 317–30.

Fryer, D. (1992) 'Psychological or material deprivation: why does unemployment have mental health consequences?', in McLaughlin, E. (ed.), *Understanding Unemployment*, London: Routledge.

Fryer, D. and Payne, R. (1984) 'Proactive behaviour in unemployment', in *Leisure Studies*, 3, 273–95.

Full Employment UK (1990) *Britain's New Underclass*, London: Full Employment UK.

Furlong, A. (1992) *Growing up in A Classless Society?*, Edinburgh: Edinburgh University Press.

——(2000) 'Introduction: youth in a changing world', in *International Social Science Journal*, 164, 129–34.

Furlong, A. and Cartmel, F. (1997) *Young People and Social Change: Individualization and Risk in Late Modernity*, London: Open University Press.

——(2004) *Vulnerable Young Men in Fragile Labour Markets*, York: Joseph Rowntree Foundation.

Future Steps (1999) *First Destinations of School-leavers*, Stockton: Future Steps.

Gallie, D. (1988) 'Employment, unemployment and social stratification', in Gallie, D. (ed.), *Employment in Modern Britain*, Oxford: Blackwell.

——(1994) 'Are the unemployed an underclass?', *Sociology*, 28, 3. 737–57.

Gayle, V. (1998) 'Structural and cultural approaches to youth: structuration theory and bridging the gap', in *Youth and Policy*, 61, 59–72.

Giddens, A. (1990) *The Consequences of Modernity*, Cambridge: Polity Press.

——(1991) *Modernity and Self-identity* Cambridge: Polity Press.

Gillborn, D. (2000) *Rationing Education: Policy, Practice, Reform and Equity*, Buckingham: Open University Press.

Gillis, J. (1974) *Youth and History*, New York: Academic Press.

Gladstone, F. (1976) *The Politics of Planning*, London: Temple Smith.

Glennerster, H., Noden, P. and Power, A. (1998) 'Poverty, social exclusion and place', paper presented at *Social Policy Association Conference*, Lincoln.

Glennerster, H., Lupton, R., Noden, P. and Power, A. (1999) *Poverty, Social Exclusion and Neighbourhood: Studying the Area Bases of Social Exclusion*, CASE paper 22, London: CASE.

Goldberg, T. (1999) *Demystifying Drugs*, Basingstoke: Macmillan.

Graham, J. and Bowling, B. (1995) *Young People and Crime*, Home Office Research Study 145, London: HMSO.

Granovetter, M. (1973) 'The strength of weak ties', *American Journal of Sociology*, 78: 1360–80.

Green, D. (1993) *Reinventing Civil Society*, London: Institute of Economic Affairs.

Griffin, C. (1985) *Typical Girls?* London: Routledge and Kegan Paul.

——(1993) *Representations of Youth*, Cambridge: Polity Press.

Grint, K. (1991) *The Sociology of Work*, Cambridge: Polity Press.

The Guardian (2002) 'Missing, possibly on a rave: the million who have left a hole in the UK's population tally', 1 October.

Gunter, A. (2004) '"Can't blame the youth": An Ethnographic Study of Black Youth in One East London Neighbourhood', PhD thesis, High Wycombe: Buckingham and Chilterns University College.

Hakim, C. (1992) 'Unemployment, marginal work and the black economy', in McLaughlin, E. (ed.), *Understanding Unemployment*, London: Routledge.

Hall, S. and Jefferson, T. (eds.) (1976) *Resistance through Rituals*, London: Hutchinson.

Hall, S., Critcher, C., Jefferson, T., Clarke, J. and Roberts, B. (1977) *Policing the Crisis: Mugging, the State and Law and Order*, London: Macmillan.

Hall, T., Coffey, A. and Williamson, H. (1999) 'Self, space and identity: youth identities and citizenship', in *British Journal of Sociology of Education*, 20, 4, 501–13.

Hall, T. (2002) 'Seventeen forever: youth, adulthood and the young unemployed', Working Paper Series no. 30, School of Social Sciences, Cardiff University.

Halsey, A. H. (1992) 'Foreword' to Dennis, N. and Erdos, G., *Families without Fatherhood*, London: Institute for Economic Affairs.

Hammersley, M. (1992) *What's Wrong with Ethnography?*, London: Routledge.

Harding, P. and Jenkins, R. (1989) *The Myth of the Hidden Economy*, Milton Keynes: Open University Press.

Harvey, D. (1989) *The Condition of Postmodernity*, Oxford: Blackwell.

Hayden, C. 'Exclusion or inclusion?' Social Policy Association Conference, University of Teesside.

Heath, A. (1992) 'The attitudes of the underclass', in Smith, D. (ed.), *Understanding the Underclass*, London: Policy Studies Institute.

Heath, S. and Kenyon, L. (2001) 'Young adults and shared household living', in Helve, H. and Wallace, C. (eds.), *Youth, Citizenship and Empowerment*, Aldershot: Ashgate.

Hebdige, D. (1979) *Subculture: The Meaning of Style*, New York: Methuen.

——(1988) *Hiding in the Light*, London: Comedia/Routlege.

Herrnstein, R. and Murray, C. (1994) *The Bell Curve*, New York: The Free Press.

Hills, J. (2002) 'Does a focus on "social exclusion" change the policy response?', in Hills, J., Le Grand, J. and Piachaud, D. (eds.), *Understanding Social Exclusion*, Oxford: Oxford University Press.

Hills, J., Le Grand, J. and Piachaud, D. (eds.) (2002) *Understanding Social Exclusion*, Oxford: Oxford University Press.

Hirst, P. (1994) *Associative Democracy and New Forms of Economic and Social Governance*, Cambridge: Polity Press.

HMSO (2000) *Social Focus on Young People*, London: HMSO.

HM Treasury (1999) *The Modernisation of Britain's Tax and Benefit System, no. 4: Tackling Poverty and Social Exclusion*, March, London: HM Treasury.

Hobbs, D. (1994) 'Mannish boys: Danny, Chris, crime, masculinity and business', in Newburn, T. and Stanko, E. (eds.), *Just Boys Doing Business? Men, Masculinities and Crime*, London: Routledge.

Hobcraft, J. (1998) 'Intergenerational and Life-course Transmission of Social Exclusion' CASE paper 15, London, CASE/LSE.

——(2002) 'Social exclusion and the generations', in Hills, J., Le Grand, J. and Piachaud, D. (eds.), *Understanding Social Exclusion*, Oxford: Oxford University Press.

Hobcraft, J. and Kiernan, K. (1999) 'Childhood Poverty, Early Motherhood and Adult Social Exclusion', CASE paper 28, London, CASE/LSE.

Hodkinson, P. (2002) *Goth: Identity, Style and Subculture*. Oxford: Berg.

Hodkinson, P. and Sparkes, A. (1997) 'Careership: a sociological theory of career decision making', in *British Journal of Sociology of Education*, 18, 1, 29–44.

Holden, C. (1999) 'Globalization, social exclusion and Labour's new work ethic', in *Critical Social Policy*, 19, 4, 529–38.

Hollands, R. (1990) *The Long Transition: Class, Culture and Youth Training*, Basingstoke: Macmillan.

——(1995) *Friday Night, Saturday Night: Youth Cultural Identification in the Post-industrial City*, Newcastle: University of Newcastle upon Tyne.

——(2002) 'Divisions in the dark: youth cultures, transitions and segmented consumption spaces in the night-time economy' *Journal of Youth Studies*, 5, 2, 153–71.

Holman, B. (1994/5) 'Urban youth – not an underclass', *Youth and Policy*, 47, 69–78.

Home Office (2003) 'Government cracking crime in 'Kelby"', *Press Release*, www.drugs.gov.uk/news, accessed 1 September 2003.

Hough, M. (1996) *Problem Drug Use and Criminal Justice*, London: Home Office Drugs Prevention Initiative.

House of Commons Education and Skills Committee (2003) *Government Response to the Committee's Seventh Report of 2002–3: Secondary Education – Pupil Achievement*, London: The Stationery Office.

Howieson, C. (2003) *Destinations of Early Leavers: Evidence from the Scottish School Leavers Study*, Special CES Briefing no. 28, Edinburgh; Centre for Educational Sociology.

Hudson, R. (1986) 'Sunset over the Tees', *New Socialist*, September, 13.

Hudson, R. (1989a) 'Labour market changes and new forms of work in old industrial regions', in *Environment and Planning D: Society and Space*, 7, 5–30.

——(1989b) *Wrecking a Region: State Policy, Party Politics and Regional Change in North-east England*: London: Pion Press.

Hutton, W. (1995) *The State We're In*, London: Jonathan Cape.

Institute for Social and Economic Research (ISER) (2004) *Taking the Long View: the ISER Report 2003/4*, Colchester: University of Essex.

Istance, D., Rees, G. and Williamson, H. (1994) *Young People not in Education, Training or Employment in South Glamorgan*, Cardiff: South Glamorgan Training and Enterprise Council/University of Wales, Cardiff.

Jahoda, M. (1982) *Employment and Unemployment: A Social Psychological Analysis*, Cambridge: Cambridge University Press.

James, A. and Prout, A. (eds.) (1990) *Constructing and Reconstructing Childhood*, London: Falmer Press.

Jeffs, T. and Smith, M. (1996) 'Getting the dirtbags off the street: curfews and other solutions to juvenile crime', in *Youth and Policy*, 53, 1–14.

——(1998) 'The problem of "youth" for youth work', *Youth and Policy*, 62, 45–66.

Johnston, L., MacDonald, R., Mason, P., Ridley, L. and Webster, C. (2000) *Snakes & Ladders: Young People, Transitions & Social Exclusion*, Bristol: Policy Press.

Jones Finer, C. and Nellis, M. (eds.) (1998) *Crime and Social Exclusion*, Oxford: Blackwell.

Jones, G. (1988) 'Integrating process and structure in the concept of youth: a case study for secondary analysis', in *The Sociological Review*, 36, 706–32.

——(1997) 'Youth homelessness and the "underclass"' in MacDonald, R. (ed.), *Youth, the 'Underclass' and Social Exclusion*, London: Routledge.

——(2002) *The Youth Divide*, York: Joseph Rowntree Foundation/York Publishing Services.

Jones, G. and Wallace, C. (1992) *Youth, Family and Citizenship*, Buckingham: Open University Press.

Jordan, B. (1998) *A Theory of Poverty and Social Exclusion*, Cambridge; Polity Press.

Jordan, B. and Redley, P. (1994) 'Polarisation, the underclass and the welfare state', *Work, Employment and Society*, 8, 2, 153–76.

Joseph Rowntree Foundation (ed.) (2004) *Overcoming Disadvantage: An Agenda for the Next Twenty Years*, York: Joseph Rowntree Foundation.

Kalra, V., Fieldhouse, E. and Alam, S. (2001) 'Avoiding the New Deal', *Youth and Policy*, 72.

Kasarda, J. (1989) 'Urban industrial transition and the underclass', *Annals of the American Academy of the Political and Social Sciences*, 50, 1, 26–47.

Kay, T. (1996) 'Women's work and women's worth: the leisure implications of women's changing employment patterns', in *Leisure Studies*, 15, 49–64.

Kearns, A. and Parkinson, M. (2001) 'The significance of neighbourhood', *Urban Studies*, 38, 12, 2103–10.

Kelby Borough Council (1999) *A Strategy for Reducing Crime and Disorder 1999–2002*, Cleveland: Kelby Borough Council.

Kelby Partnership (2003) *Evaluation Project and Community Strategy Performance Indicators*, Kelby Borough Council, July.

Kelvin, P. and Jarrett, J. (1985) *Unemployment: Its Social Psychological Effects*, Cambridge: Cambridge University Press.

Kleinman, M. (1998) 'Include me out? the new politics of place and poverty', CASE paper 11, London: London School of Economics.

Kiernan, K. (2002) 'Disadvantage and demography – chicken and egg?', in Hills, J., Le Grand, J. and Piachaud, D. (eds.), *Understanding Social Exclusion*, Oxford: Oxford University Press.

Kingston, P. (2003) 'Train in vain', *The Guardian*, 18 November.

Kinsey, R. (1993) 'Innocent underclass', *New Statesman and Society*, 5, 16–17.

Lakey, J., Barnes, H. and Parry, J. (2001) *Getting a Chance: Employment Support for Young People with Multiple Disadvantages*, York: JRF/York Publishing Services.

Lash, S. and Urry, J. (1987) *The End of Organized Capitalism*: Oxford: Blackwell.

Lash, J. (1994) 'Reflexivity and its doubles', in Beck, U., Giddens, A. and Lash, S. (eds.), *Reflexive Modernization*, Cambridge: Polity Press.

Laub, J. and Sampson, R. (2003) *Shared Beginnings, Divergent Lives: Delinquent Boys to Aged 70*, Cambridge, MA: Harvard University Press.

Lauder, H. (1999) *Trading in Futures: Why Markets in Education Don't Work*, Buckingham: Open University Press.

Lawless, P., Martin, R. and Hardy, S. (1998) *Unemployment and Social Exclusion: Landscapes of Labour Inequality*, London: Jessica Kingsley/RSA.

Learning and Skills Council (2003) *Directory of Opportunities: Modern Apprenticeships*, Tees Valley: Learning and Skills Council.

Lee, A. and Hills, J. (1998) *New Cycles of Disadvantage?* Report on a conference organised by CASE on behalf of ESRC for HM Treasury, CASE Report 1, London: CASE.

Lee, P. and Murie, A. (1997) *Poverty, Housing Tenure and Social Exclusion*, Bristol: Policy Press.

Lee, D. (1991) 'Poor work and poor institutions: training and the youth labour market', in Brown, P. and Scase, R. (eds.), *Poor Work: Disadvantage and the Division of Labour*, Milton Keynes: Open University Press.

Legard, R., Woodfield, K. and White, C. (2001) 'Staying away or staying on? A qualitative evaluation of the education maintenance allowance', *Research Brief 256*, London: DfEE.

Le Grand, J. (1998) 'Social exclusion in Britain today', paper given at ESRC seminar *Future Britain*, London.

Levitas, R. (1996) 'The concept of social exclusion and the new Durkheimian hegemony', *Critical Social Policy*, 46: 5–20.

Levitas, R. (1998) *The Inclusive Society? Social Exclusion and New Labour*, Basingstoke: Macmillan.

Lewis, O. (1966) *La Vida*, New York: Random House.

Lister, R. (2004) *Poverty*, Oxford: Blackwell.

Lister, R., Middleton, S., Smith, N., Vincent, J. and Cox, L. (2002) 'Negotiating transitions to citizenship', *ESRC Youth, Citizenship and Social Change Research Briefing*, 5.

Little, M. (1990) *Young Men in Prison*, Aldershot: Dartmouth.

Littlewood, P. and Herkhommer, S. (1999) 'Identifying social exclusion', in Littlewood, P. with Glorieux, I., Herkhommer, S. and Jonsson, I. (eds.), *Social Exclusion in Europe*, Aldershot: Ashgate.

Lloyd, T. (1999) *Young Men's Attitudes to Gender and Work*, JRF Findings no. 559, York: JRF.

Loader, I. (1996) *Youth, Policing and Democracy*, Basingstoke: Macmillan.

Lock, M. (1945) *County Borough of 'Kelby' Survey and Plan*, Yorkshire: Kelby Corporation.

Lupton, R. (2003) 'Neighbourhood effects: can we measure them and does it matter?', CASE paper 73, London: LSE.

Lupton, R. and Power, A. (2002) 'Social exclusion and neighbourhoods', in Hills, J., Le Grand, J. and Piachaud, D. (eds.), *Understanding Social Exclusion*, Oxford: Oxford University Press.

Lupton, R., Wilson, A., May, T., Warburton, H. and Turnbull, P. (2002) *Between a Rock and a Hard Place: Drug Markets in Deprived Neighbourhoods*, Home Office Research Study 240, London: Home Office.

Lyotard, J. (1984) *The Postmodern Condition*, Manchester: Manchester University Press.

Mac an Ghaill, M. (1994) *The Making of Men: Masculinities, Sexualities and Schooling*, Buckingham: Open University Press.

MacDonald, R. (1994) 'Fiddly jobs, undeclared working and the something for nothing society', *Work, Employment and Society*, 8, 4, 507–30.

——(1996) 'Labours of love: voluntary working in a depressed local economy', *Journal of Social Policy*, 25, 1, 19–38.

——(1997a) 'Dangerous youth and the dangerous class', in MacDonald, R. (ed.), *Youth, the 'Underclass' and Social Exclusion*, London: Routledge.

——(1997b) 'Youth, social exclusion and the millennium', in MacDonald, R. (ed.), *Youth, the 'Underclass' and Social Exclusion*, London: Routledge.

——(1997c) 'Informal work, survival strategies and the idea of an underclass', in Brown, R. K. (ed.), *The Changing Shape of Work*, London: Macmillan.

——(1998) 'Youth, transitions and social exclusion: some issues for youth research in the UK', *Journal of Youth Studies*, 1, 2, 163–76.

MacDonald, R., Banks, S. and Hollands, R. (1993) 'Youth and policy in the 1990s', *Youth and Policy*, 40, 1–10.

MacDonald, R. and Coffield, F. (1991) *Risky Business? Youth and the Enterprise Culture*, Lewes: Falmer Press.

MacDonald, R. and Marsh, J. (2001) 'Disconnected youth?', *Journal of Youth Studies*, 4, 4, 373–91.

——(2002) 'Crossing the Rubicon: youth transitions, poverty drugs and social exclusion', *International Journal of Drug Policy*, 13, 27–38.

MacDonald, R., Mason, P., Shildrick, T., Webster, C., Johnston, L. and Ridley, L. (2001) 'Snakes and ladders: in defence of studies of transition', *Sociological Research On-line*, 5, 4.

MacDonald, R. and Shildrick, T. (2004) 'Street corner society', paper presented to *Leisure Studies Association Conference*, Leeds.

MacGregor, S. (2000) 'Editorial: the drugs-crime nexus', *Drugs: Education, Prevention and Policy* 7, 4, 311–15.

Macintyre, S., McIver, S. and Sooman, A. (2002) 'Area, class and health: should we be concentrating on places or people?', in Nettleton, S. and Gustaffson, U. (eds.), *The Sociology of Health and Illness Reader*, Cambridge: Polity Press.

MacKay, R. (1998) 'Unemployment as exclusion: unemployment as choice', in Lawless, P., Martin, R. and Hardy, S. (eds.), *Unemployment and Social Exclusion: Landscapes of Labour Inequality*, London: Jessica Kingsley.

Macnicol, J. (1987) 'In pursuit of the underclass', *Journal of Social Policy* 16, 3, 293–318.

——(1994) 'Is there an underclass? The lessons from America', in White, M. (ed.), *Unemployment and Public Policy in a Changing Labour Market*, London: Policy Studies Institute.

Madanipour, A., Cars, G. and Allen, J. (eds.) (1998) *Social Exclusion in European Cities: Processes, Experiences and Responses*, London: Jessica Kingsley/RSA.

Maguire, M. and Maguire, S. (1997) 'Young people and the labour market', in MacDonald, R. (ed.), *Youth, the 'Underclass' and Social Exclusion*, London: Routledge.

Maguire, M., Maguire, S. and Vincent, J. (2001) 'Implementation of the Education Maintenance Allowance pilots: the first year', *Research Brief 255*, London: DfEE.

Malbon, B. (1999) *Clubbing*, London: Routledge.

Mandelson, P. (1998) *Labour's Next Steps: Tackling Social Exclusion*, London: Labour Party.

Mann, K. (1994) 'Watching the defectives: observers of the underclass in USA, Britain and Australia', *Critical Social Policy*, 41, 79–99.

Marsden, D. and Duff, E. (1975) *Workless*, Harmondsworth: Pelican.

Marshall, B. and Macfarlane, R. (2000) *The Intermediate Labour Market: A Tool for Tackling Long-term Unemployment*, York: Joseph Rowntree Foundation.

Matza, D. (1964) *Delinquency and Drift*, New York: Wiley.

——(1969) *Becoming Deviant*, Englewood Cliffs, NJ: Prentice Hall.

May, T. (1993) *Social Research*, Milton Keynes: Open University.

McAlister, S. (2003) 'An Ethnographic Study of an "Underclass" Neighbourhood', Draft PhD Thesis, Middlesbrough: University of Teesside.

McDowell, L. (2001) *Young Men Leaving School: White, Working-class Masculinity*, Leicester: Youth Work Press.

McKnight, A. (2002) 'Low-paid work: drip-feeding the poor', in Hills, J., Le Grand, J. and Piachaud, D. (eds.), *Understanding Social Exclusion*, Oxford: Oxford University Press.

McRobbie, A. (1991) *Feminism and Youth Culture*, Basingstoke: Macmillan.

Mead, L. (1997) *From Welfare to Work: Lessons from America*, London: Institute for Economic Affairs.

Meagre, N. (2001) 'Chaos theory and youth transitions', presentation to ESRC Youth, Citizenship and Social Change Conference, Brighton.

Merton, B. (1998) *Finding the Missing*, Leicester: Youth Work Press.

Miles, S. (2000) *Youth Lifestyles in a Changing World*, Buckingham: Open University Press.

Millar, J. (2000) *The New Deals: The Experience So Far*, JRF Findings 740, York: JRF.

Mills, C. W. (1970) *The Sociological Imagination*, New York: Pelican.

Mitchell, W. and Green, E. (2002) "I don't know what I'd do without our Mam": Motherhood, identity and support networks', in *The Sociological Review*, 50, 1, 1–22.

Mitchell, R., Shaw, M. and Dorling, D. (2000) *Inequalities in Life and Death*, Bristol: Policy Press.

Mizen, P. (2003) *The Changing State of Youth*, Basingstoke: Palgrave.

Morris, L. (1993) 'Is there a British underclass?', *International Journal of Urban and Regional Research*, 17, 3, 404–13.

——(1994) *Dangerous Classes*, London: Routledge.

——(1995) *Social Divisions*, London: UCL Press.

Morris, L. and Irwin, S. (1992) 'Employment histories and the concept of an underclass', *Sociology*, 26, 401–20.

Morrow, V. (2001) 'Young people's explanations and experiences of social exclusion', *International Journal of Sociology and Social Policy*, 21, 4, 37–63.

——(2004) 'Networks and neighbourhoods', in Phillipson, C., Allan, G. and Morgan, D. (eds.), *Social Networks and Social Exclusion*, Aldershot: Ashgate.

Muggleton, D. (1997) 'The Post-subculturalist', in Redhead, S. (ed.), *The Clubcultures Reader*. Oxford: Blackwell.

——(2000) *Inside Subculture*, Oxford: Berg.

Muncie, J. (1999) *Youth and Crime*, London: Sage.

Munro, K. (1999) *Research for Change: Young People, Youth Justice and the Use of Custody in Teesside*, Teesside: Children's Society.

Murad, N. (2002a) 'Gulity victims', in Chamberlayne, P., Rustin, M. and Wengraf, T. (eds.), *Biography and Social Exclusion in Europe*, Bristol: Policy Press.

——(2002b) 'The shortest way out of work', in Chamberlayne, P., Rustin, M. and Wengraf, T. (eds.), *Biography and Social Exclusion in Europe*, Bristol: Policy Press.

Murie, A. (1998) 'Linking housing changes to crime', in Jones Finer, C. and Nellis, M. (eds.), *Crime and Social Exclusion*, Oxford: Blackwell.

Murray, C. (1984) *Losing Ground*, New York: Basic Books.

——(1990) *The Emerging British Underclass*, London: Institute of Economic.

——(1994) *Underclass: the Crisis Deepens*, London: Institute of Economic Affairs.

——(1999) *The Underclass Revisited*, American Enterprise Institute, www.aei.org/scholars/murray.htm (accessed 29 September 2002).

——(2000) 'Baby beware', *The Sunday Times*, 13 February.

National Audit Office (2002) *The New Deal for Young People*, Report by the Comptroller and Auditor General, HC 639, London: The Stationery Office.

Nicolaus, M. (1968) 'Fat cat sociology', Remarks made at the American Sociological Association Conference, New University Conference.

Noon, M. and Blyton, P. (1997) *The Realities of Work*, Basingstoke: Macmillan.

O' Donnell, K. and Sharpe, S. (2000) *Uncertain Masculinities*, London: Routledge.

Ofsted (1998) *Report on 'East Kelby' Schools*, London: DfEE.

Osler, A., Street, C., Lall, M. and Vincent, K. (2002) *Not a Problem? Girls and School Exclusion*, London: National Children's Bureau.

Osmond, J. and Mugaseth, J. (2004) 'Community approaches to poverty in Wales', in Joseph Rowntree Foundation (ed.), *Overcoming Disadvantage: An Agenda for the Next Twenty Years*, York: Joseph Rowntree Foundation.

Page, D. (2000) *Communities in the Balance*, York: Joseph Rowntree Foundation.

Pai, H. and Leigh, D. (2004) 'Tragic death that uncovered the shadowy world of Britain's hidden Chinese workers', *The Guardian*, 13 January.

Pakulski, J. and Waters, M. (1996) *The Death of Social Class*, London: Sage.

Parker, H., Aldridge, J. and Egginton, R. (2001) *UK Drugs Unlimited*. London: Palgrave.

Parker, H., Aldridge, J. and Measham, F. (1998b) *Illegal Leisure*, London: Routledge.

Parker, H., Bury, C. and Eggington, R. (1998a) *New Heroin Outbreaks amongst Young People in England and Wales*, Police Research Group Paper 92, London: Home Office.

Parker, H., Measham, F. and Aldridge, J. (1995) *Drug Futures: Changing Patterns of Drug Use amongst English Youth*, London: ISDD.

Parker, H. and Newcombe, R. (1987) 'Heroin Use and Acquisitive Crime in an English Commmunity', *British Journal of Sociology*, 38, 3, 331–50.

Parkin, M. (1979) *Marxism and Class Theory*, London: Tavistock.

Pavis, S. and Cunnigham-Burley, S. (1999) 'Male street youth culture: understanding the context of health-related behaviours', in *Helath Education Research*, 14, 5, 583–96.

Payne, J. and Payne, C. (1994) 'Recession, restructuring and the fate of the unemployed: evidence in the underclass debate', *Sociology*, 28, 1, 1–21.

Pearce, J. (2003) *'It's someone taking part of you': A Study of Young Women and Sexual Exploitation*, London: National Children's Bureau/JRF.

Pearson, G. (1983) *Hooligan: A History of Respectable Fears*, London: Macmillan.

Pearson, G., Gilman, M. and McIver, S. (1987) *Young People and Heroin: An Examination of Heroin Use in the North of England*, London: Health Education Council.

Perri 6 (1997) *Escaping Poverty: From Safety Nets to Networks of Opportunity*, London: Demos.

Perri 6 et al. (1997) *The Substance of Youth*, York: Joseph Rowntree Foundation.

Perrons, D. (1998) 'Gender as a form of social exclusion', in Lawless, P., Martin, R. and Hardy, S. (eds.), *Unemployment and Social Exclusion*, London: Jessica Kingsley.

Phillipson, C., Allan, G. and Morgan, D. (eds.) (2004) *Social Networks and Social Exclusion*, Aldershot: Ashgate.

Phoenix, A. (1991) *Young Mothers?*, Cambridge: Polity Press.

Phoenix, J. (2002) 'In the name of protection: youth prostitution policy reforms in England and Wales', in *Critical Social Policy*, 22, 2, 353–75.

Pilkington, H. and Johnson, R. (2003) 'Peripheral youth: relations of identity and power in global/local context', *European Journal of Cultural Studies*, 6, 3, 239–83.

Pleace, N. (1998) 'Single homelessness as social exclusion: the unique and the extreme', in Jones Finer, C. and Nellis, M. (eds.), *Crime and Social Exclusion*, Oxford: Blackwell.

Plewis, I. (1998) 'Inequalities, targets and zones', in *New Economy*, 5, 2, 104–8.

Power, A. (1998) 'Social exclusion and poor neighbourhoods', in Lee, A. and Hills, J. (eds.), *New Cycles of Disadvantage?*, Case report 9, London: LSE.

——(1999) *Estates on the Edge*, London: Routledge.

The Prince's Trust (2004) 'New report reveals gaps in local support for the hardest to reach', Press Release, London: Prince's Trust.

Putnam, D. (1995) 'Bowling alone: America's declining social capital', *Journal of Democracy*, 6, 1, 65–78.

——(1996) 'The strange disappearance of civic America', *American Prospect*, Winter, 34–48.

——(2000) *Bowling Alone*, New York: Simon and Schuster.

Quinton, D., Pollock, S. and Golding, J. (2002) 'The transition to fatherhood of young men', *ESRC Youth, Citizenship and Social Change Research Briefing*, 8.

Raffe, D. (1990) 'The context of the Youth Training Scheme', in Gleeson, D. (ed.), *Training and its Alternatives*, Milton Keynes: Open University Press.

Raffe, D. (2003) *Young People not in Education, Training or Employment*, Special CES Briefing no. 29, Edinburgh: Centre for Educational Sociology.

Raffo, C. and Reeves, M. (2000) 'Youth transitions and social exclusion: developments in social capital theory', *Journal of Youth Studies*, 3, 2, 147–66.

Rapoport, R. and Rapoport, R. (1975) *Leisure and the Family Life Cycle*, London: Routledge and Kegan Paul.

Reay, D. (2003) 'Class, authenticity and the transition to higher education for mature students', *The Sociological Review*, 50, 3, 398–418.

Redhead, S. (ed.) (1993) *Rave off: Politics and Deviance in Contemporary Culture*, Aldershot: Avebury.

——(1997) *The Club Cultures Reader*, Oxford: Blackwell.

Rees, G., Fevre, R., Furlong, J. and Gorard, S. (1997) 'History, place and the learning society', *Journal of Education Policy*, 12, 6, 485–98.

Regan, S. and Robinson, P. (2004) 'Loud and clear: an open and persistent poverty strategy', in Joseph Rowntree Foundation (ed.) (2004) *Overcoming Disadvantage: An Agenda for the Next Twenty Years*, York: Joseph Rowntree Foundation.

Richardson, L. and Mumford, K. (2002) 'Community, neighbourhood and social infrastructure', in Hills, J., Le Grand, J. and Piachaud, D. (eds.), *Understanding Social Exclusion*, Oxford: Oxford University Press.

Riddell, S., Baron, S. and Wilson, A. (1999) *End of Award Report*, ESRC: Swindon.

Ridge, T. (2002) *Childhood Poverty and Social Exclusion: From a Child's Perspective*, Bristol: Policy Press.

Rifkin, J. (1995) *The End of Work*, New York: Putnams.

Riseborough, G. (1993) 'The gobbo barmy army', in Bates, I. and Riseborough, G. (eds.), *Youth and Inequality*, Milton Keynes: Open University Press.

Rizzini, I., Barker, G. and Cassaniga, N. (2002) 'From street children to all children', in Tienda, M. and Wilson, W. J. (eds.), *Youth in Cities: A Cross-National Perspective*, Cambridge: Cambridge University Press.

Roberts, B. (2002) *Biographical Research*, Milton Keynes: Open University Press.

Roberts, K. (1984) *School Leavers and Their Prospects*, Milton Keynes: Open University Press.

——(1995) *Youth and Employment in Modern Britain*, Milton Keynes: Open University Press.

——(1997a) 'Is there a youth underclass? The evidence from youth research', MacDonald, R. (ed.), *Youth, the 'Underclass' and Social Exclusion*, London: Routledge.

——(1997b) 'Structure and agency: the new youth research agenda', in Bynner, J., Chisholm, L. and Furlong, A. (eds.), *Youth, Citizenship and Social Change in a European Context*, Aldershot: Ashgate.

——(1999) *Leisure in Contemporary Society*, Wallingford: CABI Publsihing.

——(2000) 'The sociology of youth: problems, priorities and methods', paper given to British Sociological Association Youth Study Group Conference, University of Surrey, July.

——(2001) *Class in Modern Britain*, London: Palgrave.

Roberts, K., Campbell, R. and Furlong, A. (1990) 'Class and gender divisions among young adults at leisure', in Wallace, C. and Cross, M. (eds.), *Youth in Transition*, Basingstoke: Falmer Press.

Roberts, K. and Parsell, G. (1992) 'The stratification of youth training', *British Journal of Education and Work*, 5, 65–83.

Robinson, C. (2000) 'Creating space, creating self: street frequenting youth in the city and suburbs', *Journal of Youth Studies*, 3, 4, 429–43.

Robinson, F. (1990) *The Great North?* A Special Report for BBC North-east, Newcastle.

Robinson, F. and Gregson, N. (1992) 'The "underclass": class apart?', *Critical Social Policy*, 34, 38–51.

Room, G. (1995) *Beyond the Threshold: The Measurement and Analysis of Social Exclusion*, Bristol: Policy Press.

Rudd, P. and Evans, K. (1998) 'Structure and agency in youth transitions: student experiences of vocational further education', in *Journal of Youth Studies*, 1, 1, 39–62.

Rugg, J. (ed.) (1999) *Young People, Housing and Social Policy*, London: Routledge.

Rugg, J., Ford, J. and Burrows, R. (2004) 'Housing advantage? The role of student renting in the constitution of housing biographies in the UK', *Journal of Youth Studies*, 7, 1, 19–34.

Runciman, W. G. (1990) 'How many classes are there in contemporary British society?', *Sociology*, 24, 378–96.

Rustin, M. and Chamberlayne, P. (2002) 'Introduction', in Chamberlayne, P., Rustin, M. and Wengraf, T. (eds.), *Biography and Social Exclusion in Europe*, Bristol: Policy Press.

Rutherford, A. (1992) *Growing out of Crime: The New Era*, London: Waterside Press.

Rutter, M. and Madge, N. (1976) *Cycles of Disadvantage*, London: Heinemann.

Salo, H. (2003) 'Negotiating gender and personhood in new South Africa', *European Journal of Cultural Studies*, 6, 3, 345–565.

Sampson, R. and Laub, R. (1993) *Crime in the Making*, London: Harvard University Press.

Schuller, T. (2004) *The Benefits of Learning*, London: Routledge.

Shildrick, T. (2000) 'Youth culture, the "underclass" and social exclusion', *Scottish Youth Issues Journal*, 1, 1, 9–30.

——(2002) 'Young people, illicit drug use and the question of normalisation', *Journal of Youth Studies*, 5, 1, 35–48.

——(2003) '"Spectaculars", "Trackers" and "Ordinary" Youth: Youth Culture, Illicit Drug Use and Social Class', PhD Thesis, Middlesbrough: University of Teesside.

Shiner, M. and Newburn, T. (1997) 'Definitely, maybe not: the normalisation of recreational drug use amongst young people', *Sociology* 31, 3, 1–19.

——(1999) 'Taking tea with Noel: the place and meaning of drug use in everyday life', in South, N., *Drugs, Controls and Everyday Life*. London: Sage.

Sibley, D. (1995) *Geographies of Exclusion*, London: Routledge.

Silver, H. (1995) 'Reconceptualising social disadvantage', in Rodgers, G., Gore, C. and Figueiredo, J. (eds.), *Social Exclusion: Rhetoric, Reality, Responses*, Geneva: ILO.

Simpson, D. and Cieslik, M. (2000) 'Expanding study support nationally: implications from an evaluation of the East Middlesbrough Education Action Zone's programme', *Educational Studies*, 26, 4, 503–15.

Simpson, M. (2003) 'The relationship between drug use and crime', *International Journal of Drug Policy*, 14, 307–19.

——(2004) 'A Qualitative Study of the Drugs-Crime Relationship in a North-eastern Town', PhD thesis, Middlesbrough: University of Teesside.

Skeggs, B. (1997) *Formations of Class and Gender*, London: Sage.

Skelton, T. (2002) 'Research on youth transitions: some critical interventions', in Cieslik, M. and Pollock, G. (eds.), *Young People in Risk Society*, Aldershot: Ashgate.

Smith, D. (ed.) (1992) *Understanding the Underclass*, London: Policy Studies Institute.

Smith, D. and McVie, S. (2003) 'Theory and method in the Edinburgh study of youth transitions and crime', *British Journal of Criminology*, 43, 169–95.

Smith, D. and Stewart, J. (1998) 'Probation and social exclusion', in Jones Finer, C. and Nellis, M. (eds.), *Crime and Social Exclusion*, Oxford: Blackwell.

Social Exclusion Unit (1997) *Tackling Truancy*, London: Social Exclusion Unit.

——(1998) Bringing Britain Together: A National Strategy for Neighbourhood Renewal, London: Social Exclusion Unit.

——(1999a) Bridging the Gap, London: Social Exclusion Unit.

——(1999b) *Teenage Pregnancy*, London: Social Exclusion Unit.

——(2000) *Report of Policy Action Team 12: Young People*, London: Social Exclusion Unit.

——(2004) *Tackling Social Exclusion: Taking Stock and Looking to the Future*, London: Office of the Deputy Prime Minister.

South, N. (1999) 'Debating drugs and everyday life: normalisation, prohibition and otherness', in South, N. (ed.), *Drugs: Cultures, Controls and Everyday Life*, London: Sage.

Spano, A. (2002) 'Premodernity and postmodernity in southern Italy', in Chamberlayne, P., Rustin, M. and Wengraf, T. (eds.), *Biography and Social Exclusion in Europe*, Bristol: Policy Press.

Spicker, P. (1997) 'Exclusion', *Journal of Common Market Studies*, 35, 1, 133–43.

Stenson, K. and Watt, P. (1998) 'The street: It's a bit dodgy round there', in Skelton, T. and Valentine, G. (eds.), *Cool Places: Geographies of Youth Culture*, London: Routledge.

Stephen, D. and Squires, P. (2003) '"Adults don't realize how sheltered they are". A contribution to the debate on youth transitions from some voices on the margin', *Journal of Youth Studies*, 6, 2, 145–64.

Strathdee, R. (2001) 'Change in social capital and "risk" in school to work transitions', *Work, Employment and Society*, 15, 2, 1–16.

Tabberer, S. et al. (2000) *Teenage Pregnancy and Choice*, York: Joseph Rowntree Foundation.

Taylor, I. (1999) *Crime in Context*, Cambridge: Polity Press.

Tees Valley Training and Enterprise Council (2000) *Labour Market Information: Monthly*, Teesside TEC.

Thomson, R. (2000) 'Dream on: the logic of sexual practice', *Journal of Youth Studies*, 3, 4, 407–27.

Thomson, R., Hollands, J., Henderson, S., McGrellis, S. and Bell, R. (2002a) 'Inventing adulthoods: young people's strategies for transition', *ESRC Youth, Citizenship and Social Change Research Briefing*, 13.

Thomson, R., Bell, R., Holland, J., Henderson, S., McGrellis, S. and Sharpe, S. (2002b) 'Critical moments: choice, chance and opportunity in young people's narratives of transition', *Sociology*, 36, 2, 335–54.

Thornton, S. (1995) *Club Cultures*, Cambridge: Polity.

Townsend, P. (1979) *Poverty in the United Kingdom*, Harmondsworth: Penguin.

Toynbee, P. (2003) *Hard Work: Life in Low-pay Britain*, London: Bloomsbury.

Turner, K. (2004) 'Young women's views on teenage motherhood', *Journal of Youth Studies*, 7, 2, 221–38.

Turok, I. and Edge, N. (1999) *The Jobs Gap in Britain's Cities*, Bristol: Policy Press.

Valentine, G., Skelton, T. and Chambers, D. (1998) 'Cool places', in Skelton, T. and Valentine, G. (eds.), *Cool Places: Geographies of Youth Culture*, London: Routledge.

Valentine, G., Skelton, T. and Butler, R. (2002) 'Understanding marginalisation among young people', *ESRC Youth, Citizenship and Social Change Research Briefing*, no. 11, Brighton: TSA.

Wacquant, L. (1993) 'Urban outcasts: stigma and division in the Black American ghetto and the French urban periphery', *International Journal of Urban and Regional Studies*, 17, 3, 366–83.

Walker, A. (1990) 'Blaming the victims', in Murray, C., *Underclass: The Crisis Deepens*, London: Institute for Economic Affairs.

Walker, S. and Barton, L. (eds.) (1986) *Youth, Unemployment and Schooling*, Milton Keynes: Open University Press.

Wallace, C. (1986) 'From girls and boys to women and men', in Walker, S. and Barton, L. (eds.), *Youth, Unemployment and Schooling*, Milton Keynes: Open University Press.

Wallace, C. and Kovacheva, S. (1998) *Youth in Society*, Basingstoke: Macmillan.

Waters, M. (2001) *Globalisation* (second edition), London: Routledge.

Watt, P. and Jacobs, K. (2000) 'Discourses of social exclusion: an analysis of "Bringing Britain Together: a National Strategy for Neighbourhood Renewal"', *Housing, Theory and Society*, 17, 14–26.

Webster, C., Simpson, D., Abbas, A., Cieslik, M., MacDonald, R., Shildrick, T. and Simpson, M. (2003) 'A critical case study of extended criminal and drug using careers: social capital and social exclusion', American Criminological Society Conference, Denver, Colorado.

Webster, C., Simpson, D., MacDonald, R., Abbas, A., Cieslik, M., Shildrick, T. and Simpson, M. (2004) *Poor Transitions: Social Exclusion and Young Adults*, Bristol: Policy Press.

Weiner, G., Arnot, M. and David, M. (1997) 'Is the future female?', in Halsey, A., Lauder, H., Brown, P. and Stuart Wells, A. (eds.), *Education, Culture, Economy*, Oxford: Oxford University Press.

Westergaard, J. (1992) 'About and beyond the underclass: some notes on influences of social climate on British sociology', *Sociology*, 26, 575–87.

White, M. and Forth, J. (1998) *Pathways through Unemployment: The Effects of a Flexible Labour Market*, York: JRF.

Wicks, R. (2004) 'Labour's unfinished business', in Joseph Rowntree Foundation (ed.) (2004) *Overcoming Disadvantage: An Agenda for the Next Twenty Years*, York: Joseph Rowntree Foundation.

Williamson, H., (1997) 'Status zer0 youth and the "underclass": some considerations', in MacDonald, R. (ed.), *Youth, the 'Underclass' and Social Exclusion*, London: Routledge.

Willis, P. (1977) *Learning to Labour: How Working Class Kids Get Working Class Jobs*, London: Saxon House.

Wilson, W. J. (1987) *The Truly Disadvantaged*, Chicago: University of Chicago Press.
——(1996) *When Work Disappears*, New York: Knopf.
Whyte, W. F. (1943/1981) *Street Corner Society*, Chicago: University of Chicago Press.
Wynn, J. and Dwyer, P. (1999) 'New directions in research on youth in transition', *Journal of Youth Studies*, 2, 1, 5–22.
Wood, M. and Vamplew, C. (1999) *Neighbourhood Images in Teesside: Regeneration or Decline?*, York: JRF/York Publishing Services.
Young, J. (1999) *The Exclusive Society*, London, Sage.

Index

Note: Page numbers in bold indicate the most extensive/significant discussion of that topic.